Edward Ryan

The History of the Effects of Religion on Mankind

In countries ancient and modern, barbarous and civilized

Edward Ryan

The History of the Effects of Religion on Mankind
In countries ancient and modern, barbarous and civilized

ISBN/EAN: 9783337427276

Printed in Europe, USA, Canada, Australia, Japan

Cover: Foto ©Lupo / pixelio.de

More available books at **www.hansebooks.com**

THE

HISTORY

OF THE

EFFECTS OF RELIGION

ON

MANKIND;

IN COUNTRIES, ANCIENT AND MODERN,
BARBAROUS AND CIVILIZED.

CONTAINING,

Sect. I. The Expediency of true Religion in civilized States, with the Origin and Effects of Pagan Superstitions.

Sect. II. The Effects of Judaism on the Hebrews themselves, and on the Sentiments of Pagans.

Sect. III. Tendency and real Effects of the Christian Code.

Sect. IV. Origin, Progress, and Effects of Mahometanism.

By the Rev. EDWARD RYAN, B. D.

HAUD SCIO, AN PIETATE ADVERSUS DEOS SUBLATA, FIDES ETIAM,
ET SOCIETAS HUMANI GENERIS, ET UNA EXCELLENTISSIMA
VIRTUS, JUSTITIA TOLLATUR.
      Tully de Nat. Deor. Lib. I. Cap. ii.

LONDON:
PRINTED FOR J. F. AND C. RIVINGTON, N° 62,
ST. PAUL'S CHURCH YARD.
M DCC LXXXVIII.

TO THE

Right Rev. ROBERT FOWLER, D.D.

Lord Archbishop of DUBLIN.

MY LORD,

TO whom could this work be so properly dedicated as to the friend and protector of its author? Accept it then, my Lord, as the offering of respect, esteem, and gratitude. It is the only return I can make, for the many favours and marks of attention with which I have been honoured by your grace; favours not a little enhanced by the free and generous manner in which they were conferred. Exclusive of these considerations, the rectitude with which you, my Lord, discharge the duties of archbishop, should in itself be a sufficient inducement to submit this work to your grace's protection; nor can I doubt the patronage of him, whose conduct has ever evinced the sincerest wishes for the advancement of religion. You, my Lord, have at all times displayed a desire of distinguishing merit, by your approbation and protection;

tection; and have laudably encouraged your clergy to the faithful difcharge of their duty, by various marks of attention and regard. Were I fkilled in panegyric, I could point out many virtues in your grace's private character of hufband, father, friend, &c. &c. but the virtues which you fo eminently practife in your public ftation, more peculiarly demand a public acknowledgment; which cannot, in juftice, be withheld by him, who has the honour to fubfcribe himfelf

Your Grace's moft dutiful,

Moft obliged,

And moft devoted Servant,

EDWARD RYAN.

PREFACE.

THE subject of this work originated from a question proposed, in the University of Dublin, by the Provost and Fellows in the year 1775, entitled " A Dissertation on the Influence of Religion on Civil Society." Four months were allowed for the disquisition; and a premium was offered to the author of the best dissertation. The right honourable John Hely Hutchinson, the Provost, has attended more than any of his predecessors, to this mode of encouraging literary compositions; and we have reason shortly to expect excellent works, from men who have been taught early to arrange their ideas, to write correctly, and to direct their studies to important subjects. The author's dissertation, on that question, was honoured with a premium by that learned Society; and, in the year 1780, he was encouraged, and prevailed on by the late Dr. Foresayth, who was eminent for erudition, to enlarge on the subject. The author often lamented

PREFACE.

that some of the most learned and ingenious Fellows of that University, did not undertake the task; and assures his readers, that if he had foreseen the difficulties which were to be encountered, and the degree of judgment and information which would be necessary in this disquisition, he would not have engaged in this work, from a despair of doing justice to so important an enquiry. Conscious that a treatise, which elucidates theology by history, will be more read than dry dissertations on religion and morality; the Author has blended theology with policy, and the doctrines of all religions with history, both ancient and modern, civil and ecclesiastical. In order to reduce this work to a moderate size, sentences short and deemed expressive, have been preferred to well turned periods; and those religious tenets are selected, which had an influence on policy and morals, on the condition of individuals, and the welfare of barbarous, as well as civilized states. By this selection many important questions are discussed in three octavos; the first of which exhibits the *effects* of *Natural, Pagan, Jewish, Christian,* and *Mahometan* religions. The next two volumes will,

PREFACE.

will, doubtless, be more interesting to many readers, as they contain the history of events less remote. This history, in some cases, detects, without controversy, false systems of religion; and shews that doctrines, which tend to the detriment of society, and have operated according to their tendency, could not have been dictated, by a wise and good God. On the contrary, the real and solid advantages, which have resulted from the Gospel; and the many evils which arose from breaches of its precepts, should attach men to it, and induce the enemies of religion to give it a fair hearing. Candidates for the clerical profession might derive much useful and necessary information from a treatise of this kind, which refers to some of the best authors on each subject; and comprises, within a narrow compass, the fruits of many years close study and research. Yet they who read for the purpose of censure will, doubtless, be gratified, in perusing this work; for though it is supported by history, and, in general, by arguments which cannot be controverted; " yet it is not armed at all points for battle, nor capable of standing the test of a captious controversy." Can-

PREFACE.

did and learned readers will readily excuse trifling imperfections, in a work useful in its tendency, and extensive in its information; but severity is chiefly to be apprehended from men of superficial knowledge, who possess, or think they possess some taste in composition; while they want judgment, and information for a work of this nature. The author of this tract has pointed out errors, in writers far superior to him in understanding and knowledge; and must expect the same treatment, from some who are, perhaps, inferior to him in both these respects. But he has not animadverted on any writers, except those who held erroneous opinions, which clashed with his system; or who held tenets subversive of morality and detrimental to society. If he has, like other writers, maintained such doctrines; or voluntarily perverted the books which he consulted; he neither deserves, nor desires the indulgence of his readers. If Criticks should attack him, he has determined not to suffer an answer to interrupt the progress of his two succeeding volumes; but will postpone his defence to the conclusion of the Third. The Author could not conclude

this

PREFACE.

this Preface, without expressing his acknowledgments to several men of learning, who have each read one or more Sections of this volume, and favoured him with their remarks. He is much indebted to Dr. Agar, Lord Archbishop of Cashel, for his judicious observations respecting the arrangement; and to Dr. Woodward, Lord Bishop of Cloyne, for perusing this entire volume, and suggesting many inportant ideas in the course of this treatise. He is also indebted to Dr. Bathurst, Canon of Christ Church, Oxford; and to Dr. Dobbin, Dr. Dabzac, Dr. J. Kearney, Dr. Young, Messrs. Barrat, Burrowes, Elrington, Graves, (Fellows of the University of Dublin) and other learned men, who have each read particular Sections of it, and honoured him with their observations.

CONTENTS.

SECTION I.

EXPEDIENCY OF TRUE RELIGION TO CIVILIZED STATES, WITH THE ORIGIN AND EFFECTS OF PAGAN SUPERSTITIONS.

The origin and establishment of civil society.—The expediency and defects of human laws.—Human sanctions imperfect.—Pagan legislators employed religion to remedy the defects of human laws.—Tendency of natural religion to prevent crimes and enforce oaths.—Its tendency with respect to judges and witnesses, princes and their subjects.—Source of religious knowledge among some ancient nations. —Effects of that religion, usually called natural, on the ancient Chinese.—Effects of it on the ancient Persians.—Effects of it on the ancient Indians.— Question relative to the origin and effects of paganism.—Anubis and Sphinx, Egyptian symbols, not real beings.—Osiris and Neptune, symbols, not real beings.—Isis, Ceres, Diana, and Venus.— Mars, Hercules, Vulcan, Apollo, taken from Horus an Egyptian symbol.—Muses, Graces, Pallas, Pales taken from the figures of Isis.—Symbols and funeral ceremonies of the Egyptians the source of fables.—Fable of the Giants and Proserpine.—Mercury,

CONTENTS.

cury, Memnon and Bacchus.—*Origin of the worship of animals, of augury and other superstitions. —Origin of idolatry and the worship of false Gods.—Brucker's opinion examined.—Causes of obscurity in Heathen Mythology.—Cicero's opinion examined.—Effects of paganism in Egypt.—Popular religion of other Pagan nations.—Paganism productive of impurity, adultery and drunkenness. —Paganism a source of cruelty. The same subject continued.—Pagan priests and players did not restrain vice in the Roman empire.—Philosophers did not restrain vice by precept or example.—Pagan lawgivers inculcated some virtues.—Paganism a mere political contrivance.—Heathen oracles.—Some particular effects of paganism in Heathen governments.—Effects of various Pagan superstitions.—Paganism assisted the Romans in extending their conquests.—Superstition contributed to the destruction of the Roman empire.—The state of religion among Pagans, proves the necessity of supernatural assistance.* Page 1.

SECTION II.

Effects of Judaism on the Hebrews themselves, and on the sentiments of Pagans.

Design of the miracles of Moses and of his whole law. —Intention and effects of the sabbath.—Of the Hebrew

CONTENTS.

Hebrew festivals.—Of the sabbatical year, jubilee and laws of usury.—Of clean and unclean beasts and the place of worship.—Means employed to procure respect for God.—Of the tabernacle and temple.—Of sacrifices and lustrations.—Tendency of the theocracy and of temporal sanctions.—Effects of those sanctions in the time of judges.—Effects of them in the time of kings.—Intention of particular laws and rites of Judaism.—The same subject continued.—The same subject continued.—General tendency of the Mosaic rites, precepts, and prohibitions. —The Mosaic rites and institutions local and temporary.—Laws of Moses preferable to those of Pagan lawgivers.—His writings of divine authority.—Temporal sanctions prove his divine commission.—The truth of his account confirmed by Bryant.—Judaism imperfect.—Judaism prepared men for the gospel.—Hebrew writings useful in chronology and history.—Mosaic account of the creation tends to remove some errors of naturalists.— Jews and their tenets known to ancient Pagans.— Hebrews and Heathens relate the same facts.—Plato borrowed from the Hebrews.—Orpheus, Homer, Solon and others borrowed from them.—Greeks indebted to them by the testimony of the learned.— Ancient philosophers borrowed their theology.— Greek philosophers were plagiaries.—Their absurdities prove that they borrowed their theology.—Divine attributes not investigated by reason.—Brucker errs in denying that Heathens borrowed from Hebrews.

CONTENTS.

brews. *The same subject continued.—He errs in denying that Plato borrowed from them. He errs with respect to the similitude of Jewish and Pagan dogmas.—Whether the law allowed of human sacrifices.—How far it was lawful to eject and destroy the Canaanites.—The election of the Hebrews no argument of divine partiality.* Page 89

SECTION III.

TENDENCY AND EFFECTS OF THE CHRISTIAN RELIGION.

Doctrines and motives of the gospel.—Lord Kaims's idea of universal benevolence.—His opinion of the malignant affections.—Bolingbroke approves of the moral system of Christians.—Gospel motives to obedience preferable to any other.—The practices of barbarous states prove the expediency of the Christian system.—The gospel tends to abolish the evils of revenge among Barbarians.—Cruelty and murder among uncivilized states.—Excellence of the gospel proved from the bad effects of violating its precepts in Peru and other places.—Bad effects of violating it in the English colonies of the West and East Indies.—Effects of violating it in Denmark, Ireland, Poland and Russia.—Effects of modern Paganism prove the excellent tendency of the gospel.—The gospel

CONTENTS.

gospel tends to remove the bad effects of false ideas of futurity.—It tends to abolish austerities and other effects of superstition.—Effects of Paganism at Malabar, Narsinga, and other places.—Effects of Paganism in North and South America.—Some superstitions productive of gentleness among Indians and Peruvians.—Frauds in China, Arrakan, and other places.—Frauds in Peru, Congo, Loango, and other places.—Frauds in Whidah, Guinea, and other places. —Frauds in Japan and other places.—Frauds of priests marks of false religion—Difficult to ascertain the actual effects of the gospel.—The gospel abolished divorce and polygamy.—It mitigated the rigours of servitude.—Its teachers preserved justice and checked warriors.—Gospel abolished barbarous practices.—It abolished the fights of gladiators.— —It rendered Britons, Scots, Gauls and Irish less barbarous.—It checked cruelty in China and Japan. —It abolished human sacrifices and other cruelties in many places.—Also idolatry and cruelty in Germany, Paraguay, and Canary islands.—It diffused knowledge and abolished some bad effects of superstition.—Its teachers preserved learning.—The example of Christians taught Pagans kindness to the distressed.—Gospel rendered its first proselytes true and honest;—patient, constant and chaste.—Corrected pride and vanity.—Improved the old Roman laws.—Calumnies against Christians and the gospel serviceable to both.—Christians falsely accused of incest and devouring infants.—Of being atheists and

CONTENTS.

and authors of public calamities.—Of turbulence.—Of being poor and ignorant.—And useless members of society.—Tertullian and Justin Martyr prove mankind reformed by the gospel.—The same proved by other authors.—Julian and Pliny admit the virtues of Christians.—An assertion of Mr. Gibbon examined.—Animadversions on Dr. Priestley's 56th lecture. Page 184

SECTION IV.

ON THE ORIGIN, PROGRESS, AND EFFECTS OF MAHOMETANISM.

Enquiry into the origin of Mahometanism, useful and curious.—State of religion in Arabia, and the disputes of Christian churches favoured Mahomet's designs.—Imbecility of neighbouring nations, and the political state of Arabia contributed to his success.—Means employed in propagating his religion.—The same subject continued.—Parts of the Koran designed to extricate him from some difficulty or gratify some passion.—Character of Mahomet.—He abolished some superstitious and barbarous practices of Pagan Arabs.—Many of his doctrines borrowed, and inferior to those in the originals.—His unborrowed opinions false, contradictory and ridiculous.—His paradise and hell.—Paradise and other doctrines contributed to his successes.—Death of Mahomet, and establishment of the Caliphat.—

Maho-

CONTENTS.

Mahometanism assisted Caled in reducing Persia and other places.—It assisted him in reducing Damascus.—It assisted Obeidah in reducing Hems, Jerusalem, and other places.—All Syria, Egypt, and part of Persia, submit to the Saracens in the Caliphat of Omar.—Other places submitted to them in his Caliphat.—Other causes concurred with Mahometanism in promoting the conquests of the Saracens.—Comparison of Christianity and Mahometanism in the tendency and effects of their doctrines.—Comparison of the lives and doctrines of Christ and Mahomet.—Difficulty of making apostates from Mahometanism.—Despotism an effect of the conquests of the Saracens.—The Koran secures private property to individuals.—Ignorance an effect of Mahometanism.—Revenge, illiberality, and extortion effects of it.—Effects of the doctrine of Predestination.—Effects of Mahometan devotions on individuals and communities.—Effects of Mahometanism prove the excellent tendency of Christianity. Page 297

THE HISTORY

OF THE

EFFECTS OF RELIGION

ON

MANKIND.

SECT. I.

Expediency of true Religion to civilized States, with the Origin and Effects of Pagan Superstitions.

SOME moralists, enquiring into the origin and advantages of civil institutions, have exhibited a picture of a state of nature, which never existed, except in their own fertile imaginations. In this state, they have supposed a considerable number of men destitute of every just notion of property, maiming, murdering and plundering each other. These men, by exaggerated descriptions of the evils of this fantastic state, probably intended

The origin and establishment of civil society.

SECT. I. intended to compliment legiflators and founders of ftates. But the hypothefis of thefe moralifts is repugnant to reafon, and to the moft ancient account of the origin of mankind. The hiftory of the Hebrew lawgiver affures us, that mankind fprung from a fingle pair, who muft have kept their children fubject to parental government, and inculcated both moral and focial duties. As mankind multiplied, the ties of blood were gradually loofened, men's private interefts were feparated, and, as we may reafonably fuppofe, feveral fmall focieties were formed independent of each other. But thefe focieties, being refpectively in the condition afcribed to individuals in a ftate of nature, muft have been fubject to the evils refulting from that ftate. Should any difpute arife between two families, or between two members of different families, we may guefs the confequences: for want of a common judge, prejudice and felf-love muft render men obftinate, warp the judgment, and magnify offences to fuch a degree, that the conteft naturally terminates in riot and bloodfhed. To avoid thefe inconveniences, and to obtain all the advantages of a focial ftate, individuals and tribes judged it expedient to unite in fociety. Before fuch union they enjoyed uncontroled liberty, and were fubject to no earthly jurifdiction but parental. However, as this liberty was uncertain in its duration, and liable to encroachments; it is reafonable to fuppofe, that men

would

would cheerfully refign part of it; in order to preferve the remainder inviolate. This refignation was made by the eftablifhment of civil polity, which deprived man of his original independence, and of all right of avenging himfelf; and fubjected him to fuch laws, as were enacted by general confent for the common intereft. Nor was it difficult to prevail on men to affociate together, and unite in focieties. Their weaknefs, their wants, and the many evils, to which they were expofed, required it; while a propenfity to propagation and a love of their offspring made fuch focieties defirable and ufeful. The Roman orator (a) acquaints us, that even mifanthropes feek for the fociety of men, to whom they might communicate their thoughts, and difcharge their malice on the reft of mankind. The diverfity of talents produced a reciprocal dependence amongft men, the faculty of fpeech, which is ufelefs out of fociety, fitted them for it; a defire of praife prompted them to it (b); and all thefe circumftances concur in proclaiming it to be the divine will, that men fhould enter into a focial ftate; for, what reafon and human neceffities dictate, we may be fully perfuaded is the divine will. A late ingenious writer maintains, that man is a compound of unfocial affections as well as focial;

(a) De Amicitia, cap. 23.   (b) See Tucker's Treatife on Government, Part II. c. 1.

SECT. I. and that the former are as natural to man as the latter. That averfion to ftrangers makes a branch of our nature, exifts among individuals in private life, flames high between neighbouring tribes, and is vifible even in infancy. That favage nations who are gentle, juft, good-natured and grateful to thofe of their own tribe are falfe and faithlefs to ftrangers and foreigners. "That Europeans, who vifited fome iflands of the South-Sea, found the natives with arms in their hands, refolute to prevent their landing. That among the Koriacks, bordering on Kamfcatka, murder within the tribe is feverely punifhed; while the murder of a ftranger is not minded." But, might not the averfion fubfifting among neighbouring tribes be afcribed to quarrels, which are unavoidable, where property is undetermined, and no written laws to terminate difputes? It fhould not be confidered as a proof of unfocial affections, that favages arm themfelves to repel Europeans, who were generally known to vifit their coafts, not to gratify curiofity, but to difturb their tranquility and ftrip them of their poffeffions. Nor is it fair to judge of human nature from favages, who act more from example and felf-defence, than from the refinements of reafon. Had this writer perufed the works of the benevolent Cumberland, he could not have maintained, the malignant affections to be natural to man, without attempting to refute him; efpecially, as the argument from

favages,

savages, who are as narrow in their affections, as in their education; cannot overthrow the reasonings of that prelate, which are founded on the nature of man and on his obligations to virtue. Even Lord Kaims produces instances, in the same Sketch, of disinterested benevolence among nations and tribes, who possibly were strangers to the violence of invaders. This writer asserts, that "the inhabitants of some southern islands appear to have little or no aversion to strangers; and that among the Celtæ it was capital to kill a stranger, whereas the killing a citizen was but banishment (*c*).

Expediency and defects of human laws.

Both reason and respectable authorities (*d*) evince, that human laws were instituted to prevent injustice, to protect the weak, to restrain the turbulent, to encourage virtue, and to promote the peace and interest of society. If human laws do not uniformly produce those salutary effects, the original intention of entering into society is so fa frustrated, as those laws are defective. But the following observations, borrowed chiefly from the writings of a learned bishop (*e*), fully prove that human laws are not sufficiently coercive, nor productive of all the advantages, which they were intended to produce. Human laws, being the compositions of weak, prejudiced or interested

---

(*c*) Book II. Sketch 1.   (*d*) Hor. Lib. I. Sat. iii. 111. Tully de Leg. Lib. I. cap. 22. and Lib. II. cap. 5.
(*e*) Warburton's Divine Legation, Book I. sect. 2.

SECT. I. men, are not always juft, and when juft, cannot provide againft all diforders in a ftate: many grievances neceffarily efcaping the forefight of the wifeft legiflators. They are frequently ambiguous, equivocal and liable to mifinterpretation, and the plaineft and moft fimple are often wrefted from their obvious meaning and intention. Political laws, ever attentive to the external actions of men, forbid only fuch enormities as are evidently pernicious to fociety, and plainly deftructive of human happinefs. They take no cognizance of trifling errors, which fometimes lead to, or terminate in, ferious mifchiefs: do not prohibit ingratitude, detraction, and a breach of promife; nor reprefs pride, avarice, ambition, envy, malice and revenge fo deftructive of the peace and welfare of fociety. There are feveral virtues, which the civil magiftrate cannot enforce by penal laws; without confiderable inconvenience. Were men conftrained to hofpitality, liberality, truth, beneficence, gratitude, fincerity and other duties, it muft deftroy the merit of thofe many virtues, the free exercife of which conftitutes the good and amiable character. In a word human laws do not compel men to the practice of thofe virtues; a man may omit the duties of imperfect obligation, without dread of the civil magiftrate; though they contribute to the happinefs and ornament of fociety. Civil inftitutions cannot reftrain fuch irregularities, as refult from

our

our natural appetites; and are so far from effecting this important and desirable end, that civil polity rather inflames and quickens than controls the passions. In a laborious state of unimproved nature, mens wants are few, and their appetites moderate; while improved civil society creates artificial wants, and numberless contests arise from avarice and luxury. Upon the whole, it is evident, that human laws, considered as a system of rules for the benefit of society, are not always just, universal, and determinate; do not restrain intemperance, regulate the thoughts, meliorate the heart nor promote the general practice of virtue.

The insufficiency of human laws will more fully appear, from a consideration of their sanctions. So useful are rewards and punishments in enforcing obedience to laws, and so necessary for the support of governments; that it has been a question among moralists, whether rewards or punishments are the most cogent motives to an observance of them. The controversy points out the necessity of uniting them; and we find that legislators in their speculative schemes have really done so. But that laws must be imperfect, with respect to rewards and punishments, will appear evident from the following observations. The civil magistrate cannot always clearly prove the crime against offenders, who frequently evade the law and escape its penalties. Should an offender even be convicted, he still hopes for impunity from the lenity

Human sanctions imperfect.

SECT. I. or corruption of the civil magiftrate: and fhould he be punifhed, the penalty is frequently too fevere for the offence. Were penal laws lefs fevere, delinquents of the fecond clafs, fuch as thieves, robbers, &c. who often efcape the punifhment juftly merited by their crimes, might be encouraged to the perpetration of offences, ftill more heinous and dangerous to fociety. For this reafon capital punifhments are wifely denounced, againft fuch as are convicted; as the feverity of punifhments fhould more than balance the hope of impunity and the uncertainty of detection. As to the fanction of laws by rewards, it is obvious that it could not be eftablifhed in any government; becaufe, according to an eminent Englifh lawyer (*f*), " were the exercife of every virtue to be enforced by the propofal of particular rewards, it would be impoffible for any ftate, to furnifh ftock for fo profufe a bounty." The payment of fuch rewards, by taxes levied on the people, would be impoffible; no nation being able to bribe every member to an obfervance of its laws. Since then rewards and punifhments are the bafis of human laws, and " the very hinges upon which all government turns;" and fince civil inftitutions are, in numberlefs inftances, deftitute of thofe fupports; it is evident, that without fome other prop, the fabric of human laws muft, in fome

(*f*) Blackftone's Commentaries, Introd. fect. 2.

degree,

degree, be unsupported, and so far fail of the end which they propose.

Having taken a cursory view of the defects of penal laws, it will be necessary to point out some remedy, for those defects and imperfections. History acquaints us, that founders of states have employed religion, as the most effectual means of supplying the defects of laws, and weakness of their authority. No regular government has ever been established without some form of religion; as if the former was defective without the latter, and the one was a necessary appendage to the other. Theseus (*g*) committed the care of religion and the interpretation of sacred matters to the nobility: Lycurgus (*h*) consulted Apollo, previous to his political institutions; and Solon (*i*), and the laws of the twelve tables, were not inattentive to religion. These and other lawgivers inculcated a notion of some superior beings, who were to influence men's actions, by the powerful motives of hope and fear. These men did not take a superficial view of human nature, like many ancient and modern unbelievers; but were acquainted with the tempers and capacities of mankind, from experience and intercourse with the world. The legislators of every state, conscious of their own insufficiency in conducting their political plans, and finding the minds of their sub-

Pagan legislators, assisted by their religion endeavoured to remedy the defect of human laws.

(*g*) Plutarch's Lives.   (*h*) Ibid.   (*i*) Ibid.

jects

jects impreſſed with ſome ideas of religion, judged it expedient, to give the religious principle ſuch a direction, as might advance their deſigns. For this purpoſe they eſtabliſhed a mode of worſhip calculated to ſupport the civil magiſtrate in his office, and to inſpire a reſpect for laws, ſuppoſed to be dictated by ſome deity, whom the people were taught to reverence. In order to accompliſh this end they pretended to an intercourſe with ſome deity, from whom they profeſſed to have received their laws and ordinances. The Egyptian legiſlators pretended to have received their laws from Amaſis and Mnemes: Zoroaſter the Bactrian from Veſta; the Cretans, Minos and Rhadamanthus from Jupiter; Lycurgus from Apollo; Romulus from Conſus, and Numa from Egeria. To perpetuate thoſe laws, and procure an unfeigned obedience to them, they kept this perſuaſion alive, by the pompous parade of rites and ceremonies, which never fail to have a powerful effect on the minds of the multitude. Games were celebrated, temples erected, ſolemn rites inſtituted in honour of thoſe gods, under whoſe protection they affected to place their civil as well as religious rights, and to whom, as their guardians, they had recourſe in all emergencies.

Tendency of natural religion to prevent crimes. Having pointed out the defects of human laws, and the means employed by legiſlators to rectify them; I ſhall in the courſe of this ſection conſider the influence of thoſe means on human kind, and proceed immediately to shew, what effect true religion is calculated to produce, on the morals of men in polished and barbarous states, and how it remedies the imperfections of civil establishments. By true religion I mean, a sense of the being and attributes of God, discovered by reason, revelation, tradition, or by all of them together. Refined ideas of the deity have been derived, with some probability, from ancient tradition; with certainty, from the Mosaic and prophetic writings; and obscurely, if at all, from the deductions of reason, as will appear in the second section. Those three kinds of religion, according as we judge them to be borrowed from reason, revelation and patriarchal religion, I call natural, revealed, and Noachian; and shall consider, in the course of this work, the tendency and effects of these, on the morals of individuals, and on the welfare of communities. It is evident, that a lively sense of the divine attributes, as understood by the patriarchs and prophets, and afterwards taught by the wisest and most ancient sages, must enforce morality and remedy the defects already pointed out in the laws of every country. The most important human laws are founded on natural; and denounce civil penalties, on crimes already prohibited by the laws of nature or of God. For this reason, though a criminal should escape here the punishment due to his offences; yet, if possessed of the religious principle, he cannot expect

SECT. I.

pect to escape the all-seeing eye of the Supreme Being whose justice requires him to punish offenders.

Its tendency with respect to judges and witnesses, sovereigns and their subjects.

The validity of oaths is founded on a sense of the omnipresence and justice of God; and the expediency of those solemn appeals will appear, from considering their influence upon judges and witnesses, upon sovereigns and their subjects. Civil laws being often ambiguous, sometimes obscure, and seldom universal; in all these cases, the decision depends much on the integrity of the judge, whose duty and oath require him to supply deficiences, and elucidate obscurities, by a fair and simple interpretation; by an impartial application of laws to particular cases; and by attending to the original intention and spirit of the legislator. The veracity of witnesses, cited in courts of justice, also depends much upon their sentiments of religion: the more disinterested men are, the more credible; and none surely are more disinterested, than the truly religious; who consider a present unjust advantage as trifling and mean, compared with that, which is future and eternal. Hence it appears, that religion is a powerful preventive of corruption in judges, and the most effectual means, which the civil magistrate has ever devised, for the advancement of truth, in matters relative to life and property. Nor is religion less useful to princes and their subjects: what can add more weight to the authority of a

supreme

supreme magistrate, or more dignity to his office; than a full assurance of his piety and impartiality in dispensing justice, and enforcing the laws? " So natural, says Hooker (*l*), is the union of religion with justice, that we may boldly deem there is neither, where both are not." The faithful execution of laws depends, in some measure, upon the sacred oath, whereby the prince is bound to administer them with equity, and to act according to the trust reposed in him by his people. A supreme magistrate might perhaps, by the dread of his power, compel his subjects to an observance of his laws; but without a conscientious concurrence of the will, no sincere obedience is to be expected. The religious principle tends to render sovereigns mild and just in their administration; and subjects loyal and obedient to their prince. " Such is the force which religion hath, to qualify all sorts of men, and to render them in public affairs the more serviceable; governors the apter to rule with conscience, inferiors, for conscience sake, the more willing to obey (*m*)." " A prince who loves and fears religion, says Montesquieu (*n*), is a lion who stoops to the hand that strokes, or to the voice that appeases him: he, who fears and hates religion, is like the wild beast that growls and bites the chain which prevents his flying on the passenger: he, who has

(*l*) Eccl. Polity, Book V. Sect. I. (*m*) Ibid.
(*n*) Spirit of Laws, Book XXIV. Chap. II.

no religion at all, is that terrible animal who perceives his liberty only, when he tears to pieces and devours." Since then religion is so useful in states, where prince and people are directed by standing laws; how much more useful must it be in despotic governments, where the sovereign is absolute; and where the people have no security from oppression, but in the humanity of the prince? What can so humanize the despot's heart, or so effectually restrain him from exchanging his scepter for an iron rod; as a strong sense of a being, to whom he must account for his actions, and who will reward or punish him according to his works?

<small>Source of religious knowledge among some ancient nations.</small>

If we take a view of the opinions entertained of God, by some ancient nations, and examine their effects; we shall find their ideas of the deity tolerably refined, and their moral practice such, as might naturally be expected from a strict adherence to the precepts of true religion. It is universally acknowledged, that Ham, one of Noah's sons, had settled in Egypt after the deluge. Being about one hundred years old, he was acquainted with religion, morality, agriculture and arts of the antediluvian world; and well qualified to instruct his family, and descendants in the knowledge and practice of them. It is natural to suppose, that Noah, the second father of mankind, had impressed on the minds of his children, a strong sense of the attributes of God and the necessity

cessity of morality. His escape, from the general destruction, must have made him contemplate the goodness and forbearance of God, with pleasure and gratitude; and his power, wisdom and goodness, with awe, wonder, and dread of offending. He must have told his family, that the antediluvian world was incorrigibly wicked, and destroyed, not only for the punishment of their crimes, but for an example to posterity. The pride of being a favourite of heaven must have made this miraculous flood, the vices of mankind, and the attributes of God, his favourite theme and subject of conversation: so that his disciples must have been well instructed in religious and moral precepts, and have conveyed each of them, the same instruction to his children and descendants. We are not sufficiently acquainted with the history of nations thus instructed, to point out accurately the influence of pure religion on the lives of individuals and the state of society. But it is highly probable, that different nations observed differently the precepts of religion, and that some observed them strictly, while others degenerated into vice, superstition and idolatry. We find vestiges of Noachian or perhaps revealed religion among some ancient nations, and such morals as might be expected from men whose minds were impressed with true ideas of a deity.

It

SECT. I.

Effects of that religion, usually called natural, in the ancient Chinese.

It appears from the testimony of Numenius (o), quoted by Eusebius, that the Bramins, Jews, Magi, and Egyptians, he might have also said the Chinese, had nearly the same notions of a Supreme Being. Nor is it improbable; since all sprung from the same stock, and the Noachian traditions were uncorrupted in all nations, for some time after the deluge. The primitive Chinese had refined ideas of the attributes of God; and worshiped him, under the title of Shangti or Tyen. They considered him as eternal, and always active, the sovereign emperor, intelligent, incomprehensible, omnipotent; the self-existent unity, which produced all things by his power, just, good and merciful; who rewards or punishes either here, or hereafter; whose justice is love, and whose punishments are mercies (p). This people continued a long time pure, in their religious system, and moral practice; most of their emperors were pious, learned, just and generous; and one of them was so exemplary in his manners, that he permitted his subjects, to write on a table, exposed to public view, any thing reprehensible in his conduct. As the religion of China lasted longer pure than in other countries; so they excelled other nations, in wisdom, virtue and duration of their monarchy (q). The Chinese, in pro-

(o) Ramsay's Philosophical Principles of Religion, Vol. II. Chap. I. (p) Ibid.
(q) Mod. Univ. Hist. Vol. III. folio, Introd. to Hist. of China.

cefs of time, degenerated into superstition and vice, notwithstanding the endeavours of Confucius to restore the purity of the original worship. After the death of this reformer, the idolatry of Fo was spread over a considerable part of India, Tartary, and China; and the Chinese became false and fraudulent, whether from a decay of religion, or some other cause, I shall not pretend to determine.

According to the same author, extant in Eusebius's time, the Persian Magi considered the Supreme Being eternal, uncreated, incorruptible, incorporeal and uncompounded, the greatest and best of beings, creator of soul and body, of light and darkness, and prior to both (*r*). The Medes and Persians who were sprung from Shem, Noah's son, probably retained, for some time, the ancient patriarchial religion and customs without any considerable alteration. Zoroaster reformed the religion of the Persians from any corruptions that had crept into it, and might have been enabled to do so from his acquaintance with the Hebrews, during the Babylonish captivity, and from his knowledge of the Old Testament (*s*). The learned Hyde affirms, that the ancient Persians are the only nation upon earth, except the Jews and their ancestors, who retained from the deluge, to his own time, the knowledge and wor-

(*r*) Ramsay's Philof. Principles of Religion, Vol. II. Chap. i.
(*s*) Hyde's Hist. Relig. Veterum Persarum, Cap. i. and xxii.

ship of the true God; with some slight mixtures of idolatry and superstition. They have been accused by Christians and Mahometans of ignorance of God, and the worship of fire; Hyde, though he admits they paid great homage to this element, yet denies they prayed to it; and maintains, that they always worshipped the true God with sincerity and ardour (*t*). The moral system and manners of Persians were such as might be expected from persons, who had formed true ideas of the divine attributes. Their Sadder (*v*), or sacred book, abounds with excellent moral precepts, blended indeed with false opinions; and requires them to begin the day with prayer, praises and thanksgivings unto God; to be chaste in their bodies, honest in their dealings, and to shun pleasure, pride, robbery, and revenge (*u*). This people were temperate in their festivals, grave and austere in their deportment; it was deemed criminal in a plebeian to commit fornication, and even the monarch was not allowed to get drunk, more than once a year (*w*).

Effects of natural religion on the ancient Indians.

The ancient Indians held an opinion, that the governor of the world pervades it as a soul; that he is immortal and bountiful, and knoweth, ruleth and preserveth all things; that the human soul is a particle of the divine, survives the body, and re-

(*t*) Hyde, Cap. viii.   (*v*) Ibid. prope finem.
(*u* Bruckeri Hist. Critica de Philosophia Persarum, Lib. II. Cap. xv.   (*w*) Hyde, Cap. xxxiv.

turns

turns to God to be rewarded or punished (*x*). From the Verdam, or Sacred Book of the Indians it appears, that they believed in a supreme being, who protects all things by viceroys or inferior deities; is simple, invisible, immutable, eternal, wise, holy, true, good, just and merciful (*y*). The morality of the Indians was so sublime and pure, and had such a tendency to subdue the passions, and induce men to the practice of many virtues; that Brucker (*z*), from a partiality for the Greek philosophy, seems to suspect; that the doctines ascribed to them, were borrowed from the Greek schools and the precepts of the Gospel. The Indian philosophy required men to extirpate evil desires and criminal indulgences, and to lead lives of innocence and austerity. Their practice was, in general, conformable to their principles; the Indians were so austere, that some secluded themselves from society, to shun occasions of sin, and to practise virtue retired from the world. Others abstained from wine, and animal food, and performed several acts of patience and self-denial; while some despised even death, though administered in torments. The ancient Bramins, or priests, were remarkably rigid; and acquired great influence with prince and people, not only for

(*x*) Bruckeri de philosophia Indorum, Lib. II. Cap. iv. Sect. 6.
(*y*) Ramsay, Ch. i. of God's Existence and Attributes.
(*z*) Bruckeri, Lib. II. Cap. iv. Sect. 4. and 7.

SECT. I.

their continence and hardiness; but for their skill in prophesy, and interceding with the Gods in time of public calamity. Being sent for by Alexander the Great, who had conquered their country; they treated him with contempt, disobeyed his summons, and desired he would come to them, if an interview was necessary (a). From what has been said it appears, that the ancient Chinese, Persians and Indians, who entertained sublime ideas of God though blended with false opinions, were virtuous in practice, and that some of them were moral, even to a degree of austerity. With respect to the Egyptians, we know little of their religion and morality, in the early ages of that nation: but we may judge from analogy, that they continued for some time religious and virtuous; and know to a certainty, that in the time of Moses they were actually sunk in superstition and vice.

Question relative to the origin and effects of Paganism.

Having marked the tendency of true religion, and its salutary effects in some ancient kingdoms; I proceed to point out the mischiefs that have arisen, from ignorance or corruptions of the precepts which it enjoins. The history of these mischiefs, when exhibited, will furnish an argument of the excellence of that religion, which would prevent or remove them. True religion naturally prevents false opinions, and the various inconveniences which flow from them to individuals and communities: did men practise its precepts, these

(a) Bruckeri, Sect. 7.

incon-

inconveniences would have been removed; and many of them actually were abolished, in countries enlightened by the Jewish and Christian revelations. It might be expected, in point of order, that I should exhibit the effects of the patriarchal religion, and of that system of superstition which prevailed in the world, before the promulgation of the law. But, as history is not sufficiently clear on either of these points, I am obliged to confine myself to the effects of true and false religion, subsequent to that period. It appears from the history of almost all nations, that men entertain some ideas of divine worship; and that the human mind, unless properly directed, has generally attached itself to unworthy objects; the worship of which has been detrimental to society. Before I describe the effects of Pagan superstitions, it will be necessary to enquire into the origin of idolatry, and into the motives which prompted men to so abominable a practice. This enquiry, while it gratifies the curiosity of many readers, will enable them to understand, more thoroughly, the rise of Heathen superstitions; and the effects which they produced, on the conduct of the Gentiles. It is not easy to determine this question, in a satisfactory manner; as both ancient and modern authors are confused on the subject. Herodotus, Diodorus Siculus and Plutarch, differ from each other, and are obscure in explaining the rise of heathenism: while no modern mythologist has, in my opinion, treated it with so much clearness and appearance of probability, as Abbe Le Pluche; from whose writings I have extracted, what seems to me the most natural account of the origin of idolatry. I do not affirm, that this author's hypothesis is every where well founded; nay, it is admitted, that he sometimes pushes his argument too far, like all systematic writers; yet does his general history of the rise and progress of idolatry appear more natural, than that of any other writer, who has treated on this subject. But, as I have made only a short extract from his history of the Heavens; I refer my readers for a more ample account to Le Pluche's work or to Lilius Gyraldus, to whom he is chiefly indebted for information on this subject. A late author (*b*) justly celebrated for erudition, adopts Plutarch's opinion of the Egyptian Mythology, which Le Pluche had condemned as fabulous and groundless: had the learned Brucker read the history of the Heavens, he could not have differed from the ingenious Abbe, without attempting to refute him. They who desire further information on this subject, should also consult Banier, Bryant, and other writers, who are learned on this topic, though not so clear, upon the whole, as the author whose system I have adopted.

(*b*) Bruckeri Hist. Crit. de philosophia Egyptiorum, Cap. vii. Sect. 14.

SECT. 1.

All Mythologists are agreed, that we are to seek in Egypt for the origin of idolatry; and that in this fertile soil, it was nurtured and matured. But, though agreed in the soil and parents, which gave birth to the monster; yet they differ, in accounting for the manner of its production, and in tracing its strides, through so many nations of the earth. Le Pluche proves, that the Egyptians had several figures exposed to public view, which were intended, as an almanack or calendar, to divide the year, regulate the seasons, mark the times of sowing, the inundation or retreat of the Nile, and other important concerns. These figures were called symbols or hieroglyphics; and served as a language to express their wants, to retain the memory of past events, and to convey, in a short and popular way, various kinds of instruction. The primitive intention of them was, to remind men to glorify God; to acquaint them with the progress of the sun, the approach of the dog-days, and many particulars relative to husbandry. The safety of the Egyptians, and their success in agriculture, depended on the direction of the winds, the height of terraces, and the rising of the dog-star; and all these things were denoted by figures of birds and beasts, and of men, women and children in different dresses and attitudes, according to different circumstances. It was a general observation in Egypt, that the hawk flew from North to South, at the approach of mild weather; and there-

Anubis and Sphinx Egyptian symbols not real beings.

SECT. I. therefore the figure of that bird was thought a proper emblem of Etesian winds, which blew in that direction, about the summer solstice (c). The whoop was a bird which followed the course of the Nile, as it retired within its banks; and fed on new-born insects, that were generated from its mud. The figure of this bird, exhibited in public, was looked upon as a notice, that the waters were subsiding, and proclaimed the time of surveying and sowing their lands (d). The Nile overflowed soon after the sun had entered into Syrius; and the Egyptians called that star the dog-star, for its vigilance, and exhibited a symbol to give warning of the inundation. This figure, called Anubis, had the head of a dog, a vigilant animal, to guard them against the flood; a pot on his arms, to denote provisions; wings on his feet, that they may fly to their terraces; and this symbol was accompanied with a tortoise or duck, an amphibious bird, that lives by the water side; to express the situation of the Egyptians during the flood (e). The Sphinx was a public sign, which acquainted them, how high they were to raise their terraces, to escape the inundation: this figure had the face of a virgin, and the body of a lion couching; to express the inactivity which prevailed during the flood, and the time that elapsed, while the sun was passing through Leo and Virgo (f).

(c) Hist. of Heavens, Book I. Ch. i. N° 8.   (d) Ibid.
(e) Ibid. N° 7.   (f) Ibid. N° 8.

All

of Religion on Mankind.

All ancient nations, by a common custom, met at the New-moons, to offer up their praises and thankſgivings to God for his goodneſs and beneficence. The Egyptians did ſo, and filled the places where they met, with ſignificant figures expreſſive of an intelligence which gives heat and ſplendour to the ſun, fertility to the earth, and ſucceſs to induſtry. The principal of theſe figures were, at firſt, employed to expreſs the attributes of the Deity, and the regulations of huſbandry; but were afterwards made inſtruments of ſuperſtition and idolatry. The Egyptians made the ſun, the grandeſt viſible object, the emblem of the Almighty; repreſented it by a circle in their religious aſſemblies; proſtrated themſelves before it; and called that figure, which was only the ſymbol of God, the Eternal, the Father of Life, the Mighty, the moſt High. But the mind being, in all public acts of devotion, intent on the ſun and on that circle which was its emblem; they ſoon forgot God, aſcribed to the ſun thoſe attributes, and at length confounded the creature with the creator. They alſo repreſented the governor of the world, by the figure of a man bearing a ſceptre; ſometimes by that of a coachman with a whip; and called thoſe different figures Oſiris; a word which, in the original, ſignifies inſpector, leader, king, ſoul of the world and governor of the ſtars: all of which being attributes of the Deity; thoſe figures muſt have been intended as

SECT. I.

Oſiris and Neptune ſymbols not real beings.

emblems

SECT. I. emblems of them (g). The Egyptians, in process of time, miftook their moft diftinguifhed figure for the father of their nation; and afcribed to him feveral particulars of the hiftory of Ham. Finding the circle, the fymbol of God and of the fun, on the forehead of Ofiris, they confounded him with them; and afcribed divinity to Ham or Ammon, the father and founder of the kingdom of Egypt. Thofe figures had different appendages, to exprefs the attributes of the deity; ferpents or eels, which were fymbols of life and health in Egypt, denoted that God was the author of thofe advantages; and figures of fruitful plants were annexed to the circle or fphere, to mark the bounties of Providence. They had a figure of Ofiris, exhibited in public, to denote the annual return of trading fhips and merchandife; and called this figure Pofeidon or Neptune; words which fignify the provifion of maritime countries, and the arrival of fleets: this fymbol was afterwards fuppofed to be the figure of a god who delighted in the fea (h).

Ifis, Ceres, Diana and Venus.

The Egyptians had feveral female figures, each of which was called Ifis: one of them, with a fickle in her hand, denoted harveft; another, in a different drefs, was exhibited, when they met at their feafts, to return thanks to God for the

(g) Hift. of Heavens, Book I. ch. ii. N° 1. (h) Ibid. Book I. ch. i. N° 5.

fruits

fruits of the earth. At the feasts of new or full moons, they placed a crescent or full moon over the head of the symbol; they proclaimed a plentiful year, by an Isis surrounded with a multitude of breasts; and, on a year of scarcity, exposed an Isis with a single breast, which probably gave rise, to the fable of the Amazons (*i*). The Egyptian Isis was the same with the Phenician and Sicilian Ceres, the Demeter of the Greeks and Diana of the Ephesians. A figure of Isis, which marked the productions of the earth, was called Diana, and looked on as a terrestrial deity; sometimes, Diana was considered as the moon, from the crescent she wore; and sometimes, as the queen of hell; because, being for some time invisible about new moon, she was supposed to have then visited the regions of the dead. The poets have represented Diana as chaste; and yet are so inconsistent, as to mention her nightly visits to the shepherd Endymion; the origin of which calumny was as follows. It was usual to celebrate the ancient state of mankind, before the flood, near some beautiful grotto or fountain, called Endymion; and to place an Isis there, together with another figure, called Horus, the symbol of work. Endymion was the place where the figure of Diana was deposited; and the poets have represented it as a man, whom Diana was accused

(*i*) Hist. of Heavens, Book I. ch. i. Nº 10.

of visiting in the night (*k*). There was a figure of Isis, with a child in its lap, which was considered as the symbol of a fruitful woman; this figure was afterwards metamorphosed into a goddess, wholly employed, in disposing men and animals to propagation. This goddess was afterwards called Venus, from the girls who prostituted themselves in her temple, and who were called Venoth, in the language of the Phenicians (*l*).

Mars, Hercules, Vulcan, Apollo taken from Horus an Egyptian symbol.

The Egyptians had several figures, exhibited to public view, expressive of the successive operations of industry, and the state of agriculture; and they called each of them Horus, a word which signifies, in the original, husbandry or skill in agriculture. Sometimes they exhibited the symbol of a full grown man, at other times that of a child, and sometimes that of a youth. The different dresses of the same figure taught them when to begin, and when to end their annual works; and suggested every precaution that was necessary to accomplish them. Horus, with his hands and feet encumbered, and as it were swathed up, marked the inactivity which prevailed during the inundation; the figures were exhibited more free and disengaged in their limbs, as the waters subsided; and Horus asleep was the emblem of repose and rest from labour (*m*). When the

---

(*k*) Hist. of Heavens, Book I. ch. ii. N° 12.
(*l*) Ibid. N° 14.   (*m*) Ibid. Book I. ch. i. N° 10.

Egyp-

Egyptians were preparing for war, they dressed Horus in a military garb, and entitled him the formidable: this symbol was afterwards considered as the figure of a warrior, and assumed different names in diverse countries; Afis among the Syrians, Horus among the Gauls, Ares among the Greeks, and Mars among the Latins. The Thracians, and other warlike nations took him for an ancient worthy of their country, who assisted them in war (*n*). The figure of Horus armed with a club, and exhibited in public, gave notice, that the valiant were going to engage in an expedition, against some wild beast or notorious robber. This public sign, called Hercules, signified the eminent in war; but was afterwards mistaken for the statue of an hero, who was employed in the destruction of robbers and monsters (*o*). Horus, dressed like a blacksmith, was the emblem of mechanic arts, and called Vulcan, a word signifying work dispatched. When war was proclaimed, they separated the symbol of Vulcan from that of Isis, and substituted in its room that of Mars; which gave rise to the fable of Vulcan's jealousy, and the criminal correspondence of Venus and Mars (*p*). The figure of Horus armed with arrows and vanquishing the monster Python, expressed the retreat of the Nile, and the victory

(*n*) Hist. of Heavens, Book I. ch. ii. N° 20.
(*o*) Ibid.   (*p*) Ibid. N° 22.

SECT. I. of husbandry, in spite of the inundation. When this symbol was transported into the island Delos, it gave occasion to the fable of Apollo killing Python, and to the Pythian games afterwards celebrated in this and other places (*q*). Some figures of Horus were expressive of the works that were to be done in each season; and therefore Apollo was reported to have pronounced oracles, to have been acquainted with, and to have foretold future events (*r*).

Muses, Graces, Pallas, Pales, taken from the figures of Isis.

Egypt was free from inundation for nine months, and overflowed for three; and the Egyptians had nine different figures of Isis, to mark the first days of the nine, and three other figures to denote the three months of inundation. The nine figures gave rise to the fable of the Nine Muses, and the other three to the story of the Three Graces. We cannot entertain a doubt of the truth of this opinion; when we consider, that the original words translated Muses and Graces signify respectively safe from waters, and divorce or interruption of the correspondence between the cities, during the flood. The figure of Apollo, with his harp, was taken from that of Horus or husbandry, delighting himself with music, at the retreat of the waters; and we find the Nine Muses under the direction of Apollo, as those nine months

(*q*) Hist. of Heavens, Book I. ch. ii. N° 19.
(*r*) Ibid. No. 29.

were

were employed in works of induftry (s). It appears from the names and functions of the Athenian Pallas and the Sabine Pales, that they were taken from the Ifis of the Egyptians. Pales gave laws to the hufbandmen of Italy; Pallas taught the Athenians agriculture: and both thefe names fignify public order; in allufion to the functions of Ifis, who regulated the feafons by various figns peculiar to each. At Sais in Egypt a figure of Ifis was exhibited, as a public fign; to proclaim the marching of troops and levying of foldiers. The Athenians, who were a colony from Egypt, armed their Pallas in imitation of this figure; and borrowed the manufacture of linen from the inhabitants of Sais. The Egyptian Ifis bore in her hand a weaver's beam; and therefore the Athenians imagined that their goddefs taught them the manufacture of linen, the making of ftuffs, and the invention of arts (t).

The Egyptians had a figure, called Saturn, the fymbol of juftice, which was afterwards confidered as a real perfon by the Greeks, Romans and other nations. Homer fpeaks of him as quick-fighted in punifhing criminals, and he has been reprefented as fond of being worfhipped, by the effufion of human blood. To mark the end of the old and beginning of the new year, they painted an old man who feemed to bite off the head of

Symbols and funeral ceremonies of the Egyptians the fource of fables.

(s) Hift. of Heavens, Book I. ch. ii. N° 29.
(t) Ibid. N° 15.

his

his son; which gave rise to the fable of Saturn's devouring his own children (*u*). The funeral ceremonies of the Egyptians, and the symbols employed on the occasion, at first conveyed useful instructions relative to the state of the dead: but these symbols were afterwards considered as pictures of the treatment of the deceased in the next world. There was a burial ground near Memphis, on the borders of the lake Ackerusia, at the shore of which, certain judges enquired into the conduct of the deceased. If a man had not paid his debts, or had violated the laws, his body was left unburied, or probably was thrown into a sink called Tartarus (*w*). If no accuser appeared, or only a false accuser, his friends praised his respect for religion, equity, chastity and other virtues; conveyed his corpse over the lake into a plain called Elysium, embellished with brooks, groves and other rural ornaments, thrice sprinkled sand over it, gave three cries, and bid adieu to the dead. To express this in symbolic language they had a figure called Charon, which represented an incorruptible waterman who ferried over such only, as could stand the test. At the entrance of Elysium, they placed the figure of a dog with three heads, called Cerberus; a word signifying the cries of the grave: and they had

(*u*) Hist. of Heavens, Book I. ch. ii. N° 39.
(*w*) Ibid. Book I. ch. i. N° 17.

another

of Religion on Mankind.

another called Pluto, a symbol of the deliverance of the just; which was afterwards transformed into a god, who presided over hell (*x*). At places where carcasses were thrown, they exhibited a leaking vessel, into which water was incessantly poured, and many other figures frightful to behold; that of a man tied to a wheel which constantly turned; of another whose heart was perpetually gnawed by a vulture; and of one who rolled a stone up a hill without intermission, which returned immediately to furnish him with employment (*y*). These were probably symbols of incessant and endless tortures, to which the wicked were exposed; while the virtuous were conveyed into the mansions of the happy.

Fable of the Giants and Proserpine.

The descendants of Noah represented the dreadful effects resulting from the flood by symbols; and their principal feasts related to the dismal alteration experienced after the deluge. They denoted this event, by the figure of a water-monster, which rose from under ground; and by figures of monstrous giants that sprung out of the earth, to dethrone Osiris; whose names were Briareus, Othus, Ephialtes, Enceladus, Mimas, Porphyrion, and Rhecus. These figures marked the disorders that followed the flood, and the unhappy state of mankind after that period. Their names, translated in the order in which they are

(*x*) Hist. of Heavens, Book I. Chap. ii. N° 2.
(*y*) Ibid. Book I. Chap. i. N° 17.

D   written,

SECT. I. written, signify loss of serenity, diversity of seasons, gatherings of clouds unknown before, the havocks occasioned by inundations, earthquakes, great rains and storms. According to the fable, Osiris defeated those giants; and his son Horus, the symbol of industry, assumed the head and claws of a lion, to resist Rhecus, or the wind, which destroyed his hopes. This part of the fable intimated, that they could not avoid the dreadful effects of Rhecus, or the wind, but by watching the sun's entrance into the sign Leo (z). The Egyptians had a figure of Isis, which represented the ancient state of the earth disordered by the flood; this symbol regretted the loss of her former fecundity, the want of food to nourish, and of fire to warm and light the people. This figure, afterwards called Ceres, gave rise to the fable of that goddess lighting torches, and with grief and diligence seeking her daughter Proserpine; a word which signifies corn lost among a crowd of weeds (a).

Mercury, Memnon and Bacchus.

The observance of the dog-star procured the Egyptians an abundance of corn; and this people enriched themselves by selling to foreigners. For this reason, the figure of Anubis was often accompanied with a full purse; and men styled it the dealer, the cunning, or only commerce. This symbol was called Camillus among the Hetrurians,

(z) Hist. of Heavens, Book I. Ch. i. N° 14.
(a) Ibid. Book I. Ch. ii. N° 45.

Janus,

Janus, among the Latins, Hermes, among the Greeks, and Mercury, among the Phenicians. This figure, from being a public sign, was converted into the god of commerce and intrigue: holding in its hand a long pole to meafure the rifing of the waters; it was afterwards taken for a leader, an ambaffador or an orator. The wings on his feet, at firſt intended to remind them to fly to their terraces, made them miſtake him for a meſſenger. The fable of the Statue of Memnon, daily uttering a found at funrife, arofe from the fymbol of Horus, exhibited in public, which directed the huſbandman, what works were to be done every day in the year (b). When the Egyptians commemorated the infancy of huſbandry after the flood, they repreſented it by the fymbol of Horus or a child: and the Greeks, who imitated the Egyptians in their repreſentations, took this fymbolic child for a real one, the fon of Semele, and called Bacchus in Italy, and Dionyfus in Greece, from the expreſſions of forrow made ufe of at this folemnity. That Horus and Bacchus were the fame, appears from the writings of the poets, who afcribe to Bacchus all the attributes of Horus, and the operations of induſtry. It was huſbandry, and not any man that ever exiſted, which guarded againſt inundations of rivers and tides (c); extracted rivers of wine, milk and ho-

(b) Hiſt. of Heavens, Book I. Ch. ii. N° 26.
(c) Hor. Lib. II. Ode xix.

SECT. I.

ney from barren soil, and vanquished Rhecus, or the wind, by observing the sun's entrance into the sign Leo (d).

Origin of the worship of animals, of augury and other superstitions.

We shall find, that animal worship, augury and other superstitions, had a similar foundation. It was usual with the ancient Egyptians to lead about, at their feasts, certain animals of the same name with the sign, into which the sun entered at that season. The harvest was ended at Thebes, when the sun entered Aries; at Memphis, when he entered Taurus; and at Mendes, when he entered into the Kids. They led about, at their respective feasts, these animals; and in process of time worshipped the ram at Thebes, the ox at Memphis, and goats at Mendes. At the great feast of Isis, a living dog walked foremost in the procession as the emblem of the dog-star; which gave rise to the reverence paid to dogs in many parts of Egypt. Every beast used in their ceremonies, in time became objects of adoration, as the ram, kids, bulls, goats, fishes, serpents, crocodiles, wolves, and several others; and even plants were worshipped, whose foliage was added to the figures of those animals (e). The ancient Egyptians never embarked, sowed or planted, without consulting the figures of birds, which served as weathercocks, to mark the direction of winds and changes of the weather. The hawk, whoop, Numidian

(d) Le Pluche, Book I. Ch. ii. N° 45.
(e) Ibid. Book I. Ch. ii. N° 41, 42.

hen

hen and Ibis, were public symbols which represent- SECT. I.
ed certain winds and gave intelligence about the
weather, the success of husbandry, navigation,
trade, war and other undertakings. In process
of time they forgot the original import of those
figures; and consulted real chickens and other
birds at Rome and other places about future events.
The husbandman or traveller no longer observed
the symbols, in order to know how the winds
blew; but waited until some bird appeared, to
give the wished-for information; and imagined
that birds, which accidentally crossed the air, were
messengers of the gods to acquaint them of their
intentions. Even the appendages of the principal figures were converted into instruments of
idolatry: the symbols Osiris, Isis, Horus and Anubis sometimes held a scepter; at other times an
horn to call the people together; sometimes a president's crook to denote a feast where he presided;
sometimes a pole to measure the Nile; a reed to
signify the support of the vine; and a distaff to
mark the helps afforded by the loom. The import of these symbols was in time forgotten; and
the scepter, hook and other appendages of the
principal figures, were considered as instruments in
prognosticating events. Even flutes, lyres, and
other musical instruments, employed in their feasts,
were mistaken for instruments of divination; various dresses of the same figure gave birth to a
new god; and gods were multiplied as much as

symbols,

SECT. I.

Origin of idolatry and the worship of false gods.

symbols, by the interpretation of philosophers and embellishment of poets (*f*).

Le Pluche proves, with a tolerable degree of clearness, that other figures had a similar intention; and that the entire group of heathen gods and goddesses originated in Egypt from the use of symbols. That, the Cretans and other nations adopted them, with some variations in attire, name or attributes; that the Phenicians and others, who came to Egypt for corn, introduced them into Europe and Asia; and that the Greeks and Romans transformed them into so many gods and goddesses, demigods and heroes, to whom they ascribed genealogies and historical events. At first, there was nothing mysterious in symbols; they were significant and expressive of their wants, and like a language which every person understood. After the invention of letters, the symbolic language became obsolete, and priests and learned men retained the use of symbols at feasts, burials, and in the outward ceremonies of religion. But in general the original intention of them was forgotten, and men stupidly gazed at them, without understanding their meaning. Interpreters explained them variously, as best suited their fancies or interests; and to these men we may ascribe the extravagant stories of heroes and demigods, which never existed except in the imaginations of men. Had they any foundation in nature, the

(*f*) Le Pluche, Book I. Ch. iii. N° 1.

heathen

heathen mythology could not have fo abounded with errors, fables and contradictions of expofitors. Symbols were the alphabet of the ancients; and it is as abfurd to feek in nature for any creature like the Sphinx or Anubis, as to enquire into the genealogy of any letter in the alphabet. It may feem extraordinary, that the Egyptians fhould miftake the original meaning of the fymbol of the feafons, which annually returned and was frequently renewed. But it is obvious, that as the old Egyptian year confifted of three hundred and fixty-five days, without intercalation; the feafts and feafons muft have been gradually difplaced. When the fymbols no longer expreffed the feafons, or the works and feafts proper to them; men naturally forgot that they related to them, or were intended to regulate them (*g*). The author of the Philofophical Principles of Religion is of opinion, that the defcendants of Noah engraved on ftone, in hieroglyphics, the doctrines of religion and other important truths; dreading another deluge, and thinking this a furer method, than oral tradition, to convey information to pofterity. This writer maintains, that in time men forgot the true import of thofe facred fymbols, and gradually fell into idolatry and fuperftition (*h*).

A learned author affirms, that the firft founder of Egyptian erudition engraved on pillars his laws; Brucker's opinion examined.

(*g*) Le Pluche, Book I. Ch. i. N° 8.
(*h*) Ramfay, Vol. II. Introd.

SECT. I. and expressed them by figures of animals and other parts of nature, that they might not be loft or forgotten. That symbols were at first invented to elucidate and not to obscure doctrines; not to make religion mysterious, but to render its sublime and intellectual ideas familiar to the vulgar. So far Brucker and Ramsay concur in opinion with the ingenious Abbé; but the former differs from Le Pluche, with respect to the foundation of Egyptian theology, and the origin of idolatry in other nations. Brucker adopts Plutarch's opinion, that the most ancient gods of Egypt were men deified for the benefits conferred by them on mankind. He denies that the Egyptians supposed mere men to be gods, but says they believed a divine energy to have pervaded the universe, some effluvia or particles of which reside in men, who surpassed themselves in genius and useful inventions. He also contends, that Egyptians worshipped the sun, stars and planets as useful to men, animated by some divine influence, and the chief residence of the deity. He owns that the ignorant worshipped the stars and sun without reserve, while the wise considered them only as his throne and residence (*i*). I have rejected the opinion of this very learned writer as founded on hypothesis, and unsupported by a single conclusive or even probable argument. Osiris, Isis and others, whom Le

(*i*) Brucker de philosophia Ægyptiorum, Cap. vii. Sect. 8 and 14.

Pluche

Pluche proves to have never exifted, Brucker fuppofes to be real perfons, who flourifhed in Egypt. He denies that Egyptians worfhipped mere men, and yet admits that wife, good and ufeful men were objects of their veneration. This author, confcious of his own inability to explain the fignification of fymbols, affigns feveral caufes of difficulty and obfcurity in them. He afferts, that Egypt underwent feveral changes from inundations, which obliged the ancient inhabitants to migrate; and from the invafions of foreigners, who introduced new cuftoms and new doctrines into that country. The Egyptians being ridiculed by foreigners, for the worfhip of the fun, ftars, heroes and animals; the ingenious attempts to explain their fuperftitions have added to the obfcurity (*k*). Priefts alfo contributed to render hieroglyphics obfure, by explaining them in a manner which was calculated to impofe on an ignorant and fervile people, and to promote their own intereft and that of their rulers (*l*). Poets too contributed to render the heathen mythology obfcure, by celebrating the fame of heroes in hyperbolic language; and by afcribing to them the attributes of the Supreme Being. To thefe heroes, the divines, who were poets, fung praifes in verfe, with which fort of compofition, among the ancients, fable and fiction were always found united.

(*k*) Brucker de philofophia Æpyptiorum, Cap. vii. Sect. 12.
(*l*) Ibid. Sect. 2.

SECT. I.

Causes of obscurity in heathen mythology.

When once the fabulous age of the poets began, the sense of ancient symbols was disfigured; the most sublime truths were turned into extravagant visions; and in time, the original import of hieroglyphics was lost or forgotten, in the numerous interpretations of expositors. Historical interpreters imagined, that the fictions of poets contained the genuine history of kings and generals; and applied to these, as to real personages, what had been related of kings and heroes in the fables of poets. Physiologists interpreted symbols, in a physical way, by the different parts and operations of nature, of which they thought them emblems or representations. The Stoics, says Seneca (*m*), represent the several functions of the Supreme Being, under different names; sometimes they call him Bacchus, the father and fountain of all beings; Hercules, because indefatigable and invincible; and Mercury, from the reason, order and wisdom of his proceedings. St. Augustine (*n*) assures us, that the true God assumed different names, according to the effects which he produced. " In the ethereal spaces he is called Jupiter, in the air Juno, in the sea Neptune, in the earth Pluto, in hell Proserpine, in the element of fire Vulcan, in the sun Phœbus, in divination Apollo, in war Mars, in the forest Diana, and in the sciences Minerva; all that crowd of gods and

(*m*) De Beneficiis, Cap. xii.   (*n*) De Civ. Dei, Lib. IV. Cap. x.

goddesses are only the same Jupiter whose different powers and attributes are differently expressed." Anaximander, Democritus, Epicurus, Lucretius, and all the materialists thus understood symbols, contrary to the spirit of those ancient hieroglyphics. These men considered the combats of the gods, with the Titans, as allegories expressive of the different changes and discord of the elements; and the effects of those explanations were fable and impiety (*o*). Some refined philosophers as Zoroaster, Pythagoras, Socrates and Plato, explained the symbols and fables of the poets in a theological way, and maintained, that they represented things spiritual and divine. Certain Jews and Christians held, that heathen mythology was founded upon the writings of the Hebrews, and on the history of that people; that Osiris and Jupiter were Adam; Isis and Juno, Eve; Tubalcain, Vulcan; Bacchus, Noah; that Apollo, Adonis, Mythras, Mars, Mercury and Hercules were Abraham, Moses, Joshua; and, in short, that all the Jewish heroes were gods of the Gentiles. This system, though defended by the learned Bochart, Vossius, Huet, Thomasin, Gale and other writers, is improbable and ill-founded for many reasons; but for one especially, that Heathens, who hated the Hebrews, were unlikely

(*o*) Ramsay, Vol. II. Introd.

SECT. I. to deify their legislators, or pay divine honours to the worthies of that nation (*p*).

Cicero's opinion examined. Some have imagined that poets, who give life and energy to things inanimate, have encreased the number of popular deities, by giving the name of some god to things salutary and useful to mankind: to the earth Ceres, to the sea Neptune, and to the air Juno. Cicero (*q*) affirms that the Egyptians worshipped no beast, except for the advantages derived from it to society; as the Ibis, for preserving the country from the plague, and devouring winged serpents brought thither from the desarts of Lybia. And as poets, by magnifying the achievements of heroes, and ascribing divine attributes to them, caused men to erect altars and monuments in honour of them; so painters and sculptors seconded the fiction, and contributed, not a little, to the establishment of those errors. Tully (*r*) assures us, that men formed ideas of Jupiter, Juno and the rest of the gods, from images and statues presented to their senses by painters and statuaries. I admit that poets, painters and sculptors, by their fables and representations, have confirmed and riveted the errors of the people: but the Roman orator does not explain the origin of idolatry, nor shew what gave rise to poetical fables and representations of

(*p*) Ramsay, Vol. II. Introd. Sect. 12.
(*q*) De Nat. Deorum, Lib. I. Cap. xxxvi.
(*r*) Ibid. Cap. xxix.

their

their gods. He shews indeed, that the people were misled by poets and artists; but gives no hint of the source of error in those men themselves. It is admitted, that poets and painters are apt to indulge their fancies, and accustomed to exaggerate; but usually borrow from nature or history the outlines of their work: what foundation then was there in nature for the Sphinx or Chimera, or in history for the fabulous account of Jupiter and Juno? Le Pluche has cleared up the difficulty, told us what suggested those ideas to poets and painters, and explained the origin of Pagan superstitions.

Having enquired into the origin and progress of idolatry, I proceed to examine the effects of the superstitious opinions entertained in Egypt, Greece, Italy, and other Gentile nations less polished and civilized. In treating this subject, I shall not trouble my readers with the fables and genealogies of the Heathen gods and goddesses, which are known to every school-boy; but shall make such observations on the popular religion of the Pagans, as may enable men to perceive its tendency and effects, and the necessity of revelation to abolish or prevent its pernicious influence. The ancient Egyptians celebrated several feasts, in honour of their gods; at which were exhibited many scenes of cruelty and disorder. In the feast of Isis, they tumbled an ass down a precipice; in that of Mars, they fought furiously with clubs; and in the feasts

of

of Bacchus, they indulged freely in riot and debauchery (s). Nothing could be more abfurd than the worſhip paid by the Egyptians to cats, dogs, wolves, crocodiles, and ſeveral kinds of beaſts. They had lands ſet apart for their maintenance; and perſons of diſtinction attended them; who were reſpected for being engaged in that ſacred office. If any of theſe animals was killed with deſign, the offender was inſtantly put to death; if involuntarily, he was puniſhed at the diſcretion of the prieſts; when dead they were lamented, and their funerals celebrated with great expence and ſolemnity. The ancient Egyptians had ſo ſuperſtitious a veneration for a cat, that the killing this animal undeſignedly was puniſhed with death (t). Diodorus Siculus aſſures us, that the populace were ſo enraged at a Roman, who accidentally killed a cat, that neither the authority of the king, nor reſpect for the Roman name, could ſave him from deſtruction: they even choſe to eat each other, in a ſeaſon of famine, rather than kill one of thoſe ſacred animals (u). There was a ſpotted calf kept at Memphis, in beautiful fields; all whoſe motions were judged ominous and prophetical; and to which offerings were made under the title of Apis. This idol was

(s) Roſs's Religion of all Nations, Sect. 2.
(t) Ancient Univ. Hiſt. Vol. I. folio, Book I. Ch. iii.
(u) Broughton's Dict. Art. Ælurus.

consulted, by observing into which of two chambers, prepared for him, he entered; and prognostics were drawn from his accepting or declining food that was offered him. They prevented the indecency of his death, by drowning him; interred him with devotion mixed with sorrow; and then sought for a calf with similar spots. They had also a sacred ox, at Heliopolis, which brought crowds thither, to offer up their devotions; and priests encouraged those frauds from motives of interest (*w*). The principal gods of Egypt were worshipped all over the kingdom; while the worship of inferior deities was not universal, but confined to particular cities and provinces. Several cities were denominated from the gods or animals worshipped in them, as Diospolis, Heliopolis, and Cynopolis; almost every city worshipped a different idol, and the inhabitants of some eat the animals reverenced by others. Diodorus Siculus affirms, that this diversity of worship was a source of disturbances; and that those dissensions were fomented by kings, in order to divide the turbulent into adverse sects, to keep them employed in religious contention, and thus to prevent conspiracies against them (*x*). Cambyses the Persian monarch, in his war against Egypt, laid siege to Pelusium; and, finding his

(*w*) Hist. of the Heavens, Book I. Ch. ii. N° 42.
(*x*) Ancient Univ. Hist. Vol. I. folio, Book I. Ch. iii. Sect. 1.

troops galled by the enemies arrows, made use of a stratagem which succeeded admirably. He placed in the front of his army a multitude of cats, dogs, sheep, and other sacred animals: protected by these, he advanced with safety to the garrison, and made himself master of it; the Egyptians being afraid, even to throw a dart (*y*). Hence it is evident, that the superstitions of Egypt had a considerable influence on the policy of that country, and the temper of its inhabitants; while they did not in the least improve the morals of the people. Juvenal (*z*) thus describes the superstitions of Egypt and the effects of them, in his fifteenth satire:

> Quis nescit, Volusi Bithynice, qualia demens
> Ægyptus portenta colat? Crocodilon adorat
> Pars hæc: illa pavet saturam serpentibus Ibim.
> Illic cæruleos, hic piscem fluminis, illic
> Oppida tota canem venerantur, nemo Dianam.
> Porrum et cæpe nefas violare, ac frangere morsu.
> O Sanctas gentes, quibus hæc nascuntur in hortis
> Numina! Lanatis animalibus abstinet omnis
> Mensa. Nefas illic fætum jugulare capellæ;
> Carnibus humanis vesci licet.

> Fish-gods you'll meet with fins and scales o'ergrown:
> Diana's dogs ador'd in ev'ry town;
> Her dogs have temples, but the goddess none.
> 'Tis mortal sin an onion to devour;
> Each clove of garlick has a sacred pow'r:

(*y*) Polyænus Strategematum, Lib. VII. Cap. ix.
(*z*) Beginning of Satire, and Dryden's Translation.

> Religious nations sure and bless'd abodes,
> Where ev'ry orchard is o'ergrown with gods.
> To kill, is murder, sacrilege to eat
> A kid or lamb—man's flesh is lawful meat!

Heathen nations attributed to their gods anger, fear, grief, jealousy, and several passions and imperfections unworthy of the divine nature. Tertullian (*a*) asks the Gentiles the following questions: is there any of your deities equal in wisdom to Socrates, in justice to Aristides, in war to Themistocles, in greatness to Alexander, in prosperity to Polycrates, in eloquence to Demosthenes? which of them is so grave or wise as Cato, so excellent a soldier as Scipio, so mighty as Pompey, so rich as Crassus, or so eloquent as Cicero? The Heathen religion did not promote the honour of God, or the good of his creatures; the gods of the Gentiles were rather branded for their vices, than distinguished for their virtues; and patronized impurity by their lives and actions. They were guilty of adultery and incest, stole, murdered, and committed the most unnatural crimes: according to the popular religion, Mercury was a thief, Venus a prostitute, Bacchus a drunkard, and Jove dethroned his father Saturn, who had murdered his own offspring, and who was delighted with sacrifices of little children. Homer, though he calls Jupiter father and king

Popular religion of other Pagan nations.

(*a*) Apolog. Cap. x. xi.

of gods, counsellor, deliverer, defender of houses and cities; yet makes him guilty of incest with his sister Juno and his daughter Minerva; of pederasty with Ganymede, and of ravishing Europa and several others. According to the theology of this poet, the father of men and gods is the author of strife (*b*); encourages the Trojans to perjury by his daughter Venus; loves Sarpedon and Hector and grieves for them (*c*). The other gods conspired against Jupiter and would have bound him with chains had they not dreaded Briareus (*d*). Mars and Venus are wounded by Diomede; gods and goddesses are armed against each other; and Jupiter expresses a more ardent passion for his wife Juno, than he ever did for any of his wives or mistresses before (*e*). This god lay with Alcmena in the shape of her husband: and Minerva assisted Ulysses to hide his money in a cave, and to wrestle with a beggar (*f*). So unworthy were the ideas which the Tyrians entertained of their gods, that they chained the statue of Hercules, that he might not desert to Alexander the Great who besieged them (*g*): while the Persians adored Arimanius the author of evil; the Greeks their Cacodemons, and the Latins their Vejoves (*h*). Hea-

---

(*b*) Iliad IV. 34.   (*c*) Iliad XVI. 433, and XXII. 168.   (*d*) Iliad I. 399.   (*e*) Iliad XIV. 315.   (*f*) Odyss. Lib. XIII.   (*g*) Quin. Curt. Lib. IV. cap. xiv.   (*h*) De Nat. Deorum, Lib. III. Sect. xxiv.

thens made offerings to a fever, winds, and to every thing that could hurt them; and Theseus and Alexander the Great sacrificed to fear, that their troops might not be terrified on the _y of battle. Titus Tatius worshipped the goddess Cloacina, and both Greeks and Romans erected temples to contumely, impudence, and licentiousness (*i*). The gods of the Gentiles were so impure, obscene and detestable, that Julius Africanus advised their votaries, to convert their temples into theatres, and their players into priests; that they might sing the amours and impieties of their gods. Plato condemned the Pagan theology, and the genealogies of the gods, by Hesiod and Homer, as false and impolitic; and maintained that, though true, they ought not to be published; as tending to debauch the morals of youth, and encouraging revenge, murder, rapes, drukenness, theft, and rebellion against parents. This philosopher condemns Homer, for representing the Gods as constantly engaged in feuds and contention; and asserts, that poetical fables ought to serve the wise purposes of policy or morals (*k*). Cicero applauds Plato for banishing Homer and other poets from his imaginary republic; " Since even their absurdities do mischief by the pleasantness of the stile in which they are written: these men introduced gods inflamed with anger and

(*i*) Tully de Leg. Lib. II. cap. xi. and xvii.
(*k*) Eusebii Præp. Evang. Lib. XIII. ch. ii.

SECT. I. lust; and exhibited their wars, wounds, hatred, dissensions, births, deaths, complaints, lamentations, their excessive intemperance, adulteries, fetters, copulations with mortals, and men sprung from immortal gods (*l*)." Such was part of " the beautiful mythology which, according to Mr. Gibbon, pervades and animates the compositions of Homer, Virgil, and other poets," though the most impure and deformed that fancy could devise! This historian represents Pagan worship as consisting of sacrifices, processions, spectacles, feasts, good humour and elegant arts, and omits every circumstance which proves it a system of lust, cruelty, and immorality. Had the historian of the Roman empire known, that Plato and Cicero had condemned this system, he might perhaps have had some deference for their authority, and not have censured the fathers for reprehending the poets. I cannot suppose this writer so depraved in taste and morals, as to be enamoured of paganism, and to call its rites elegant ceremonies and innocent devotions, had he examined its deformity or the effects which it produced. It will presently appear, that these effects were such as might naturally have been expected from their opinions of their gods. The author of the Jewish letters (*m*) briefly sums up these effects in the fol-

(*l*) De Nat. Deorum, Lib. I. Sect. xvi. and Tusculan Quest. Lib. II. ch. xi.   (*m*) Part III. Letter I. Sect. iii.

lowing

lowing words: "Here behold a sacrifice of female modesty; there human blood flows upon the altars, and the dearest victims expire in those flames which superstition has lighted up. A little further violence is offered to nature, by brutal love; every where the people live in shocking ignorance, and the philosopher in error and uncertainty." It will now appear that these and other crimes were the genuine fruits of Heathen superstitions.

An universal corruption of manners was the natural consequence of Heathen theology; the morals of Heathens were such, as might reasonably be expected from the conceptions which they formed of adulterous, incestuous, and impure gods; whom they thought it laudable to imitate in all their abominations. The Pagan gods being guilty of enormous crimes, their votaries suited their worship and practice to the ideas which they entertained of them. He who wished to commit adultery was encouraged by the example of Jupiter, he that was delighted with unnatural love, viewed Ganymede in Jove's embraces, or Hiacinthus in Apollo's; and the horror of incest was extenuated, if not excused, by the marriage of Jupiter to his sister Juno. Venus, the patroness of strumpets, promoted numberless adulteries, rapes and incests by her example and suggestions: she had a son by her brother Mercury (*n*), and

Impurity, adultery and drunkenness, effects of Paganism.

(*n*) Tooke's Pantheon, Part II. Ch. vii. Sect. 2.

incited

SECT. I. incited and assisted Nictimene (o) and Myrrha (p) to commit incest with their fathers. The Romans, who boasted a descent from her son Eneas, erected temples in honour of her, and she was the chief goddess worshipped at Rome, by all females. Harlots worshipped her for gain, pure virgins for beauty, matrons for concord with their husbands, widows for husbands, and all for fecundity (q). The Athenians, Chians, Thracians and others, originally worshipped Cotytto, the goddess of wantonness, with the most lewd and immodest rites; and her priests, called Baptæ, celebrated her mysteries, in the night, with dancing and all manner of obscenities. Eupolis wrote a play on the impure practices of the Baptæ, and these men, in revenge, flung him into the sea (r). The Phenician women used annually to shave their heads in token of grief, for the death of Adonis the favourite of Venus. They who refused to comply, were bound to prostitute themselves for an entire day, to all strangers that desired it; and the money was presented to her temple, where lewdness and the most impure commerce was practised, to mitigate the sorrows of the mournful goddess (s). Heathens had several lascivious figures of Jupiter, by one of which Terence's Cherea (t) was encouraged to a rape. Example is more pre-

(o) Ovid. Met. Lib. II. (p) Ibid. Lib. X. (q) Ross, Sect. 4. (r) Broughton, Art. Baptæ. (s) Anc. Univ. Hist. Vol. I. folio, Chap. vi. Sect. 1. (t) Eunuch.

valent

valent than precept, and men, difpofed to gratify their paffions, were more influenced by the actions of Jupiter, than by the doctrines of Plato, or the maxims of Cato; and never wanted the example of a God to juftify adultery, fornication, and the moft unnatural pollutions (*u*). Even the public worfhip of Pagans exhibited, in fome cafes, fcenes of lewdnefs and impurity. Priefts almoft naked, celebrated the Lupercalia in honour of Pan (*w*); and the learded Potter affirms, that fome rites employed in the Greek feftivals were impure; though confidered by fome as innocent devotions. The Locrenfes vowed, that if victorious in a war in which they were engaged, they would proftitute their virgins on the feftivals of Venus (*x*). The Aphrodifia, in honour of Venus, were celebrated in different parts of Greece with impure rites; and in her temple at Byblus in Syria, women proftituted themfelves to ftrangers on a certain day, and the hire of impurity was confecrated to that Goddefs (*y*). Such were the unhappy effects of Mr. Gibbon's innocent devotions, and of ignorance of the worfhip of the one true God! But thefe were not the only fruits of his elegant mythology; the ancient Greeks celerated night feftivals, called Nyctelia, in honour of Bacchus, with lighted torches, drinking, and

(*u*) De Civ. Dei, Lib. II. Cap. vii. (*w*) Kennet.
(*x*) Juftin, Lib. XXI. Cap. iii. (*y*) Leland's Chrift. Revelation, Part I. Chap. vii.

SECT. I. the worst of impurities; and the Romans afterwards celebrated them in Italy (z). Such scenes of licentiousness were exhibited on the festivals of Bacchus, that matrons were warned not to be present at them; and Aristippus, speaking of a chaste woman, says, she will not be corrupted, even at the Bacchanalia (a). So abominable were the rapes, poisons, and murders in Rome and other places on those feasts, that they were abolished in Rome by the Roman senate; and at Thebes by Diagondas, as Cicero (b) assures us.

Paganism a source of cruelty.

We have already proved, that Pagan superstitions produced the natural effects in some instances; and the same will appear from the following facts, with which history acquaints us. In Sparta boys were severely scourged in honour of Diana Orthia, and the cruel ceremony was performed so rigorously, that they often died on the occasion (c). The Romans, in the beginning of a war with the Gauls, buried alive two males and two females, in obedience to an oracle (d); and Porphyry affirms, that in his own time a man was slain at the feast of Jupiter Latiaris (e). The priests of Bellona offered sacrifice to that goddess, in their own blood (f); held in each hand naked swords, with

(z) Broughton, Art. Nyctelia. (a) Sext. Emp. Pyrrhoniarum, Lib. III. Cap. xxiv. (b) De Leg. Lib. II. Cap. xv. (c) Potter's Antiq. (d) Plutarch's Life of Marcellus. (e) Leland, Part I. Chap. 7. (f) Tooke, Part II. Chap. ix.

which

which they cut themselves, and wildly ran up and down like men mad or poffeffed (*g*). In time of public calamities, governors offered up children to avenging fpirits, to avert the evils which they felt, or with which they were threatened. The Carthaginians attempted to remove a peftilence by facrificing innocent children on the altars of their gods (*h*), and Agamemnon put his daughter Iphigenia to death, to appeafe the anger of Diana whofe ftag he had flain. The Phenicians were obliged to offer annual facrifices of infants to Saturn, and the ancient Carthaginians to Moloch. Among the latter people, mothers were required to attend the facrifices of their own children, to ftifle their feelings, and even to affect joy at the cries of their infants: if a tear or groan efcaped, the offering was fuppofed to lofe its merit, with thofe blood-thirfty deities. The bloody facrifices, which prevailed among the Carthaginians, had a confiderable influence on the manners of that people; they were cruel and inhuman both to friends and enemies, and callous to every fentiment of tendernefs and pity. The Druids facrificed human victims to their gods; fome they pierced with darts; others they crucified; and laid fome on piles and burned them to death. Thofe barbarous practices induced Auguftus to prohibit the religion of the Druids, and thofe cruel rites were

---

(*g*) Lact. Lib V. Cap. x. and Lib. I. Cap. xxi. (*h*) Juftin, Lib. XVIII. Cap. vi.

quite

SECT. I. quite abolished by Tiberius and Claudius (*i*). On this and other crimes of Heathens, Lactantius (*k*) makes the following very pertinent observations: How could they abstain from blood who worshipped such bloody gods as Mars and Bellona? How should they spare their parents, who worshipped Jupiter that banished his father out of heaven? Or spare their children, who adored Saturn that devoured his own children? How should they preserve chastity who worshipped a naked and adulterous goddess and common prostitute? How shall they abstain from robbery and fraud, who are acquainted with the thefts of Mercury, and teach that to deceive, is not fraud, but cunning? How shall they bridle their lusts who adore Jupiter, Hercules, Bacchus, Apollo and others, whose adulteries and impieties are acted and sung on theatres that they might be known to all? How shall they be just who are encouraged in injustice by the example of their gods." These crimes were the fruits of that system, from which Mr. Gibbon has ingeniously selected, what he calls elegant rites and innocent devotions. Strange, that he should extol a system blended with rites so detestable and hideous; while he saps the foundation of that pure and benevolent code, which tends to abolish those

---

(*i*) Suet. in Claudio, Cap. xxv. Broughton, Art. Druids, and Strabo, Lib. IV. edit. Amstelod. 1707, p. 308. (*k*) Lib. V. de Justitia.

crimes, and actually has abolished them in all countries, where it has been promulgated!

Besides the acts of cruelty already ascribed to Paganism, there are several others, equally shocking, which have originated from that source. The ancient Germans, Gauls and Britons worshipped the sun, stars and planets, and sometimes sacrificed men to their idols. The Scythians and Thracians offered every hundredth captive to Mars; the Germans paid the same compliment to Mercury; and the Cimbrian priestesses used to cut the throats of captives, that they might foretel the event of war by inspecting their bowels. The Lithuanians ripped open mens bowels, for the same purpose; and imagined they did not please the devil, unless they tortured captives before they sacrificed them (*l*). We find instances of human sacrifices, not only in barbarous countries, but even in Greece and other civilized nations. Themistocles (*m*), in order to procure the assistance of the gods against the Persians, sacrificed some captives of that nation; and Bacchus (*n*) had an altar, in Arcadia, upon which young damsels were beaten to death with rods. Achilles butchered twelve Trojan captives at the funeral of Patroclus (*o*); and Eneas, so famed for piety, offered up eight persons as sacrifices to Pallas (*p*). The inhuman sacrifices

(*l*) Ross, Sect. v.   (*m*) Plutarch's Life.   (*n*) Broughton, Art. Sacrifices.   (*o*) Homer's Iliad, xxiii. 175.   (*p*) Virgil's Æneis, x. 520.

SECT. I. offered to Moloch, Saturn, and Pagan idols; and the detestable practices in the service of Baal-Berith, Cybele, Venus, and other deities, should inspire an horror of those superstitions, and induce us to admire that religious system which is free from them; and which has abolished similar practices in all countries, where it has been introduced. The poet was prompted by bloody offerings, so common in ancient times; and by ignorance of true religion, to confound superstition and rational worship, and to impute to the latter the fruits of the former. The sacrifice of Iphigenia, at the port of Aulis, occasioned Lucretius (*q*) to make this confusion, and to ascribe to religion the fruits of superstition.

> ——————————*Sæpius olim*
> *Religio peperit scelerosa atque impia facta.*
>
> Consider that religion did, and will
> Contrive, promote, and act the greatest ill.

And again,

> *Tantum religio potuit suadere malorum.*
>
> So died this innocent, this royal maid,
> Such devilish acts religion could persuade.

Heathens have been guilty of many other crimes; but I have confined myself, in this place, to those only which were committed, in compliance with their superstitions. The crimes perpetrated in

(*q*) Lucretius, Book I. v. 84 and 102, Creech's translation.

conformity with the prejudices of the Gentiles, furnish an argument in support of that religion, which tends to remove those prejudices. The bad effects, resulting from false religion or from corruptions of the true, prove the excellence of the latter, and point out to rulers the duty of directing the minds of their subjects, to the proper object of worship, if not to obtain the advantages which naturally flow from true religion, at least to prevent the inconveniences which have arisen from false. If the land be not sowed with good seed, it will be overgrown with noxious weeds; superstition or enthusiasm will occupy the place of true religion, and be made instruments in promoting the schemes of the wicked and designing. This has been the case in Pagan countries, and even in countries, where true religion has been perverted or misunderstood; as will fully appear in the course of this history.

Perhaps it may be expected that the bad effects of Paganism were counteracted by its ministers, by theatrical performers, by the wisdom of philosophers and the policy of statesmen. We shall find, that this last was some barrier against vice and immorality; while the other three were but feeble restraints, and, in some instances, rather encouraged men in vice than deterred them from it. The heathen gods neither furnished their votaries with moral precepts, nor offered motives to the practice

Pagan priests and players did not restrain vice in the Roman empire.

practice of them: Augustine (r) denies, that Pagans ever delivered moral precepts, in the name of those gods; and challenges gainsayers to point out the places, where such precepts were read or heard by the people. The duty of Gentile priests did not require them to inculcate sobriety, purity, justice, and the social virtues; the people, on pain of displeasing the gods, frequented the temples, and attended the sacrifices and other rites; but the priests made it not their business to teach them virtue, as Locke (s) expresses it. Paganism was a compound of fable and fraud, and its priests directed mens attention to the most unworthy objects; the ghosts of persons remarkable for lewdness, bloodshed, rapine, and even to the beasts that perish. These men were so solemn in the celebration of the most ridiculous rites, and affected such gravity in the performance of the most barefaced tricks, that Cato expressed his surprise, that an haruspex, or soothsayer, could look his fellow-juggler in the face, without bursting into laughter (t). Nor did some theatrical exhibitions of the Romans, encourage modesty and purity of manners, on the decline of their republic (u). Actors worshipped Berecynthia, the mother of the gods, in the most indelicate language, and obscene gestures; and exhibited to crowded assemblies

---

(r) De Civ. Dei, Lib. II. Cap. v. and vi.   (s) Reasonableness of Christianity.   (t) De Divin. Lib. III. Cap. xxiv.   (u) De Civ. Dei, ibid.

scenes shocking to the eyes and ears of the virtuous and chaste. Yet these impure exhibitions were thought agreeable to the gods, and sometimes instituted for the purpose of appeasing them, in time of pestilence or other public calamity (*w*). It could not be expected that men should practise purity of morals, from a sense of religion, when the mother of the gods was supposed to be delighted with the impure rites of such filthy spectacles. Their theatres were schools of lewdness, where the lascivious actor recited adulteries or exhibited them, and kindled in others the passion which he represented (*x*). In Rome they devoutly celebrated plays, once a year, in honour of Flora; and harlots ran up and down the streets, by day and night, naked; expressing the most obscene gestures and filthy songs: nor were these exhibitions discountenanced, but encouraged by the magistrates of that city (*y*). Their youth were admitted to those impure pastimes; nay the sagest senators, gravest matrons, and the most rigid magistrates, were present at them. In a word, their theatrical entertainments were, in some cases, so abominable, that the ears must be defiled by hearing filthy speeches, and the eyes by seeing the lewd gestures of actors; and yet these men were rewarded, as if they had contributed largely to the service of the republic (*z*).

(*w*) De Civ. Dei, Cap. vii.   (*x*) Min. Felix, Sect. 37.
(*y*) Ken. Antiq.   (*z*) Hackwell's Apol. Book IV. Chap. vi. Sect. 1.

Nor

SECT. I.

Philosophers did not restrain vice by precept or example.

Nor were philosophers themselves always pure in their doctrines, and exemplary in their lives; on the contrary, some of the principal sages recommended and justified fornication by precept and example. Aristotle (*a*) thought it lawful, to procure abortion; and Plato (*b*), to expose children. Democritus and Epicurus condemned marriage (*c*); Plato (*d*) the Epicureans and Stoics (*e*), nay Socrates and Cato (*f*), allowed fornication and a community of wives. Aristippus (*g*) permitted pederasty, Epicurus (*h*), Zeno and the Stoics (*i*), tolerate incest; and unnatural love is authorised by the Cynics, who were shameless in their amours. Epictetus was surprised at the self-denial of Socrates, who slighted the youth and beauty of Alcibiades; and Maximus Tyrius applauds Agesilaus for only looking at, and admiring a beautiful boy. Solon allowed the love of boys, and prohibited it to slaves as too great an indulgence (*k*); and the Cretans encouraged masculine love by law, to prevent a numerous offspring (*l*). Unnatural crimes were committed in Juno's temples, in the time of

(*a*) Polit. Lib. VII. Cap. xvi. (*b*) De Rep. Lib. V. Edit. Steph. 1587, p. 461. (*c*) Clem. Alex. Strom. Lib. II. Cap. xxiii. Vol. I. Edit. Oxon. 1725, p. 503. (*d*) De Rep. Lib. VIII. (*e*) Sext. Empir. Pyrrh. Lib. III. Cap. xxiv. Edit. Antwerp, p. 526. (*f*) Tert. Apolog. Cap. xxxix. (*g*) Diog. Laert. (*h*) Theoph. Antioch. Lib. III. ad Autolych. Edit. Paris, 1636, p. 120. (*i*) Sext. Emp. ibid. p. 529. (*k*) Leland's Christ. Revel. Part I. Chap. vii. (*l*) Arist. Polit. Lib. II. Cap. x.

Julius

Julius Firmicus (*m*); and Cicero's Cotta, a man of rank and refinement, acknowledges himself guilty of the crime against nature; and justifies the deed by the authority of philosophers (*n*). This offence was committed in Rome in a barefaced manner, in Seneca's time; and the Scantinian law prohibited the public marriages of men to men; which were so common in that city, and so familiar to the satirist (*o*); that he speaks of them with less horror, than of the fights of gladiators,

> *Vicit et hoc monstrum tunicati fuscina Gracchi.*
>
> Yet Gracchus, thou degenerate son of fame,
> Thy pranks are stigmatis'd with greater blame.

Even some illustrious characters among the ancients have been guilty of suicide, and other crimes which tarnish the lustre of their brightest virtues. Brutus put himself to death; Timoleon murdered his brother upon principle; and Cato of Utica put an end to his existence; being unable to support the weight of his calamities. Cleanthes, Chrysippus, Zeno Cleombrotus and Menippus, were also guilty of suicide; the three first maintained, that the crime against nature is as allowable as fornication; while Zeno and Cleanthes held, that children may eat the flesh of parents. The Cynics

---

(*m*) De errore profanarum religionum.   (*n*) De Nat. Deor. Lib. I. Cap. xxviii.   (*o*) Juv. Sat. ii. 143, and Dryden's translation.

SECT. I. contended that parents have a right to sacrifice and devour their children, and that there is no shame in committing publicly any act of lewdness. The founder of this sect convinced the world, that he was true to his principles, by exhibiting himself in the streets in the arms of a prostitute. Aristippus, though rich, refused to maintain his children, considering them as spittle or vermin produced by his body; kept a seraglio of boys and courtezans; and maintained that a man might lawfully commit theft, sacrilege, or adultery, as a means of gratifying his brutal appetites. Xenophon practised the most unnatural pollutions with Clinias; Crates, and the female philosopher Hipparchia, cohabited publicly, and Socrates and Plato have been accused of crimes with persons of their own sex (*p*). Such were the doctrines and lives of public teachers among the Heathens! Such were the fruits of ignorance of the doctrines and motives of true religion! Philosophers, it must be admitted, enjoined a love of their country and friends, in elegant and sublime language; but their benevolence seldom went further,· they rarely extended their kindness to the rest of mankind. Socrates declared it lawful to rejoice at the misfortunes of enemies; and one of the seven wise men says, be kind to your friends, and revenge yourself on your enemies (*q*). Zeno contended,

(*p*) Skelton's Deism revealed, Dial. II.   (*q*) Young's Idolatrous Corruptions, Vol. II. Chap. iv.

that

that a man should not pardon those who offended him; and even the amiable Germanicus exhorted his friends to be revenged of those who poisoned or bewitched him (*r*). Cicero (*s*) reckons it the chief duty of justice that no man shall injure another unprovoked; and, in another part of his Offices, affirms, that a good man offends no person unless instigated by ill-usage. Even the gods of the Heathens were vindictive as well as immoral; Juno persecuted Eneas even after he had settled in Italy, and the goddess of wisdom applauds Ulysses for ungenerously exulting over his vanquished rival in his madness and distress (*t*).

SECT. I.

Ουκουν γελως ηδισος εις εχθρους γελαν.

Is it not the highest sport to laugh at enemies?

I do not deny that Plato, Epictetus, Marcus Antoninus, and few others, argued against the return of injuries; but a learned writer proves their arguments for forgiveness to be false in some respects; and that their motives to this virtue, were far inferior to those which were offered by the gospel (*u*).

It cannot be denied that Greeks, Romans, and other nations, practised some virtues highly useful to the purposes of government. Lawgivers inculcated reverence for an oath, deified truth,

Pagan lawgivers inculcated some virtues.

(*r*) Deism revealed, Dial. II. Cap. vii. and Lib. III. Cap. xix.   (*s*) De Officiis, Lib. I.   (*t*) Sophocles' Ajax Mastig. Act I. Scene i.   (*u*) Leland, Part II. Chap. x.

F 2   justice,

SECT. I.
justice, concord, fidelity, and erected temples to them. No person acquainted with Roman history can be ignorant, how strict that people were in the observance of oaths, and how averse from breaches of them. We should not be surprised, that they held oaths sacred and inviolable, who were taught, that the violation of an oath brought down the wrath of heaven upon the perjured, and branded them with infamy and disgrace on earth (*w*). That a veneration even for the false gods of the Heathens, contributed to make oaths binding, leagues obligatory, and compacts inviolable, appears from a passage of Cicero in his second book of laws. This author speaking of religion, thus expresses himself; who can deny the utility of these opinions, that knows how many things derive strength from the obligation of an oath, and what advantage the religious observance of treaties produces (*x*)? The laws of the twelve tables, as an encouragement to valour, enjoined honour, not only to those gods who have always been esteemed such; but also to Hercules, Esculapius, Romulus, Castor and Pollux, who have been deified for their merits. Those laws prohibited men to worship any vice, and required them to rank among the gods those commendable qualities by which heroes obtained heaven, as understanding, virtue, piety and fidelity (*y*). When the

(*w*) Laws of Twelve Tables.   (*x*) De Leg. Lib. II. Cap. vii.   (*y*) Laws of Twelve Tables.

Romans would imprefs a fenfe of any virtue, or abhorrence of any vice, on the minds of the people, they dedicated a temple to it. They erected temples to victory, concord and fidelity, built one to liberty, and poured out their fupplications before the altar of fear, that their troops might not be difmayed in the hour of danger. A celebrated hiftorian (z) affures us, that Numa, in order to render private contracts obligatory, deified Fidelity; built a temple to it, and inftituted facrifices in honour of it at the public expence. He expected that a regard for this virtue, diffufed through the ftate, would gradually be communicated to every individual; and was not miftaken. Faith became fo refpected, that fhe had more weight than witneffes and oaths; and the civil magiftrate, in cafes of difficulty, fometimes refted the determination of a caufe on the faith of the contending parties. Another eminent hiftorian (a), fpeaking of the Romans, fincerely regrets the degeneracy of his own countrymen, who were then on the decline; while the Romans were making large ftrides towards univerfal empire. He declares, that the ancients introduced thofe notions of the gods and of a future ftate wifely; and that the prefent generation betrayed great weaknefs in rejecting them, and appeals to facts for a proof of his affertion. " In Greece, fays he, they who

(z) Dion. Halicarn. Cap. lxxv. page 75, Edit. Oxon. 1714.
(a) Polybius, Lib. VI. Cap. xxxiv.

SECT. I. are entrusted with the public money, though it be but one talent; and though they should give a tenfold security, before twenty witnesses; yet cannot be prevailed on to keep their faith: while among the Romans, it is as rare to find any person offending in this way." It is however to be observed, that Pagan lawgivers allowed temples to Bacchus, Venus, &c. inculcated moral and social duties but imperfectly; and that these duties were not the natural effects of paganism and instruction of priests, but of political wisdom, which employed false religion in enforcing those virtues. Statesmen enjoined such virtues as were absolutely necessary to the well being of communities; political expediency engaged them, to encourage morality among those who were subject to their authority: but virtue requires a firmer basis than mere political wisdom; a support entirely independent of human institutions. When civil establishments were overturned, and the Roman government was transferred from the wise, to the vilest tyrants; then the foundation of morality was subverted, and the Romans became the most vicious, and dissolute of all people of the earth.

Paganism a mere political engine.

The wisest of the ancient Heathens employed superstition to purposes merely civil, and made it subservient to their political designs. Aided by false religion, they enforced the practice of particular virtues; were enabled to soften the manners of a rugged people, to elude the claims of factious

factious demagogues, and ufed it as an inftrument in extending their conquefts. For thefe purpofes ftatefmen, who were ignorant of true religion, encouraged fuperftition among their fubjects, built temples, raifed altars, offered facrifices, and celebrated games in honour of their gods. They did not attempt to remove vulgar errors and popular credulity; but carefully inculcated them, in order to obtain the advantages already hinted at. To excite men to great exploits, and enforce obedience to the laws and magiftrates, they taught, that fome Pagan gods had been heroes, legiflators and benefactors of mankind, who were exalted to heaven for their virtuous exertions. It appears from feveral paffages of Cicero, that the popular deities of the Heathens were but kings, and men who contributed largely to the benefit of their country. That falfe religion was cultivated in different countries to ferve purpofes of government and policy, appears from this, that the chief men generally affumed the direction of all matters relative to their fuperftitions. The dignity of the prieftly office ufually devolved upon kings, and perfons of the firft diftinction; Amphilochus and Mopfus were kings of the Argives, and alfo Augurs (b); and the Spartan princes, on their acceffion to the throne, were obliged to affume the facerdotal function. Anius was a tem-

(b) De Divin. Lib. I. Ch. xl. and xli.

SECT. I. poral prince and prieſt of Apollo (c); and Priam had his ſon Helenus and his daughter Caſſandra inſtructed, the former in augury, and the latter in propheſy. Tully (d) affirms that no perſon could be king of Perſia who was not previouſly acquainted with the diſcipline and wiſdom of the Magi. The emperor of China poſſeſſed the pontifical function, as the moſt exalted perſon to do homage to Shangti. The fifth emperor prohibited any, except emperors, to ſacrifice to the deity; and, in caſe of ſickneſs, he commanded ſome mandarin to perform that office (e). Formerly, the Japaneſe emperors were dairos or ſovereign pontiffs, and their perſons were ſo ſacred, that an oppoſition to their religious or civil decrees, was deteſted as a crime againſt God himſelf: they aſſumed blaſphemous titles, and admitted of homage bordering on idolatry (f). The Egyptian kings had their magi; the Britiſh, Gallic and Iriſh ſtates their druids: the Spartan kings their augurs; and the Athenian kings and magiſtrates their manteis. The more honourable the miniſters of religion, the greater influence they were ſuppoſed to have with the deity; to derive bleſſings upon

(c) Virg. Æneid. Lib. III. 80.
(d) De Divin. Lib. I. Cap. xli.
(e) Mod. Univ. Hiſtory, Vol. III. Folio. Introd. to Hiſtory of China.
(f) Ibid. Vol. III. and Reſnal's Settl. Vol. I. Book I.

the

the people, to deprecate the vengeance of the gods, and to avert public and private calamities.

Vandale proves, that Heathen oracles originated in the craft of priests, and in the credulity of men, who paid a blind veneration to those supposed interpreters of the will of the gods. That these oracles served as political contrivances, appears from the learned treatise of that writer, and from the answers which were usually returned to the queries of the inquisitive. The Athenians, having consulted the oracle of Apollo relative to the mode of worship that should be adopted among them, the oracle commanded them to adhere to the religion of their ancestors (*g*). Ambiguity and obscurity were their general characteristics; and priests returned such answers, as gratified the consultors, and suited their own purposes, and those of their rulers. In cases where the responses were more explicit, if the event did not correspond with the prediction, the priests ascribed the failure to some error in the interpretation, or to some defect in the mode of consulting the oracle. In the tenth year of the siege of Veii, the Roman soldiers, despairing of success, importunately desired to return home: but the Alban lake having overflowed, they were easily prevailed on to persist in the siege; as an oracle declared, that the city of Veii would be taken, the very

(*g*) Cicero de Leg. Lib. II. Cap. xvi.

year in which the lake overflowed (*b*). In all cafes priefts, initiated in religious myfteries, obferved the profoundeft fecrecy; and encouraged errors, which were beneficial to the ftate, and profitable to themfelves. We cannot entertain a doubt, that thefe jugglers turned to their own ufe, large fhares of the donations made to the temples in which they prefided. When the Romans confulted the oracle, about the overflowing of the Alban lake, we find, towards the conclufion of the Delphic anfwer, quoted at large by Livy, that the intereft of the temple and priefts was not forgotten nor difregarded. " When you have ended the war," fays the god, " and vanquifhed your enemies, bring ample offerings and donations to my temples (*i*)." Vandale (*k*) affirms, that cities, where oracles were confulted, were chiefly inhabited by inn-keepers, by fellers of frankincenfe, fpices, and beafts for facrifice; and by augurs, arufpices, priefts, poets, and other minifters of religion, who derived a fubfiftence from the lucrative traffic. Thefe impoftors difpatched emiffaries to diftant regions, to propagate the fame of oracles; and employed fpies at Rome, and other places, to obtain intelligence of the bufinefs of confultors (*l*). An extraordinary impofture was

---

(*b*) Livy, Lib. V. Cap. xv. and xvi.   (*i*) Ibid.
(*k*) Differt. I. de Oraculorum Ethnicorum Origine & Authoribus, Cap. v.
(*l*) Ibid. Cap. i.

practised by the oracle of Trophonius, on those who consulted it; he who descended into the cave of this god, to consult his oracle, was required to drink inebriating waters; and jugglers practised deceptions on him when he was thus intoxicated. While the consultor was beside himself, or otherwise unguarded; or by overhearing his prayers to Trophonius, or by intelligence of his domestics, the priests discovered his business, and were prepared in their responses (*m*). These men sometimes protracted the time, by prayers, sacrifices, ablutions and inspection of the bowels of animals; that they might, in the interval, obtain some hint of the errand of consultors. Those who desire further information with respect to oracles, I shall refer to this eminent writer, who is so learned on the subject.

Let us now take a view of the political effects of paganism, when employed, as an instrument, in the hands of legislators and rulers of states. Finding the people rough and superstitious, and themselves, for the most part, strangers to true religion and its genuine effects, lawgivers and chief magistrates took advantage of the prejudices of their subjects, and converted false religion to the useful purpose of civilization, and restraining the ferocity of rude and uncultivated societies. Livy (*n*) assures us, that this was the object of

Some particular effects of Paganism in Heathen governments.

(*m*) Dissert. I. de Oraculorum Ethnicorum Origine & Authoribus, Cap. viii. (*n*) Lib. I. Cap. xix.

Numa

SECT. I. Numa in inftituting religious rites in his infant republic. Q. Curtius (*o*) affirms, that nothing governs barbarians more effectually than falfe religion; that, when under its influence, they are more obedient to priefts than to generals; while they are cruel, fickle, and ungovernable, uninfluenced by that principle. As to the influence of paganifm in the Roman empire, I fhall be more particular, and point out its political effects in war and peace, in elections of kings and affemblies of the people. It was an eftablifhed cuftom of the Romans, in almoft every enterprize civil or military, to draw prefages of the event from the flight or chirping of birds, the entrails of beafts, the anfwers of oracles, the interpretation of dreams, and prodigies (*p*). In all thefe cafes, the priefts were interpreters, and explained every thing, as beft fuited their political convenience. Magiftrates were depofed, and public affemblies were adjourned or diffolved, when thunder and lightning came from the left. Tully (*q*) affures us, that it was unlawful to hold affemblies, while there was thunder and lightning; and infinuates, that for the fervice of the republic, they fought pretexts for difbanding the people. Livy ac-

(*o*) Lib. IV. Cap. xxxix.
(*p*) De Nat. Deor. Lib. II. Cap. lxv.
(*q*) De Divin. Lib. II. Cap. xviii.

quaints

quaints us, that the augur, at the election of Numa, having marked out the divisions of the heavens with his curved staff, and laying his right hand on Numa's head, thus addressed a prayer to Jupiter: "We pray you, father Jove, if you approve of this Numa, whose head I hold, for king of Rome, to give some sign of your approbation within those limits which I have marked out with my staff (*r*)." Among the Romans, superstition and ignorance were the bulwarks of the Patrician prerogatives, against the encroachments of the Plebeians. This latter class were perpetually instigated by seditious tribes, to extort from the nobles a share in the public offices, which had been monopolized by the Patricians. Of all their various artifices to counteract, and defeat the designs of the Plebeians; superstition was the chief; by its influence they deposed magistrates, and prorogued assemblies, which were met to enact popular laws; and by the means of this instrument they were enabled to enlarge their own authority, and abridge that of the people. In the year of Rome 356, the military tribunes were all, except one, elected from the Plebeians: the same year a plague and famine having raged at Rome, the Patricians took advantage of the terrors and credulity of the people, to inveigh against the innovation, as the cause of those disasters. They

(*r*) Lib. I. Cap. xviii.

SECT. I.

maintained, that the gods were angry at the admission of plebeians to the confular dignity; and, by this artifice, prevailed on the people to reftore the ancient mode of election, and to choofe military tribunes of the fubfequent year out of their own body (s). After Rome had been burned by the Gauls, the people, urged on by their tribunes, were with difficulty prevented from removing to Veii, and making that city the feat of empire. Camillus diverted them from their purpofe by a fpeech, the conclufion of which was a pathetic addrefs to the prejudices of a fuperftitious people. "Here, in this city, fays that general, have been preferved the facred fires of Vefta; here the fhields, fent down from heaven, have been depofited; while we remain in this city we may be certain of the protection of the gods (t)."

Effects of various Pagan superstitions.

Many of the prodigies related by Livy and Dionyfius were fo abfurd, as to impofe on the credulous vulgar only. Other phenomena, fuch as eclipfes, comets, meteors, fhowers of blood and ftones, or monftrous births, were accounted prognoftics of direful events, and have terrified whole Roman legions who were ignorant of the caufes of thofe appearances. Few generals would hazard an engagement, or undertake any expedition, without confulting the minifters of religion, who judged of the event from the eafe or difficulty with

(s) Livy, Lib. V, Cap. xiv. (t) Ibid. Cap. liv.

which a victim was led to the altar. If it struggled on receiving the blow; if it ran away; if the entrails fell out of the priest's hands; or if certain animals crossed the way to the left; in all these cases it was reckoned a certain sign of the displeasure of the gods. When an ox, led to be sacrificed, advanced with an easy air, in a right line, and without resistance, it was accounted a good omen and luckly prognostic: whereas, his resistance, his windings, and manner of falling, gave rise to several interpretations. Aruspices examined the entrails of victims, and concluded the gods approved of a project, if they were found; and condemned it, if they were defective. The Romans imagined, that the sacred chickens were never neglected without loss; nor attended to without success (*u*): and supposed that these birds could tell better when to engage, than an experienced general (*w*). In consequence of this opinion, the generals of those days were so attentive to superstitious rites, that they usually suspended an enterprise, until they consulted the chickens, and their keeper, about the event. Upon their feeding greedily, or only scattering their food, was thought to depend the success of a battle; often the fate of a kingdom or state. History acquaints us, that the commander who treated them with disrespect, was certain of being

(*u*) Minucius Fœlix, Sect. xxvi. (*w*) Bayle's Observations.

censured

SECT. I. censured as impious, and the author of public calamities. In the first Punic war, the chickens being consulted by offering them food, and the birds having declined it, Claudius Pulcher flung them, in anger, into a pool of water, that they might drink, as he expressed it, since they refused to eat. Tully (*x*), in the character of Lucilius, relates this instance of impiety, affirms that this ridicule of the gods was the cause of a defeat at sea, and of great grief to himself and country; and that the inattention of his colleague Junius to the auspices, was supposed to have occasioned the loss of a fleet in a storm: therefore, says Lucilius, Claudius Pulcher was condemned by the people and Junius put himself to death. Cicero observes, on the death of these two men, that the republic was enlarged, during the command of men who had been attentive to religion. We are told of a Jew who was present, when an augur commanded the army to halt, until he observed the flight of a bird, and drew a presage from the direction which it took. The Jew, who was but a private soldier, shot at the bird and killed it with an arrow, to convince them of the folly and absurdity of their superstitions. The augur and others, enraged at the impiety of the Jew, poured out curses and maledictions upon his head; in answer to which the Jew exclaimed, "What infatuation, to suppose that this bird, which foresaw nothing of its

(*x*) De Nat. Deorum, Lib. II. Cap. iii.

own

own death, should foretel any thing of the event of our journey (*y*).

Paganism assisted the Romans in extending their conquests.

The history of the Romans assures us, that their superstitions assisted them in extending their conquests. They rarely ventured a battle, without a strong persuasion of the approbation of the gods, signified to them, by the various means already described. Certain of the divine protection, soldiers marched into the field of battle, inspired with religious confidence; and fought with that intrepidity, which commonly ensures success. Nothing could more forcibly excite soldiers to martial achievements, than to see their generals animated by the same enthusiasm; nor so strike terror and consternation into foes, as to see adverse leaders, confident of the immediate protection of the gods, rush forward unawed by danger, unterrified by death. So great was the influence of superstition on the minds of Roman officers and soldiers, that Cicero (*z*) ascribes to it the extraordinary fortitude, with which they encountered dangers: generals often exposing themselves to certain death, rushing blindfold among their enemies, and devoting themselves to the immortal gods, for the service of the republic. The same author (*a*) asserts, that the instruments, to which the Romans were chiefly indebted for the conquest

(*y*) Eusebii Præp. Evang. Lib. IX. Cap. ii.
(*z*) De Nat. Deor. Lib. II. Cap. iii.
(*a*) De Aruspicum responsis.

SECT. I. of the world were not strength and policy, but piety and religion. Horace (*b*) ascribes victory and extent of empire to the religious principle; and in the same ode, attributes all the miseries which Italy endured to a disregard of that principle. Here I cannot avoid pointing out one very extraordinary effect of Pagan superstitions; namely, that by extending the Roman conquests they contributed to disseminate the Christian religion. The knowledge of the gospel was more rapidly diffused through one great empire, where a general communication must necessarily have subsisted, than it could possibly have been propagated through so many distinct and independent republics (*c*).

Superstition contributed to the destruction of the Roman empire.

It is a curious observation, that as superstition was instrumental in the growth of the Roman empire, so it contributed to subvert and destroy it. The truth of this observation appears, from the following facts, with which history acquaints us. Woden, a great warrior, being banished from Asia by Pompey, retired with his followers to the northern kingdoms; and conquered Norway, Sweden and Denmark. Finding his end approaching, he assembled his friends together, gave himself nine wounds in a circular form in their presence, and declared he was going to be enrolled with the other gods of Scythia, and would reward all who died intrepidly, with arms in their hands.

(*b*) Carm. Book III. Ode VI. v. 5.
(*c*) Bossuet's Hist. of the World, Part III.

By his bravery, artifices, and self-murder, he was deified after his death by a superstitious people; and his doctrines contributed to the destruction of the Roman empire (*d*). His followers called him, by way of honour, the god of armies, the father of slaughter, the depopulator, the incendiary. Warriors promised to devote a certain number of persons to him who was supposed to protect the valiant; or to choose victims to follow him to the other world, where they were to be happy. The effect of this doctrine was to render men fierce, desperate and enterprising, and to inspire an enthusiastic and sacred thirst for blood (*e*). The revenge of injuries offered to their country or parents, the Scythians considered as a sacred duty; Woden adopted this bloody doctrine and recommended it to the Cimbri, Germans and other northern nations; in order to spirit them up against the Romans, who banished him from his country. This vindictive spirit continued, a long time, rankling in their breasts, before they were enabled to gratify it by their actions: but when they had recovered the losses which they had sustained, in their wars against the Romans, they invaded the western empire, destroyed the Roman state, and fully revenged the sufferings of their ancestors (*f*). Thus the Roman empire, which owed much of its gran-

(*d*) Williams's Hist. of Northern Kingdoms, Book II.
(*e*) Resnal's Settl. Vol. II. Book I.
(*f*) Williams, ibid.

SECT. I. deur to the artifices of priests, and to rigid virtue, was utterly destroyed by the vices of the Romans, and the doctrines of this impostor. Montesquieu (g) assigns several causes of the decline of the Roman empire, and the depravity of its inhabitants; while Montagu (h) considers the " atheistical doctrines of the sect of Epicurus as the real cause of the rapid depravity of the Roman manners; as long," says this ingenious writer, " as the religious principle remained, it controled manners and checked the progress of luxury in proportion to its influence; but when atheism had corrupted this principle, the great bar to corruption was removed, and the passions were left without check or control." I admit, that the immoral principles of Epicurus tended to corrupt the manners of the Romans; and that the superstitions of this people attached them to their country, and rendered them valiant. But to support his opinion he ought to have proved, that the gods of the Heathens enjoined morality, and forbade luxury and dissoluteness of manners. If the superstition of the Romans was not a system of pure morality, I cannot comprehend, how atheism, or a disbelief of false gods, could possibly have led to vice, or depravity of manners.

The state of religion among Pagans proves the necessity of supernatural aid. I have now exhibited a few of the most striking instances of the influence of ancient Heathenism,

(g) Rise and Decline of the Roman Empire.
(h) Montagu's Rise and Fall of ancient Republics.

in some Pagan countries; and the history of every other Gentile nation will furnish numerous instances of similar effects. But as modern Paganism is less known to most readers than ancient, I shall, in my third section, point out its fruits; and conclude with a few general observations on the contents of this section. From what has been delivered, the Pagan religion appears, in many instances, to have been a system of cruelty, fraud and impurity, blended with some innocent devotions ascribed to it by Mr. Gibbon. Priests were not required by their duty, to instruct men in morality; and philosophers were insufficient to incite men to virtue, by precept or example. Some philosophers, it must be admitted, condemned the popular religion and idle fables of the poets; and entertained exalted ideas of God and his attributes: but these ideas were blended with vulgar errors and superstitious practices. The wisest sages visited the temples, whose rites and ceremonies they affected to despise; and encouraged divination and all the other artifices of statesmen. Socrates being accused of not acknowleding the gods of the republic, Xenophon (*i*) appeals to his conduct, for a refutation of the charge; since he was often seen to sacrifice in his own house, and in the temple. Besides, no person can deny that he believed in divination; since he declared, he re-

---

(*i*) Memorab. Defence of Socrates.

ceived

ceived counsel from his guardian demon, and sacrificed a cock to Esculapius, at the hour of his death. Plato (*k*) observes, that the Delphic oracle ought to direct, what gods the state should worship; and prescribe the mode of adoration. Cicero (*l*) affirms that a wise man should adhere to the sacred rites of his ancestors; and Epictetus (*m*) recommends offering up libations, sacrifices and first fruits; after the custom of his country. Since then the luminaries of the Pagan world did not oppose, but encourage the popular religion, and conformed themselves to the established worship; since, in many instances, they were ignorant of true religion, and bound by the laws to support the false; and since they wanted information to dissipate error, and authority to enforce the precepts of morality; how deplorable was the condition of the Heathen world, unassisted by some extraordinary illumination; how insuperable their ignorance, and how necessary the divine interposition? The insufficiency of philosophers, to prescribe a rational mode of worship, and to enforce their precepts by proper sanctions, proves the expedience of supernatural assistance, to extricate men from superstition and its direful effects. I now proceed to shew, that the Hebrew lawgiver delivered his people from the idolatries prevalent

(*k*) Laws, Book VIII. ipso initio.
(*l*) De Nat. Deor. Lib. III. Cap. ii.
(*m*) Enchiridion, Cap. xxxi.

in his time; and that the law, the prophets, and the judgments of God, afterwards preserved the Jews from these and other superstitions, which have already been described; while Christianity banished Paganism from many countries, and extended the benign influence of the gospel to all nations where it has been established, as will appear in the third section.

SECT. II.

EFFECTS OF JUDAISM ON THE HEBREWS THEM-
SELVES, AND ON THE SENTIMENTS OF PAGANS.

*Design of the miracles of Moses and of his whole law.
—Intention and effects of the sabbath.—Of the
Hebrew festivals.—Of the sabbatical year, jubilee
and laws of usury.—Of clean and unclean beasts
and the place of worship.—Means employed to procure respect for God.—Of the tabernacle and temple.—Of sacrifices and lustrations.—Tendency of
the theocracy and of temporal sanctions.—Effects of
those sanctions in the time of judges.—Effects of
them in the time of kings.—Intention of particular
laws and rites of Judaism.—The same subject continued.—The same subject continued.—General tendency of the Mosaic rites, precepts, and prohibitions.
—The Mosaic rites and institutions local and temporary.—Laws of Moses preferable to those of
Pagan lawgivers.—His writings of divine authority.—Temporal sanctions prove his divine commission.—The truth of his account confirmed by
Bryant.—Judaism imperfect.—Judaism prepared
men for the gospel.—Hebrew writings useful in
chronology and history.—Mosaic account of the creation tends to remove some errors of naturalists.—*
Jews

*Jews and their tenets known to ancient Pagans.—
Hebrews and Heathens relate the same facts.—
Plato borrowed from Hebrews.—Orpheus, Homer,
Solon and others borrowed from them.—Greeks indebted to them by the testimony of the learned.—
Ancient philosophers borrowed their theology. -
Greek philosophers were plagiaries.—Their absurdities prove that they borrowed their theology.—Divine attributes not investigated by reason.—Brucker
errs in denying that Heathens borrowed from Hebrews.—The same subject continued.—He errs in
denying that Plato borrowed from them.—He errs
with respect to the similitude of Jewish and Pagan
dogmas.—Whether the law allowed of human sacrifices.—How far it was lawful to eject and destroy
the Canaanites.—The election of the Hebrews no
argument of divine partiality.*

SECT. 12.

Design of the miracles of Moses and of his whole law.

OF all people of the earth, there are none to whom the attributes of God have been so clearly exhibited, as to the Hebrew nation: they were convinced of his power, by his miracles in Egypt, and by their deliverance from servitude; of his goodness and wisdom, by his compliance with their infirmities, and employing the most likely means to render them moral; and of his justice, by his rewarding the observance and punishing the violation of his laws, even in this life. In the early ages of the world, when mens understandings were unaccustomed to abstruse reasonings,

SECT. II. fonings, such extraordinary exertions of the divine attributes were absolutely necessary; since even in refined ages, it requires attention and labour to deduce these attributes either from causes or effects. God suffered Pharaoh's heart to be hardened that he should not let the Israelites go; in order to display his power to both Israelites and Egyptians, and that the former of these people should be sensible of this and other attributes, when exhibited to their senses, and felt by them experimentally. Moses dictated some laws, which were applicable to all nations, and of perpetual obligation; while others were local, and adapted to their particular circumstances, in the land of Canaan. The decalogue, though peculiarly addressed to the Israelites, is applicable to all nations, as men and citizens; while God authorised Moses to enact several political and ceremonial laws, well suited to the exigencies of his people. We are not to consider the Jewish institution, as a complete system of religion; even Moses knew it to be defective, and would have furnished a more perfect one, were it not for the hardness of their hearts. It appears from several passages of Exodus, which were prior to the Levitical law, that he wished to revive the old patriarchal system (*a*); the Hebrew doctors (*b*) maintain, that his chief design was to inculcate reverence towards

(*a*) Exod. Ch. xix. and xxv.   (*b*) Thomas Burnet de fide & officio Christianorum.

God

God and good-will to man; but finding their pronencfs to idolatry, on his return from the mount, he indulged them with numerous rites; for the purpofe of diverting them from the worfhip of idols. When they defpifed the covenant and decalogue, and manifefted an attachment to the worfhip of calves; then did the lawgiver give them a multitude of rites; in order to wean them from idolatry; and we find thefe rites condemned by the prophets as defpicable and ufelefs, when unaccompanied by juftice, mercy, and integrity of heart (c). To form a juft idea of the influence of the Jewifh code, let us take a fhort view of the feafts, rites, cuftoms, precepts and prohibitions of Mofes: fuch a view will readily convince the reader, that each and all of them tended to one great end, to promote morality; to extirpate or prevent idolatry; and to preferve a knowledge of the one true God. In treating on this fubject I fhall confider the effects of the Jewifh ordinances in the Hebrew government; and alfo the influence of the Mofaic and prophetic writings on the theology of the moft celebrated Pagan philofophers.

SECT. II.

The greater part of mankind in the early ages of the world, believed the ftars, fun, moon and other planets, to be eternal; and confidered thefe and other parts of the vifible world as chief objects of adoration. To remove the opinion of the

Intention and effects of the fabbath.

(c) Pfalm v. Ifai. i. Jer. vi. 20. Hofea vi. 6. Micah vi. 8.

eternity

SECT. II. eternity of the world, Mofes affures the Ifraelites that God created thofe things which Gentile nations deemed eternal and divine; and that the fabbath was inftituted to commemorate the creation, and to induce men to look upon created things as unworthy of their worfhip (*d*). That the prevention of idolatry was the primary end of its inftitution, appears from feveral paffages of the Old Teftament: men are exhorted to fhun idols in the fame paffages of fcripture which enjoin an obfervance of the fabbath; and the worfhip of idols and breach of the fabbath are frequently joined together in holy writ (*e*). But befides the original intention of fabbatical reft, this feftival reminded them of their deliverance from bondage; contributed to infpire them with humanity to ftrangers and domeftics; and to mitigate the rigours of fervitude in defpotic governments, where mens bodies might be worn with inceffant toil without a day of recreation (*f*). After the return of the Jews from the Babylonifh captivity they obferved the fabbath fo ftrictly, that they thought it unlawful to travel beyond a certain diftance, to kindle a fire, or drefs meat on that day; and were fo fuperftitioufly rigid in this refpect, that they declined even felf-defence when

(*d*) Spencer de legibus Hebræorum, Lib. I. Cap. iv.
(*e*) Exod. xx. 16. Exod. xxiii. 12. Lev. xxvi. 1. Ezek. xx. 18. Ezek. xxii. 8. Ezek. xxiii. 37. Malachi i. 44.
(*f*) Fiddes's Body of Divinity, Vol. II. p. 85.

attacked

attacked on the sabbath. Having experienced the inconvenience of their absurd rigour, they decreed it lawful to fight in defence of life on this day; but this decree not suffering them to destroy the enemies works, or prevent their designs until they came to execute them, Pompey forbade his soldiers to attack the Jews on the sabbath, but to employ all diligence in erecting their engines and advancing their works; by which stratagem they soon possessed themselves of the temple and city of Jerusalem (g).

Of the Hebrew festivals.

The Israelites who settled in Egypt during Joseph's administration multiplied quickly, and their descendants, a little before the time of Moses, were a warlike, rich and well-united people, indefatigable in trade, agriculture, and feeding numerous herds. The Egyptians, alarmed at their growing power, obliged them to carry heavy burdens, in order to enervate their bodies, and prevent their encrease. Pharaoh, finding this method unsuccessful, directed the midwives to destroy all the males; and, when they evaded that order, commanded even the parents to drown their male children in the river Nile. About this period, Moses was sent by God, to remonstrate with Pharaoh, about his cruelty and injustice; to conduct his people from this land of servitude; to convince that prince of his divine commission, by several miracles wrought in his presence, and by

(g) Lewis's Hebrew Antiquities, Book IV. Chap. xvi.

several

SECT. II. several successive plagues inflicted on his people. These miracles, however tremendous, did not prevail on the king to let them go; until God sent an angel to destroy the first-born of Egypt both of man and beast; while he passed over the houses of the Israelites. In consequence of this judgment, they were permitted to depart, and the Jewish lawgiver instituted the passover, to commemorate this deliverance; to remind them of the miraculous power by which it was accomplished; and of the goodness of God which they were so apt to mistrust (*h*). The feast of Pentecost celebrated the delivery of the law by Moses in fifty days after the feast of Passover: the Israelites met annually on that festival, to return thanks to God for their harvest, and to commemorate his mercies, by sacrifices and public rejoicings (*i*). On the feast of Tabernacles they returned thanks, for the fruits which they gathered in, and for the happiness which they enjoyed in commodious habitations, who formerly wandered about in the wilderness without any certain abode (*k*). The feast of New-moons, as it determined the times of the other festivals, was celebrated by the sound of trumpets; by extraordinary sacrifices (*l*); by abstinence from servile works (*m*); by attendance on divine service (*n*), and by offering the first fruits of every

(*h*) Fiddes, Vol. II. p. 86.   (*i*) Exod. xxiii. Lev. ix. 9.
(*k*) Lewis, Book IV. Chap. xx.   (*l*) Numb. xxviii. 11.
(*m*) Amos viii. 5.   (*n*) 2 Kings iv. 23.

month

month to the giver of all things. Moses limited his feasts to three, while Heathens devoted a great part of every year to the celebration of theirs; his festivals commemorated some signal benefits, while theirs were celebrated on frivolous and often on ridiculous occasions: the former were dedicated to exercises of piety as well as mirth; while those of the latter were chiefly devoted to idleness and debauchery.

SECT. II.

Besides those annual feasts, the Hebrews had other solemn times of devotion, and observed every seventh year, as a year of rest and cessation from labour. They were forbade to plow, sow or prune; and what the earth produced spontaneously that year, belonged as much to strangers, orphans, and poor, as to the proprietors of the ground (*o*). The sabbatical year inspired Israelites with humanity to strangers and slaves, and taught them their dependance on that God, who provided for them so abundantly. On this year, insolvent debtors were discharged from all debts contracted to supply the necessaries of life; and the great end of the release, was to prevent the distressed Hebrew from flying to Gentiles, and forsaking his religion. None except Israelites or proselytes of righteousness were discharged from their debts; and this privilege was refused to strangers, and even proselytes of the gate (*p*). The jubilee was en-

Of the sabbatical year, jubilee, and laws of usury.

(*o*) Lev. xxv. 4, 6. Deut. xv. 2.   (*p*) Lewis, Book IV. Chap. xxii.

joined

SECT. II. joined on every fiftieth year, and had almost the same privileges as the sabbatical, with this difference; that the sabbatical year released men from their debts, while servants were manumitted, and lands restored to old proprietors on the year of jubilee. There was no agriculture in this year, all things were in common, and to bondsmen and persons reduced to poverty, the joys of this solemnity were boundless and sincere. This season restored to them liberty and property; the prison doors were opened, slaves were released, and every man was restored to the enjoyment of his ancient possessions: all slaves and prisoners were declared free by the sound of trumpets, all lawsuits were ended, and all lands sold or mortgaged were restored to the old proprietors (*q*). The chief design of this institution, was to preserve the equality at first established in the Hebrew republic; and the great object of that equality was to attach men to a country, where their estates could not be alienated, for more than half a century, and to prevent their flying from Palestine and changing their religion; by removing all apprehension of perpetual poverty and oppression (*r*). None but Israelites or circumcised converts could enjoy the benefits of the jubilee; and even these might forfeit its benefits, if they sold their possessions to carry on trade, or for any purpose but a supply of

(*q*) Stackhouse's Body of Divinity, Sect. 4.
(*r*) Lewis, Book IV. Chap. xxiii.

their

their neceffities. The law relative to ufury was founded on their polity with refpect to property, and abfolutely unjuft with refpect to other nations; a man having as juft a right to what his money produces by trade or otherwife, as to the rent made by the induftry of others. The prohibition of ufury being founded on an equal divifion of land, there could be no reafon for it in countries where that equality did not fubfift. A people little concerned in commerce were not fuppofed to borrow, except to relieve them in diftrefs, and the prohibition was intended as an indulgence to fuch men; " if thou lend thy money to any of my people that is poor, thou fhalt not be unto him as an ufurer (*s*);" that is, thou fhalt not treat him with rigour, as is the cuftom of ufurers. In Leviticus (*t*) they were abfolutely forbade to take ufury from a brother Ifraelite reduced to poverty, or from a profelyte; but there is a paffage of Deuteronomy (*u*), which feems to tolerate ufury towards perfons who are neither Jews nor profelytes.

The Jewifh legiflator diftinguifhed between clean and unclean beafts, and excluded fome animals from the tables of Ifraelites (*w*); for the purpofe of feparating them from convivial intercourfes at the tables and feftivals of profane nations, where they might be feduced to idolatry and the worfhip

Of clean and unclean beafts and the place of worfhip.

(*s*) Exod. xxii. 25. (*t*) xxv. 35. (*u*) xxiii. 30. (*w*) Lev. xi.

SECT. II. of strange gods. This distinction must have answered the intention of the lawgiver; as men would never sit down to table together, when the dish that was delicious to one was odious to the other; and the Jew devoured the animal which the Gentile thought sacred. Ancient idolaters paid the most superstitious veneration to different animals; the Egyptians in particular worshipped oxen, sheep and goats at Memphis, Heliopolis and Mendes; some learned writers are of opinion, that Moses permitted his people to sacrifice and eat certain animals, in order to remove or prevent an opinion of their sanctity; while he prohibited others as unclean, which Heathens used in their sacrifices, and mysteries of religion (*x*). This lawgiver ordered to kill the animal at the time the Egyptians were worshipping it; to roast the flesh which that people eat raw; to eat the head which they never eat; to dress the entrails which they never dressed, but employed in divination and other purposes of superstition. Nor were the Hebrews separated from idolatrous nations, only by the distinction of meats; but by particularities of dress, language, government, customs, times, places of worship, and even by the situation of the country. The land of Palestine was fortified by nature, and almost inaccessible; which verified Balaam's prediction, " the people shall dwell alone and shall not be reckoned among the nations (*y*)."

(*x*) Lewis, Book V. Chap. xvi.   (*y*) Numb. xxiii. 9.

Heathens

Heathens believed in a multiplicity of gods who presided over woods, rivers, mountains, and valleys, and worshipped them in temples built in these places: for the prevention of this idolatrous practice Moses commanded the Israelites to worship God in one place, and to bring burnt offerings and sacrifices, and tithes and heave offerings to the place chosen by the Lord God; and threatened to cut off those who disobeyed this order. The prophet Zephaniah (z) intimates, that when idolatry shall be abolished, the worship of God shall not be confined to Jerusalem, but that it shall be lawful to worship God any where. Ancient patriarchs performed divine worship on hills or mountains, and planted them with trees, that the shade might excite devotion, and the silence of retirement inspire the worshippers with awe and reverence. Ancient Heathens perverted this innocent custom, by worshipping the sun, moon and stars on high places, by consecrating groves to their gods and heroes, and by making these groves scenes of impiety, impurity, and abominable prostitutions. To prevent such impure and idolatrous rites, Moses forbade planting trees near places of worship, commanded his people to destroy all the places, wherein idolatrous nations served their gods, to cut down their groves, and to demolish their altars and high places (a). That groves were prohibited as a preservative against idolatry, is

(z) Chap. ii, 11.   (a) Exod. xxxiv. 13.

evident

SECT. II. evident from this, that pious kings afterwards extirpated them, and apostate kings planted them (*b*).

Means employed to procure respect for God. Every precept, prohibition, rite and custom of the Israelites, their times and places of worship, and the ministers of religion, were all calculated to abolish idolatry and beget a veneration for God and his worship. In former times patriarchs, and heads of families, exercised the ministerial function; and every man offered sacrifice in fields or on tops of mountains to idols or demons. To stop this source of idolatry Moses confined the priesthood to a certain family, who were zealous in punishing idolaters, and who did not spare their own relations; from an aversion to false worship (*c*). The observance of times was also conducive to the removal of idolatry; it was usual with ancient idolaters, to devote the whole month of September to sacrifices, fasts, and other exercises of devotion; nor can Spencer see any reason why Moses should crowd so many solemnities into one month, or dedicate the same days of this month to the feasts of expiation, trumpets and tabernacles, but for the removal of idolatry. The feast of New-moons and Passover were celebrated at the times of the Pagan feasts; so that the Jews could not attend to the festivals of the Heathens; nor could any person who knew the sabbath was instituted in memory of the creation, ever worship

(*b*) Spencer de legibus Heb. Lib. I. Cap. vi.
(*c*) Ibid. Lib. II. Cap. vi.

of Religion on Mankind.

the creature instead of the Creator (*d*). The Jewish lawgiver employed various means to inspire a carnal people with respect for God, and his worship. The high-priest alone was admitted into the holy of holies, and that but once a year; no fire was used in sacrifice, but what was taken from the altar (*e*); by the command of God to Moses, a man was stoned for gathering sticks on the sabbath (*f*); and in David's time, the Lord smote Uzza, and put him to death, for inconsiderately touching the ark of the Lord (*g*). Priests were prohibited to drink wine when they entered the tabernacle, or to quit it on any pretence, until the service was performed (*h*). Their dress was to be splendid, to procure them respect; and their fortunes competent to preserve them from contempt. The deformed were excluded from the Hebrew priesthood; as a natural blemish might render their office despicable (*i*), and ministers of religion were forbade to marry a divorced woman, an harlot, or even a widow (*k*). None were allowed to enter the sanctuary, with shoes or unwashed hands, or to turn their backs on it, when going out of the tabernacle. Women after childbirth were prohibited to enter it, until they were purified; and priests and lay Jews, who had any

(*d*) Spencer, Lib. II. Cap. vi. (*e*) Lev. x. 1.
(*f*) Numb. xv. 36. (*g*) 2 Sam. vi. 6.
(*h*) Lev. x. 7. (*i*) Lev. xxi. 16.
(*k*) Lowman's Heb. Ritual, Part II. Chap. iii.

unclean-

uncleanness, were forbade to eat the flesh of sacrifices, on pain of being cut off. Moses employed various other means of restoring the knowledge of the true God, and preventing a relapse into superstition and idolatry. He separated them for forty years in the wilderness from all idolatrous nations; that they might unlearn their prejudices (*l*); destroyed multitudes of them who were incurably obstinate; extirpated the Canaanites and other neighbours who might seduce them to idolatry; and threatened to cut off all who were convicted of such seduction (*m*).

Of the tabernacle and temple. It was usual with some ancient Heathens, to carry about the images of their gods, to accompany them in their journeys, and to assist them in dangers. Some supposed these images inhabited by their gods, and chained them down in order to secure their residence; and that they might know where to invoke and address them in prayer (*n*). The prophet Amos (*o*) charges the Israelites with carrying the tabernacle of Moloch in the wilderness after the manner of the Egyptians. Moses, to abolish this custom, built a tabernacle or portable temple for the true God; in order to divert his people from that practice of idolaters: no reason can be assigned for confining the divine presence within the narrow limits of a tabernacle, or temple; but a compliance with the narrow con-

(*l*) Spencer, Lib. I. Cap. xii.   (*m*) Deut. xiii. 6. 15.
(*n*) Spencer, Diss. V. Lib. III. Cap. iii.   (*o*) Ch. v. 26.

ceptions of a grofs people, who otherwife might think him abfent or carelefs about them. To correct this erroneous opinion; Solomon, after he had built the temple, cried out in the following words, "Shall God dwell on earth? behold the heaven, and heaven of heavens cannot contain thee, much lefs this houfe which I have built." "Heaven is my throne, and the earth my footftool, fays the prophet, where is the houfe that ye build unto me?" And the apoftle fays "that Solomon built him an houfe, howbeit the Moft High dwelleth not in temples made with hands (*p*)." We cannot entertain fo unworthy an idea of God, as to fuppofe that he could be delighted with fumptuous ornaments and coftly utenfils; and the chief object of the magnificence of the temple, muft have been to gratify a carnal people, to infpire a veneration for the Being worfhipped there, and to allure them from idolatry, to the worfhip of the true God (*q*).

Mofes permitted the various facrifices ufed among the Gentiles in the worfhip of their idols, but corrected and reformed them: fome he intended as expreffions of piety and gratitude to God; fome were defigned to avert the divine anger; others to expiate offences and purify the heart; and all of them to abolifh or remove ido-

Of facrifices and luftrations.

(*p*) Ifaiah lxvi. 1. 1 Kings viii. 27. Acts vii. 47.
(*q*) Spencer, Lib. III. Diff. VI.

SECT. II. latry (r). Moses no where absolutely commanded sacrifices, but permitted them in compliance with the prejudices of his people; he knew they would offer sacrifices, and only directs them in the choice of the thing sacrificed (s), and in the object of sacrifices. The prophet Isaiah (t) asks, "Who hath required these things at your hands?" The Psalmist thinks it impious to suppose that God would be delighted with the blood of bulls or of goats; St. Paul (u) calls these and other ceremonies of the law "weak and beggarly elements;" and St. Peter affirms, that spiritual and living sacrifices can alone be acceptable to a God of holiness and purity. It must be admitted, that Abel, Cain, Noah and Abraham, offered sacrifices; but theirs were spontaneous and not enjoined. Cain offered the fruits of the earth; and Abel the firstlings of his flocks; sacrifices both different and voluntary prove that they were not required; and the prophets, to lessen all confidence in them, affirm that God did not require them, when he brought them forth out of the land of Egypt (w). Spencer maintains, that Heathens borrowed sacrifices and other rites from the patriarchs; and that, in some instances, idolatry was first built on the worship of the true God: that Moses purged these rites of every thing abominable, and changed the object, without en-

(r) Lev. xxiii. Numb. xv. 20. Lev. ii. 14. Numb. viii. 12.
(s) Lev. i. (t) i. 12. (u) Gal. iv. 9. (w) Jerem. vii. 22.

tirely

tirely abolishing them. Hence this learned writer deduces the similitude of some Pagan and Mosaic rites; and affirms, that this similitude was pleasing to the Israelites; while the smallest marks of distinction were as offensive to Heathens as rites diametrically opposite; since no sects are so averse from each other, as those which differ least, in doctrine and worship (*x*). Gentiles practised ablutions and purgations, and imagined that water, especially salt water, washed away stains from the soul as well as from the body: and Spencer can see no reason for this and other useless rites but to divert the Israelites from false worship, to the worship of the true God. The Jewish lawgiver altered and improved these rites, changed the object of them, and made them essentially distinct, while they agreed in some respects. His lustrations were simple and free from pomp, and intended to cleanse the flesh from pollutions and impurities, while those of the Heathens abounded with magical and superstitious ceremonies (*y*). Hence it is evident, that the Hebrew legislator transfused into divine worship several rites, but carefully corrected them; and rejected every impurity, so as to convert superstition into religion, and lead men from idolatry to the worship of the true God.

(*x*) Spencer, Lib. III. Diff. II.
(*y*) Ibid. Diff. III. p. 992.

The

SECT. II.

Tendency of the theocracy and of temporal sanctions.

The theocratical form of government, and temporal sanctions established among the Hebrews, tended to remove superstition and preserve them from Gentilism and the worship of idols. Their Jehovah was invested with a double authority of God and civil magistrate; and they who refused to serve him as God, thought themselves bound to obey him as king. All idolaters were considered as rebels; and several were restrained from idolatry by a threat denounced against those who were guilty of that crime (z). But an invisible king, and a theocracy appeared despicable in the eyes of a carnal people, who were accustomed to, and captivated with, all the splendor of royalty. Jehovah, it is true, appointed judges as his viceroys to direct both religious and civil affairs; but the Israelites rejected this form of government, and demanded a king who might be more indulgent to their prejudices; and denied the divine as well as political authority of their God Jehovah. Here it must be observed, that almost all the judges appointed by God were religious and good men; almost all the kings appointed by men themselves were idolatrous and tyrannical: the government of the former was mild and gentle; while under kings, they were oppressed and enslaved, as Samuel (a) forewarned them. God promised the Israelites frequently, and solemnly, a numerous

(z) Deut. Ch. xiii.   (a) 1 Sam. viii. 11.

offspring, a land flowing with milk and honey, long life and victory over their enemies, on condition of obedience; but threatens plague, famine, disease, death and defeats to those who violated his statutes. The Mosaic sanctions were accommodated to the genius of a rude, and earthly minded people, attentive only to present objects, and unlikely to be influenced by spiritual and distant considerations. The ancient Gentiles entertained an opinion, that no success was to be expected in war or agriculture, without the favour of idols or demons; and that all unprosperous events were to be imputed to their anger, when they were neglected or disregarded. The sacrifices of Pagans were intended to appease or suspend the anger of their deities; their festivals to render them propitious to their fields and orchards; or to express their gratitude for a plenteous harvest. Since then the acquisition of temporal benefits was the object of Gentile worship; it was necessary that Moses should promise temporal advantages to the observers of his laws, and threaten severe punishments to those, who implored the aid of any strange god. Temporal rewards and punishments offered by Moses, had a direct tendency to subvert the very foundation of idolatry; as he promised to bestow the blessings which they expected from their idols; and to avert the evils which they apprehended from them (*b*).

(*b*) Spencer, Lib. I. Cap. iii.

Balaam's

SECT. II.

Effects of those sanctions in the time of judges.

Balaam's advice to the Moabites proves, that peace and prosperity would necessarily attend the Israelites, whilst they were obedient to God's laws. The Moabites and Midianites having solicited Balaam to curse the Israelites, the prophet refused to curse those whom God hath blessed, but suggested the means of withdrawing the divine favour from them. Balaam advised the princes of Midian to send some beautiful females into the camp of the Israelites, in order to seduce them from the worship of the true God. The stratagem succeeded; the children of Israel, smitten with the charms of those fair idolatresses, were admitted to their embraces (*c*), bowed down to their gods, and were sorely oppressed by Midian. Joshua and his contemporaries, who had seen the miracles of Moses, served the Lord while they lived; but the next generation fell into idolatry, and were delivered by God into the hands of their enemies. Though rescued by the judges, they served other gods; and were sold into the hands of the king of Mesopotamia, who kept them in bondage eight years (*d*). When they cried unto the Lord and repented, they were delivered by Othniel who defeated that prince (*e*): having apostatized they served Eglon king of Moab eighteen years, and were rescued from this second servitude by Ehud, when they had repented of their apostacy (*f*). They soon

(*c*) Numb. xxv. 1.   (*d*) Judges Ch. iii.
(*e*) Judges iii. 10.   (*f*) Judges iii.

relapsed

relapsed into idolatry, and were sold into the hands of Jabin, who oppressed them severely for twenty years; Deborah released them from this third servitude, and God made two women chief instruments of their deliverance (*g*). Having forgot this act of mercy, they were delivered into the hands of Midian, and groaned under a more severe bondage than they had hitherto experienced; but when they cried unto the Lord, they were miraculously delivered by Gideon, who broke his father's idols and sacrificed to the true God (*h*). At Gideon's death, they relapsed into idolatry, and were sold into the hands of the Philistines and Ammonites for eighteen years (*i*); but were emancipated by Jephthah, from this fifth servitude, after they had sincerely repented (*k*). The Israelites again did evil in the sight of the Lord, in the administration of Eli; and were delivered into the hands of the Philistines, for the space of forty years. The sons of Eli committed the greatest abominations, and even debauched women at the door of the tabernacle; for which crime Eli was deprived of the high-priesthood, and his sons were cut off in one day (*l*). Samuel, who succeeded him as judge, assembled the people, and exhorted them to put away strange gods, and repent of their transgressions: having expressed solemnly all the marks of a lively repentance, God

---

(*g*) Judges Ch. iv.   (*h*) Judges Ch. vi.   (*i*) Judges Ch. x.   (*k*) Judges Ch. xi.   (*l*) 1 Sam. iv. 17.

destroyed

SECT. II. destroyed their enemies by thunder, and put an end, for that time, to their tyranny and oppression (*l*).

Effects of them in the time of kings.

The Israelites, grown weary of the government of judges, demanded a king; Samuel remonstrated against rejecting this form, but finding his remonstrances disregarded, he complied with their demand, and told them, that God gave them a king for the punishment of their offences. David, a man after God's own heart (*m*), for his adherence to his worship, tarnished the brightness of his reign by murder and adultery; and, though a sincere penitent, brought calamities upon himself, his family, and his country, by the commission of these crimes. Were it not too tedious and uninteresting, it might be proved, from the first book of Kings and the second of Chronicles, that temporal rewards and punishments were uniformly dispensed from the reign of David to the Babylonish captivity: that as often as the Hebrews fell into idolatry they were chastised, and restored to obedience by the judgments of God. They were punished for changing the government from judicial to regal, and were frequently delivered into the hands of their enemies; but were as often rescued, as they sincerely repented. This people were not influenced by rewards, nor punishments, absolutely to refrain from idolatry and vice; but their sufferings generally engaged them

(*l*) 1 Sam. Ch. vii.   (*m*) 1 Kings xv. 5.

to repent, and brought them to a sense of duty, at least for a time. Judith (*n*) sums up the effects of the obedience and disobedience of the Hebrews, in the following words; "Whilst they sinned not before God they prospered; because that God who hateth iniquity was with them; but when they departed from the way, which he appointed them, they were destroyed in many battles, and were led captives into a strange land, and the temple of their God was cast to the ground, and their cities were taken by their enemies." Such were the effects of the observance or violation of the laws of Moses! effects which accurately corresponded with the promise, and incontrovertibly prove the divine authority of the lawgiver. A short time before his death, Moses renewed the covenant between God and his people, exhorted them to obedience, and promised that they should be delivered from captivity, dispersion, or other calamity, on sincere repentance. This prediction was verified in the time of judges and kings; and we see the good effects of the divine judgments after the Babylonish captivity. A servitude of seventy years, in a strange country, at length cured them of all propensity to idolatry; there they had time to take a retrospect of a series of crimes and idolatries severely punished; saw the predictions of the prophets fulfilled, and never after relapsed into idolatry, terrified by the evils inflicted for

(*n*) Ch. v.

dis-

SECT. II. disobedience. Hence it appears, that the Mosaic penalties tended to remove superstition, and did actually remove it, at least for a time. A repetition of them had at length the desired effect, of absolutely abolishing superstition, which is the first step towards the worship of the true God. The Jews, to this day, feel the effects of the threats of their lawgiver; since they rejected their Messiah they have been dispersed and persecuted, and never constituted a nation with laws and government of their own, on account of that crime, which they never repented of. For what other offence has their God suffered them to be scattered, and oppressed, for near two thousand years, and not gathered them into their own land, according to the prediction of their lawgiver (*o*)? The hardships they have endured in that time, might convince them, that they have continued long under the rod of the Almighty, deserted and disowned by the God who poured such benefits on their ancestors, while they were obedient to his laws.

Intention of particular laws and rites of Judaism. I proceed now to point out the tendency and use of several Mosaic rites and prohibitions, which seem to have little or no connexion with religion, morals or policy: at these the infidel directs his cavils and objections; he cannot comprehend, why a pure and perfect God should enjoin such a multitude of rites and precepts, that have no moral excellence in them, and which appear to promote

(*o*) Deut. xxx.

neither

neither the honour of God, nor the advantage of his creatures. It cannot be denied, that these are ideas apt to be suggested, on a superficial view of the Levitical law, and Hebrew ritual; yet if we examine the origin and object of the Mosaic institutions, we shall find that most of them tend to prevent or remove idolatry; that none of them are immoral; that some of them conduce to the advancement of virtue, and that all of them evince the wisdom of the lawgiver, who adapts his laws to the tempers, prejudices, and circumstances of his people. It is difficult to explain the reasons of the Jewish rites and precepts at this distance of time; as many of them allude to customs which prevailed in the days of Moses, and which are now unknown to us, from our ignorance of antiquity. If we can, in many instances, vindicate the wisdom of these laws, for the times when, and the persons to whom they were prescribed; it will appear unreasonable, to condemn them in other cases, where we have not equal evidence of their wisdom and expedience. It will now appear, that some rites and precepts of the law, though unessential in themselves, were extremely useful, and even necessary, for retaining the worship of the true God, preserving the Israelites a distinct people, and for guarding them against the idolatries of surrounding neighbours. Maimonides affirms, that ancient idolaters besmeared their victims with honey, in order to render them palatable to their gods and departed heroes: Spencer (*p*) thinks that Moses was induced, by this practice, to prohibit offering honey unto the Lord; left men should suppose that he was delighted with things acceptable to the Heathen gods. The rite of boiling a kid in its mother's milk was practised by Pagans in the mysteries of their demons; they supposed these demons to be delighted with the broth, and sprinkled their trees, fields and orchards with it, in a magical way, that they might produce plentifully the ensuing year. Moses (*q*) prohibited the custom of seething a kid in its mother's milk; to abolish or prevent this superstitious practice, and not to restrain cruelty, as some commentators have vainly imagined (*r*). Pagan priests wore garments mixed of linen and woollen, to express their gratitude to certain demons, for their benign influence over their flax and sheep; and to secure their protection to their fields and flocks. The lawgiver therefore forbade his people, to wear linen and woollen together; in order to remove the mistake, that his people were indebted for these blessings to stars, or demons. That heterogeneous mixtures of linen and woollen were marks of idolatry, and instruments of superstition, appears from this circumstance; that Hebrew priests and laymen might wear both in the

(*p*) Lib. II. Cap. ix.   (*q*) Exod. xii. 5.
(*r*) Spencer, Lib. II.

service

of Religion on Mankind.

service of the tabernacle or temple, where they ran no risque of falling into idolatry (*s*).

SECT. II. *The same subject continued.*

At Pagan feasts, was exhibited a strange mixture of mirth and sorrow; the Egyptians began theirs in honour of Osiris or Adonis, with expressions of grief and sympathy with Venus for the loss of her gallant: they shaved their heads, lacerated their bodies, and carried his image in solemn procession, in honour of the idol. Solon (*t*) prohibited the Athenian women to scratch and tear themselves at the interments of their friends; and Baal's prophets cried aloud and cut themselves with knives and lancets, till the blood gushed out (*u*). Ancient idolaters considered cutting, maiming, and mangling themselves, as a rite acceptable to the infernal gods and to the spirits of the deceased. Moses forbade Israelites to make cuttings in the flesh for the dead, or print marks upon their bodies; for the purpose of abolishing or preventing such idolatrous practices. Ancient Hebrews employed these rites, as expressions of grief, at the funerals of the deceased; and therefore the lawgiver prohibited them, as they favoured of ethnicism, and led to superstition. Ancients in their funeral ceremonies used to cut their hair round, to pluck off their hair or beard, and to strew them on the corpses of the deceased, as acceptable to demons, and to the spirits of the

---

(*s*) Spencer, Lib. II. Cap. xxi.   Lewis, Book VI. Ch. xxiii.
(*t*) Plutarch.   (*u*) 1 Kings xviii. 28.

I 2   departed.

SECT. II.
departed. To remove such superstitious rites, Moses prohibited the Hebrews to " round the corners of their heads, or mar the corners of their beards (w);" it was not simple cutting or shaving their heads or beards that is here forbade; but doing it to appease demons, or to gratify the dead. Even the most scrupulous observers of the law practised these rites at funerals; the prophet Jeremiah exhorts the Hebrews to cut off their hair, and Ezekiel threatens them with baldness in token of grief (x). Ancient idolaters offered first fruits to their gods, with tears and wailing; and believed that the souls of departed friends hovered round their sepulchres, and required food for their sustenance (y). To prevent or remove such idolatrous customs, Moses commanded the Israelites to declare solemnly, that they devoted first fruits and other offerings to none but pious and charitable uses; " I have not eaten in my mourning, nor taken aught for any unclean use; nor given aught thereof for the dead; but have given to the Levite, and unto the stranger, to the fatherless and the widow (z)."

The same subject continued.
It was a custom among Phenicians, Babylonians, and other ancient nations, to appoint women for prostitution, in the temples of Venus and Priapus: adjoining these temples they had tents, where persons of both sexes prostituted themselves, in ho-

(w) Lev. xix. 27. (x) Ezek. vii. 18.
(y) Spencer, Lib. II. Cap. xxiv. (z) Deut. xxvi. 12.

nour

nour of deities, who were supposed to be delighted with impure acts, performed near their temples, or in the presence of their idols (*a*). These temples were decorated with obscene figures, of naked Jupiters, Gladiators, and other emblems of strength and lewdness; and one thousand religious prostitutes were solemnly dedicated to such filthy services at Corinth, and maintained in a temple, for the use of sailors who visited that port (*b*). Herodotus assures us, that every Babylonish woman was obliged, once in her life, to prostitute herself to some stranger openly in the temple of Venus; that beautiful women were soon dismissed from the temple; while the deformed waited sometimes for three or four years before they could satisfy the law (*c*). This historian acquaints us, that almost all nations except Egyptians and Grecians, made their temples scenes of debauchery; and that Egyptians were the first, who prohibited abominable impurities in the worship of their gods (*d*). To prevent, or abolish such impure and superstitious rites, Moses prohibited each sex to be concerned in them; " There shall be, saith he, no whore of the daughters of Israel, nor sodomite, or rather whoremaster of the sons of Israel (*e*)." That prostitution in honour of their gods, was prohibited by this law, appears from another pro-

(*a*) Strabo, Lib. VIII.   (*b*) Lewis, Book V. Ch. i.
(*c*) Herod. Lib. I.   (*d*) Herod. Lib. II.
(*e*) Deut. xxiii. 17.

hibition

SECT. II. hibition of Moses; "Do not prostitute thy daughter to cause her to be a whore;" which could only be understood of meretricious acts performed in honour of polluted idols. Baal Peor, an obscene deity, like Priapus, was the chief god of Palestine and Phenicia, whose votaries expressed their gratitude for a numerous offspring, by obscene postures, and by the indecent practice of bruising the breasts of virgins (*f*). Phenician virgins prostituted themselves in the temples of obscene deities, in the presence of their idols; and offered money, or garments obtained by meretricious practices, for the repair of temples, the maintenance of priests, or the purchase of victims (*g*). To abolish or prevent such superstitious and filthy customs, Moses prohibited females to bring the hire of an harlot into the house of the Lord; as it would be a disgrace to the temple, to admit any thing that was unchaste; and God might be supposed pleased with filthy rites, did he accept of the hire of prostitution, as an offering to his temple (*h*). The ancient Egyptians worshipped Anubis, under the form of a dog, and reverenced this animal, as the emblem of the dog-star: hence, perhaps, Moses was induced to reject from the sanctuary, the price of a dog, and forbids to bring it, as well as the price of a whore, into the house of the Lord;

(*f*) Young on Idol. Corruptions, Vol. II. Chap. i.
(*g*) Athanasius contra Gentes, Cap. xxvi. Edit. Paris, 1698.
(*h*) Spencer, Lib. II. Cap. xxiii.

and

and for the same reason, namely, because both are an abomination unto the Lord. The latter part of this verse was intended as a preservative against impurity and superstition; and we may conclude, that the former part, relative to the price of dogs, had a similar intention; especially as the word abomination generally expresses God's abhorrence of superstition and idolatry (*i*).

General tendency of the Mosaic rites, precepts, and prohibitions.

A careful view of the Hebrew ritual might readily convince us, that it tended to preserve the Hebrews from idolatry, to promote the worship of the true God, and to advance men in theological and moral knowledge. Moses prohibited many rites, which staggered the weak, and led them to, and confirmed them in, idolatry; and abolished some customs seemingly innocent, such as shaving the head round, eating over blood, wearing linen and woollen, &c. as they tended to encourage superstition and idolatry among his people. He prohibited not only impure rites, and idolatrous worship, but even acts which tended to seduce men to idolatry, such as branding their bodies, cutting their flesh, planting a grove near an altar, setting up an image, erecting painted stones, and other acts destitute of moral turpitude, and which became criminal, only by being made instruments in the worship of false gods. He opposed diametrically some Gentile institutions, to

(*i*) Spencer, Lib. II. Cap. xxiii.

SECT. II. render the Israelites odious to Pagans; while he complied with the prejudices of his own people in trifling instances, that they might not reject his more rigid, severe, and rational doctrines. It is not inconsistent with the sanctity of God to admit into his service, rites made use of in Pagan worship, provided they are improved; just as a pious king might accept of the honours paid to a tyrant, and as Heathen temples have been converted into Christian churches. It must readily be admitted, that the Jewish legislator repeatedly forbids his people to have any commerce with Gentiles, or to adopt their manners; but such passages only condemn idolatry, impurity, and every thing that clashes with good morals, and the belief of one God: and ancient Jews admitted several Heathen rites, which did not militate against morality, and the worship of the Deity (*k*). From this slight view of the Hebrew ritual, we may easily judge of its general tendency and design; even the learned Spencer thinks it impossible, to explain the reasons of all the Jewish institutions, at this distance of time, from our ignorance of antiquity.

The Mosaic rites and institutions local and temporary. It is probable, that Moses adapted his institutions to the genius of an uncultivated people, oppressed in Egypt, children in information, and accustomed to the rites of an idolatrous kingdom. He must have known the absurdity of addressing, or instructing children, as men of mature under-

(*k*) Spencer, Lib. III. Cap. xii.

standing;

standing; or peasants and mechanics, as if they were learned and refined. He enjoined several rites and precepts uneffential in themselves, for the purpose of leading them by degrees, from idolatry to true worship; just as men employ many years, in learning the rudiments of arts, and reading books, which have no intrinsic value, but as they assist in the acquisition of useful knowledge. To put it beyond all doubt that the Mosaic institutions were intended to fence against or extirpate idolatry, it may suffice to observe; that converts, who were in no danger of relapsing into Paganism, were excused from observing them. They who dreaded a relapse, were required to observe the whole law, and admitted proselytes of the covenant; while such as apprehended no danger, and promised to observe the seven precepts of Noah, were admitted proselytes of the gate, and exempted from the observance of the Hebrew ritual. That the laws of Moses were addressed to the Israelites of his own time, and not to those of after ages, appears from this; that the Jewish prophets, Christ and St. Paul, who acknowledge the divine authority of the lawgiver, censure his New-moons, solemn feasts, and other institutions, as adapted only to a gross and carnal people. St. Paul (*l*) condemns the Galatians, for desiring to be again in bondage to weak and beggarly elements; and our Saviour (*m*) says, that on the

(*l*) Gal. iv. 10. (*m*) Matt. xxii. 37.

love

SECT. II. love of God and our neighbour hang all the law and the prophets. This assertion of Christ cannot be true, unless these parts of the law, which appear to have no relation to God or man, tend to promote the interest of our neighbour, and to restore idolaters to the worship of God. Moses recommended some rites and precepts diametrically opposite to those of Pagans; while he adopted others, in compliance with the prejudices of his people. The Hebrew lawgiver, knowing that men will not adopt new rites, except they appear in the garb of old, transcribed some profane ones into his worship; but carefully reformed them, and changed their object, from idols and demons to God. Primitive Christians, sensible that prejudices were not to be removed at once, but by slow degrees, retained some Heathen and Jewish rites; and the wisest of the Protestant reformers, while they abolished the most exceptionable doctrines and rites of the Romish church, retained some trifling ones, from a tenderness for the prejudices of some ignorant converts (*n*).

<small>Laws of Moses preferable to those of Pagan lawgivers.</small>

The Hebrew ritual was not merely ceremonial, and Voltaire falsely charges it with absurdity and barbarism. We are no more to confine the divine law of the Jews, to rites and ceremonies, than the law of Christians to baptism and the Lord's supper: it does not consist entirely in show and ceremony, in washings and purifications, in offer-

(*n*) Spencer. Diss. I. Cap. i.

ings

ings of birds and beasts, as this and other writers have unfairly represented it. The Mosaic code, besides a multitude of ceremonies, requires us to believe in one God who created the world, and rules it by his providence; to love and fear him; to be grateful for his goodness, and trust in his mercy; to be just and charitable; and to love our neighbour as ourselves; it prohibits making any likeness of God, and restrains impure and vicious desires. A learned civilian (*o*) affirms, that if the laws of all other nations, except the Jewish, were put together, they are not to be compared to the old Roman laws in gravity, equity and sufficiency; and yet the Jewish laws, thus distinguished by this author, Voltaire has ignorantly presumed to censure as barbarous and absurd. If we compare Hebrew with Heathen institutions, we shall find the former preferable to the latter, in many particulars. The law forbids men to engage in war but for self-defence, or to obtain satisfaction for injuries; to enter an enemy's country, until restitution was refused; to cut down fruit trees, or commit unnecessary waste or havock of any kind. How humane was the institution of the sabbatical year, which emancipated slaves; and the Jubilee which restored old proprietors to the possessions that they had alienated? In the Mosaic code (*p*)

(*o*) Sir Thomas Ridley, Part I. Chap. i. Sect. 1.
(*p*) Exod. xxii. 21. Lev. xix. 19. Lev. xxiii. 22. Deut. xv. 7, 11. Deut. xxiii. 21. See also Maimonides De jure pauperis & peregrini, Cap. i.

there

there are many pressing exhortations to relieve the poor, the stranger, the fatherless and widow, not to be paralleled in the laws of other ancient kingdoms.—" Thou shalt not vex the stranger, nor oppress him, nor afflict the widow and fatherless child. Thou shalt not harden thine heart, nor shut thine hand from thy poor brother; thou shalt open thine hand wide unto thy brother, to thy poor, and to thy needy in thy land. When ye reap the harvest, thou shalt not wholly reap the corner of thy field, nor gather the gleanings of thy harvest; thou shalt leave them to the poor and to the stranger: thou shalt not glean thy vineyard, nor gather every grape; it shall be for the stranger, the fatherless and widow; thou shalt remember that thou wast a stranger in the land of Egypt."—Incestuous marriages so common in Egypt, Persia, Arabia, and even Greece, were prohibited by Moses, as contrary to good policy and the source of irregularities in private families (*q*). Many ancient nations had asylums for the reception of criminals which screened them from magistrates; and Moses appointed cities of refuge for the involuntary manslayer to fly to for shelter, until he was acquitted by the judges; the Mosaic institution was intended as a protection to the innocent only; while the asylums of Greeks and Romans equally protected the innocent and

(*q*) Jewish Lett. Part III. Lett. IV.

guilty.

guilty (r). In Lacedemon, even the innocent annually received a certain number of stripes, as a mark of subjection (s), and helots were murdered, to prevent their encrease; while the Jewish code guarded the lives of slaves from the tyranny of masters; and the state from the bad effects of cruelty and oppression. If a master put out the eye or broke the tooth of his slave, he was obliged to emancipate him (t); if he struck him with a stick, so that he died of the blow, he was punished or put to death. In the Hebrew republic, a woman, who killed her child, or a father who exposed his new-born infant, would have been treated as murderers; while among Greeks and Romans their laws allowed them to expose infants or put them to death. Romulus required every citizen to preserve all his males and eldest female, and permitted him to destroy his other females, and to expose weak or deformed children (u). According to the ancient Roman laws fathers might sell their children for slaves thrice, and had a power of life and death over them, as long as they lived; and Aristotle maintained, that the authority of a father over his children was so absolute, that he could do them no injustice. The old Roman laws allowed a husband to repudiate his

(r) Lewis, Book II. Chap. 13.
(s) Jewish Lett. Part III. Lett. IV.
(t) Exod. xxi. 26.
(u) Leland's Christian Revelation, Part II. Chap. x.

wife

SECT. II. wife for taking his keys; or to put her to death if taken in adultery; whilst the woman had no redress for the infidelity of her husband (w). These laws allowed creditors to exercise cruelties on debtors, and prohibited the former to load the latter with a greater weight of chains than fifteen pounds; while the Jewish code enjoins humanity even towards beasts, and forbids killing the young one, under the eye of the dam, or an animal that was pursued and took refuge in their house (x). The institutions of Lycurgus were framed for a military republic, and tended rather to render men hardy and brave, than just and benevolent. Aristotle (y) observes, that the Lacedemonians flourished in time of war, but declined in seasons of peace, as may naturally be expected from the ordinances of that lawgiver. The Jewish legislator was preferable to the Spartan in the distribution of the land; having confirmed his division by the laws of religion: according to the Mosaic code Jehovah is Lord of the land, the Israelites his vassals, and the lands, held as fiefs from him, remained unalienable in the same families, on condition of obedience (z). Plato and Aristotle did not indeed found commonwealths, like Lycurgus and Solon; yet each of them formed one in imagination, and committed it to writing: but while they laboured to shew the excellence of their

(w) Jewish Lett. Part III. Lett. IV.   (x) Deut. xxiii.
(y) Pol. ii. 7.   (z) Jewish Lett. Part III. Lett. II. Sect. 4.

genius,

genius, and the perfection of human policy, they proved incontrovertibly the weakness and imperfection of both. Plato ordained, that there should be a community of wives, among the citizens of his republic: according to which plan, all women would be common to all men; incestuous copulations must often take place; and the virtues of chastity and fidelity, as well as parental, filial, and conjugal affection, would exist but in idea. Lycurgus commanded young girls to dance naked among boys; while Plato required women, in the flower of youth, to dance, ride, wrestle, and perform all exercises naked, among young men who also wore no cloaths. It was in vain to enjoin continence to either sex, while the laws allowed a view of naked persons of each sex, which tended to kindle lust in the males, and to deprive females of that modesty which is so great a preservative of the chastity of women (*a*). Plato commands women to procure abortions, and to expose their children in certain cases; applauds unnatural and obscene love; acquits a man by law who killed his own slave, and requires him only to pay a fine, who killed the slave of another. If a person killed a freeman in anger, he was banished for two years; if deliberately he was punished with three years exile. Aristotle, who undertook to censure Plato, and other lawgivers, was also defective in his laws, for the reformation of manners, and the

(*a*) Hackwell's Apology, Book IV. Chap. ii. Sect. 3.

SECT. II. good of the commonwealth. If a man had as many children as he could maintain, Aristotle ordered his wife to procure abortion, and parents to expose weak or deformed children (*b*). These laws tended to render men cruel and inhuman; since, as Lactantius (*c*) observes, it could not be expected, that he should spare other mens children, who spared not his own. Aristotle prohibited lascivious pictures, lest young persons should be corrupted by the sight of them; but excepted the images of certain gods in whom custom allowed licentiousness: how absurd, says Lactantius, to take away all other wanton representations, whilst he allowed the lascivious pictures of the gods, which corrupt much more?

Mosaic writings of divine authority.

We shall not be surprised at the superior excellence of the Mosaic laws, when we consider, that the author of them was commissioned by God. The following considerations ought fully to acquit this lawgiver of all suspicion of fraud and imposture: it would have been impossible for him to have deceived the Israelites by pretended miracles, and equally impossible for any other person after him, to deceive a whole nation. The lawgiver relates miracles said to have been wrought publicly, in the sight of Israelites and Egyptians, and which every man would have rejected had they not been performed; at least, it could not be expected, that a whole nation would unani-

(*b*) Arist. Pol. vii. 16.   (*c*) Lib. VI. Cap. xx.

mously

mously agree in such an imposture. Nor could a forgery be imposed on the Jews at any subsequent period; since men who were continually rebelling, and disposed to deny the divine authority of Moses, would naturally have said of his miracles, These are marvellous things, but we never heard of them before. Would a rebellious and stiff-necked people submit to circumcision, or expensive sacrifices; or consecrate to God the first fruits of their ground, and the first-born of their cattle; had they not believed those laws divine, and been eye-witnesses of the miracles wrought to confirm them? The Hebrew festivals are standing monuments of the reality of these miracles; the wisdom of proverbs far transcending Heathen morality in brevity and clearness; the harmony of the inspired writers, and the accomplishment of prophesies, prove those books to be of divine authority. This lawgiver required the lands to rest every seventh year, and promised that every sixth year should produce abundantly for two years: had not his divine commission enabled him to fulfil this promise, his people must have been starved and his imposture detected. They who doubt or deny his divine authority, allow him to be a wise lawgiver; and is it to be supposed that such a man would weaken the authority of a wise code, by blending it with an account of miracles, which every man knew had never been performed? Moses describes the faults as well as virtues of Abraham, Isaac, Jacob,

SECT. II. and other heroes of his history; conceals not the envy and murmuring of his sister Miriam, the idolatry of his brother, nor disguises his own unadvised thoughts which none but God and himself could know. He was modest and free from vanity, and though he commanded armies, and obtained victories, he observes a total silence about his own grandeur and exploits. He settled the office of high-priest in his brother's family, and left not his own children any office of honour or emolument, but that of simple Levites; while he appointed Joshua to conduct the Israelites into the promised land (*d*). Some think it impossible to resist the evidence of miracles, and cannot believe that the Israelites would have worshipped idols, had they seen the wonders related by Moses. But miracles do not absolutely determine the will; and we have the testimony of a philosopher, that he himself would have resisted them though he had seen them with his eyes. " Make the lame to walk, the dumb to speak, or raise the dead, says he, and I shall not be shaken by this." Such was the opinion of this free-thinker relative to miracles; while others of his fraternity differ from him, and maintain the impossibility of resisting their force (*e*)!

Temporal sanctions prove his divine commission. A cursory view of the Jewish history, while it convinces us, that obedience was attended with rewards, and disobedience with punishments, proves

(*d*) Philo de vita Mosis, and Joseph. Antiq. Lib. II. Cap. v.
(*e*) Jewish Lett. VI.

at the same time the divine authority of Moses, and the influence of his promises and threats on the condition of his people. Of all institutions none so strongly marks the divine legislator as temporal sanctions: in the course of this world, rewards and punishments are not uniformly dispensed, according to the merits or demerits of individuals or nations; there is not an inseparable connexion between obedience and rewards, disobedience and punishments in this life. All other lawgivers have employed future sanctions to excite men to the observance of their laws and ordinances: but Moses accommodated his to the tempers and capacities of his people. He promised to reward or punish, with national prosperity or national judgments, the observance or violation of his laws, and his promises were performed; nor could any, except a divine lawgiver, fulfil such promises. It has been proved, in the preceding section, that other lawgivers could not reward obedience to their laws; that their power extended only to the punishment of individuals, and not to the chastisement of a whole people, who became vicious and disobedient; this was that privilege of the Jewish lawgiver which distinguished him from all other legislators, and proved his commission from God and his wisdom from heaven (*f*). The Israelites could not be strangers to future

(*f*) Warburton's divine Legation, passim.

SECT. II.

sanctions from Abraham and the patriarchs (g); nor did Moses inculcate them to enforce obedience to his political institutions; but employed those, which were more likely to operate on a sensual people, affected only by present objects. He knew, that men who were not kept within the bounds of duty by present rewards and punishments, would be little influenced by those that are future and remote.

The truth of his account confirmed by Bryant.

A learned and ingenious writer maintains, that Janus, Saturn, Orus, Poseidon, Zeuth, Osiris, Prometheus, and other names of Heathen gods and heroes, were different titles of Noah, and that the mythology of these is nearly the same with the history of that patriarch, as related by Moses. He proves that several Pagan fables referred to Noah, the ark and deluge; and deduces the certainty of this event, from several vestiges of it to be traced in the mythology of the ancients. According to this writer, Isis, Rhea, Atargatis, were emblems of the ark, and an ark or ship was employed in the rites of Isis and Osiris, in the Dionusia, and other festivals celebrated by Pagans. The dove, that announced the subsidence of the waters, was held sacred by many nations; while the raven, which disappointed their hopes, was generally esteemed a bird of ill omen. The bow, that token of covenant between God and man, according to the Mosaic account, was reverenced for many ages;

(g) Stackhouse's Body of Divinity, Sect. 3.

and

and we find this token and covenant referred to by Hesiod, Homer, Parmenides, and other ancient writers (*h*). Hesiod (*i*) alludes to this covenant, and calls it the great oath; and affirms, that this oath was iris or the rainbow, to which the deity appealed, when any of the inferior deities were guilty of a falshood. Homer (*k*) compares the colours in Agamemnon's cuirass to those of the iris, and affirms it was placed in the heavens as a sign to mankind.

——εκατερθ ιρισσιν εοικοτες ἃς τε Κρονιων
Εν νεφεϊ στηριξε τερας μεροπων ανθρωπων.

Jove's wondrous bow of three celestial dyes,
Plac'd as a sign to man amid the skies.

Homer (*l*) speaks of this phenomenon nearly in the same manner in other passages of his works. Hence we may conclude, that Pagans borrowed from Moses, or derived from one source those rites, customs and opinions, which resembled each other, and were common to all nations. The latter was the opinion of Bryant, who maintains, that this similarity subsisted universally in the most ancient nations, and argues from thence for the truth of the Mosaic account. This learned writer contends, that a resemblance prevailing universally

(*h*) Bryant's Mythology, Vol. II. 4to. p. 349.
(*i*) Theog. V. 780.   (*k*) Iliad, xi. 27.
(*l*) Iliad, xvii. 547, and Hymn to Selene, quoted by Bryant, ibid.

SECT. II. between Pagan fables, and the plain narrative of Moses, proves incontrovertibly the truth of the latter; since if originally false, it would not have been so widely diffused; and ancient nations would not have agreed with it, and with each other, in so many particulars.

Judaism imperfect. From what has been said of the divine commission of Moses, we might naturally expect, that Judaism should be a perfect code, to all the purposes of religion and morals; and would not be disappointed in our expectations. The Mosaic law, though imperfect in itself, was perfect in its kind, had the perfection intended by its author, and answered the purposes for which it was designed. Even the most exceptionable parts of the law tended to divert men from the worship of false gods, to separate them from idolatrous nations who were likely to seduce them, and reminded them of their obligations to the true God. The prevention of idolatry was its grand object; but when that end was attained, the ritual part was repealed, and the moral part, including the worship of God in spirit and in truth, was retained and insisted upon. The Hebrew code was not intended for all mankind, but for this people; not as a perfect law, but as a means to a more perfect; not to last for ever, but to the coming of the Messiah. Rites unnecessary for the first two thousand years of the world, and abolished at Christ's appearance, must have been local and temporary;

temporary; nor was the Hebrew ritual sufficiently general, to oblige all mankind: it does not mention a covenant between God and mankind, but between God and the Israelites, and requires duties, which none but Israelites could perform, with convenience or propriety; such as repairing thrice a year, to particular places appointed for God's worship, and the celebration of feasts, in commemoration of benefits conferred on that people. Even the decalogue was addressed to this people, and to them only; as appears from the preamble; " Hear, O Israel, I am the Lord thy God who brought thee out of the land of Egypt, out of the house of bondage." The rewards and punishments of the Mosaic laws were prosperity or adversity in the land of Canaan; which sanctions were applicable to the Jews only, and could not extend to the rest of mankind. For these reasons, the Hebrew revelation was not intended for the mass of mankind, who could not observe its laws, nor be influenced by its sanctions. But the law was not only local and temporary, but likewise defective in many other particulars: it rigourously commanded the observance of times, places, sacrifices, oblations and corporal purgations; while it enforced but feebly the duties of justice, charity, purity of heart, patience, temperance, and other virtues. Its encouragements to virtue, and restraints on vice, were not sufficiently strong; it is doubtful whether it even mentions a future state; it is certain

SECT. II. tain it is not clear upon the subject. The law promises no supernatural aid to enable men to conquer the frailties of their nature, and to free them from the bondage of sin and corruption; and offers to transgressors no hope of pardon and mercy, these strong motives to amendment and preventives of despair. The law does not hint at the plan of redemption, except perhaps by types; and is silent on the different kinds of worship, such as praise, thanksgiving, confession and prayer (*l*). So imperfect a revelation could not have been perpetual; " had the first covenant been faultless, there would have been no place found for the second," as the apostle (*m*) expresses it. But the Hebrew code was perfected and all its defects were remedied, by the Christian dispensation, which added some parts that were of eternal obligation, as will appear in the next section.

Judaism prepared men for the gospel.

But Judaism tended not only to abolish superstition, but contributed to the reception of Christianity in the world. The Mosaic and prophetic writings prepared the Jews for Christ's coming, and disposed them to admit him as their Messiah, when the predictions concerning him were so exactly fulfilled. One great effect of the Jewish code was, to shew the connexion between the Hebrew and Christian dispensations, and to serve as a preparative to a more perfect scheme of religion. Moses, and other sacred writers, point expresly at a

(*l*) Barrow's Serm. XV. (*m*) Heb. viii.

Messiah,

SECT. II.

Messiah, to rescue men from sin and superstition; the law and the prophets may be considered as an introduction to Christianity; the Jewish ritual, though weak and imperfect in itself, suited the circumstances of the Hebrews, and disposed men to receive that better religion, which was to be revealed, at the coming of the Messiah. The ritual prepared the Jews for the alterations which were to take place at Christ's appearance, and the apostles proved from the law and the prophets that Christ was the Messiah. The apostles repeatedly explained ritual expressions in a figurative way, considered some Mosaic rites as types, and urged them as arguments that Christ was the Messiah. St. Paul, in his epistle to the Hebrews, employed Jewish rites, to elucidate and confirm the doctrines of Christianity: and since the ritual answered the purpose of enforcing the truth of the gospel, this was possibly one of its designs: especially, as the same prophetic spirit, which at first devised rites, as useful in a literal sense, might have had a view to the use of them in future times (*n*).

The Hebrew writings were not only useful, in preventing idolatry and preparing men for the gospel; but in supplying defects in the chronology of the ancients, in directing naturalists in their researches, and in furnishing some Pagans with refined ideas of the attributes of God. Without

Hebrew writings useful in chronology and history.

(*n*) Lowman's Hebrew Ritual, Part III. Chap. iii.

the

SECT. II. the sacred records, we should have no exact account of time from the creation, to near the Christian æra, and Newton employs them in his chronology as supplements to profane history, which was so defective without them. A learned Heathen was of opinion, that if men knew the origin of the world they should calculate from thence; Varro divides time into uncertain, fabulous and historical: from the creation to the flood uncertain; from the flood to the first olympiad fabulous; and from thence to his own time historical (*o*). The æra of the olympiads commenced above three thousand years after the creation; of which period we have no historical account, which can be relied on, except from the scriptures. Without this source of information, we must be ignorant of ancient history from the creation to the beginning of the Persian empire; a period little less than three thousand years. Herodotus wrote about the time of Xerxes; Thucydides and Xenophon long after this period: nor is there any profane history extant, except some dubious fragments, but what was written after the deliverance of the Jews from the Babylonish captivity. Profane histories furnish no true narratives of events prior to this deliverance, and to the beginning of the Persian empire, as I have already observed. The books of Berosus the Chaldean, Manetho the Egyptian, Sanchoniathon the Phenician,

(*o*) Censorinus de Die Natali, Cap. xxi.

of Religion on Mankind. 139

SECT. II.

cian, and Megasthenes the Indian, are either lost or counterfeit; and though authentic, were written in the time of Ptolemy Philadelphus. "There is nothing, says Julius Africanus, quoted by Eusebius (*p*), accurately written in history by the Greeks before the olympiads; all things said to have happened before that time are confused and incoherent." Thucydides (*q*) begins his history with the Peloponnesian war; because matters preceding that period were known only by conjecture: and Plutarch (*r*) goes no farther back than Theseus; all before his time being but fable and fiction. The annals of the Romans previous to the burning of Rome by the Gauls were lost at that time; and as to the Scythians and other Barbarians, we know little of them, except from the Greeks and Romans, whose accounts are so frequently blended with fable and falshood.

We may judge of the excellence of the Mosaic system from the inconveniences which have resulted from ignorance, disbelief, or neglect of it. The Hebrew lawgiver affirms, that God created the earth, sea, birds, beasts and fishes for the convenience of mankind: had naturalists embraced this account, and exercised their talents in discovering the laws which prevail in the system, instead of creating worlds out of their own imagina-

Mosaic account of the creation tends to remove some errors of naturalists.

(*p*) Eusebii Præp. Evang. Lib. X. Cap. x.
(*q*) De Bello Pelop. Lib. I.
(*r*) Life of Theseus.

tions,

SECT. II. tions, their time might have been ufefully employed; whereas, by deviating from this account, we find nothing but errors and abfurdities among poets and philofophers. Ariftotle, Epicurus, Gaffendus, Des Cartes, and other materialifts, afcribe every thing to matter and motion, and fee no neceffity for the divine interpofition in the fabric of the univerfe; whereas if they had followed the Mofaic account they might have been more fuccefsful in their theories; and have feen in the contemplation of the world manifold inftances of the power, wifdom and goodnefs of God (s). Thofe who wifh to be acquainted with the fictions of philofophers, concerning the ftructure of the heavens and the earth, I refer to a learned writer (t), who exhibits their different whims, relative to the chaos and primitive matter. Mofes, on the contrary, does not fuppofe a world made without a God, nor material beings transformed into fpiritual, by their own power, nor beings to exift which never exifted, fuch as fauns, nymphs, &c.: his fcheme, though grand and majeftic, is yet fimple; not contrary to reafon or experience; unlike the abfurd and confufed accounts of the cofmogonies of the Pagans (u). Newton, by agreeing with the infpired writer concerning the production of the feveral elements,

(s) See Ray's Wifdom of God in the Creation—Galen de Ufu Part.—Derham's Phyfico-theology—and Boyle on final Caufes.
(t) Le Pluche's Hift. of Heavens, Book II.
(u) Winder's Hift. of Knowledge, Vol. II. Chap. viii.

and

and the motion and organization of the whole, has devised a theory which will last for ever; while the systems of fantastic writers are forgotten or disregarded. This prince of philosophers, by adopting the Mosaic account, has investigated the laws which prevail in our system, and proved them the best that could possibly have been contrived; thus exerting his abilities, to the glory of God and good of man, and not employing them against his Creator, like some ancient and modern unbelievers.

In order to prove, that Heathens borrowed theological information from Hebrews, it will be necessary to shew, that some Pagan historians, philosophers, lawgivers and poets, had opportunities of being acquainted with the writings of the Jews, or with the people themselves. We have the testimony of Aristobulus, that the books of Moses were translated into Greek before Alexander the Great; nor can we entertain a doubt, that the works of Moses and the prophets were known to Heathens before they were translated. Demetrius Phalereus, a peripatetic, wrote in praise of the Old Testament, and persuaded Ptolemy Philadelphus to employ seventy-two learned men to translate it from the Hebrew into the Greek tongue. The Jews were well known to the Greeks at the time of Xerxes; since Cherillus, who was more ancient than Herodotus, says, that they assisted

Jews and their tenets known to ancient Pagans.

that

that prince in his expedition against Greece (*w*). Josephus (*x*) assures us, that when Ptolemy Euergetes took possession of Syria by force, he did not sacrifice to the Egyptian gods for his victory, but went to Jerusalem, and offered sacrifice to God, according to the custom of the Hebrews. This historian (*y*) proves, by various other arguments, that the Greeks were known to the Jews, and might have learned from them their doctrines and practices. Agatharchides derides the Jews for resting on every seventh day from war, agriculture and commerce: and Theophilus, Theodotus, Mnaseas, Aristophanes, Euhemerus, Conon, Zopyrion, and other Greek writers, make mention of the Jews, though guilty of mistakes concerning them, for want of an accurate knowledge of the sacred writings (*z*). The Jews, by their traffic with the Phenicians, might have become known to the Greeks (*a*); and their several captivities must have disseminated their tenets among Heathen nations. Their impatience under servitude might have induced some captives to fly to other countries; while the singularity of their customs must have excited the curiosity of their masters, to enquire into the doctrines of a people, who were proud of being favourites of heaven, even while

---

(*w*) Joseph. contra Ap. Lib. I. Sect. 22.   (*x*) Ibid. Lib. II. Sect. 5.   (*y*) Ibid. Lib. I. Sect. 22.
(*z*) Ibid. Sect. 22.   (*a*) Ibid.

they laboured under oppression. The Chaldeans might have learned the Hebrew theology, during the seventy years in which the Jews were captives in Babylon: when Daniel had interpreted the king's dream, the king made him ruler of the province of Babylon, and cried out, " Your God is a God of gods, a Lord of kings, and a revealer of secrets (*b*)." The most learned and curious had opportunities of acquiring a knowledge of the Hebrew doctrines from this chief president; nor could any man be ashamed of learning from a prime minister, as Winder (*c*) expresses it. A friendship and intercourse having subsisted for a time, between the Egyptians and Jews, by Solomon's marriage to an Egyptian princess, and by the commerce which was carried on between the two nations, it is probable, that the Egyptians borrowed from the Hebrews, though they did not acknowledge the favour. The friendship between the two countries was of short continuance; and we are not to suppose, that Egyptians, who valued themselves on knowledge, would own their obligations to the Hebrews, after they had quarrelled with that people (*d*). Diodorus Siculus maintains, that Orpheus, Musæus, Melampus, Dedalus, Homer, Lycurgus, Solon, Plato, Pythagoras, Thales, Eudoxus, Democritus, and other

(*b*) Daniel ii. Ch. vii. Sect. 3.
(*c*) Hist. of Knowledge, Vol. II.
(*d*) Ibid.

famous

SECT. II. famous men, visited Egypt, in order to converse with the priests and learn their mysteries (*e*). Pythagoras resided twenty-two years in that country, submitted to be circumcised, in order to be initiated in their religious mysteries, and expressed himself in the symbolic manner in use among the Egyptians (*f*). Can it then be supposed, that a man who travelled for information, and endured so dangerous and painful an operation, in quest of knowledge, would miss any opportunity of seeking for it, wherever it could be found? Inquisitive Heathens had opportunities of learning, at least through the Egyptians, any knowledge possessed by the Hebrews; and it seems probable, that they availed themselves of these opportunities. Not only Jews and Christians, but also Pagans; not only divines and ecclesiastics, but laymen and lawyers have maintained, that the ancient Pagan philosophers were indebted to the Jews, for some sublime ideas of God; while others as warmly contend, that they derived their knowledge of these things from reason, or tradition from the patriarchs.

Hebrews and Heathens relate the same facts. Egyptian, Phenician and Chaldean authors testify, that the first men lived long; and the ingenious author of the History of Knowledge proves, that in the accounts of Diodorus Siculus, Berosus and Sanchoniathon, are to be found some traces

(*e*) Steuchus de Perenni Philosophia, Lib. VII. Cap. viii.
(*f*) Ibid.

of the Mosaic history of the creation, though their accounts are far inferior to that of Moses, in evidence and simplicity. Berosus a Chaldean, affirms, that many fled to the top of a mountain in Armenia, at the time of the deluge; and Abidienus assures us, that Sissithrus fled to Armenia in a ship, and was overtaken by a flood; that, after it had subsided, birds being repeatedly sent out returned, the third time, with feet marked with mud (*g*). Moses writes of the tower of Babel and the confusion of languages; and Pagan authors report, that giants built a lofty tower for ascending into heaven; that the gods in anger demolished this tower, and confounded the language of the builders (*h*). So great was the resemblance of the Mosaic and fabulous account in this instance, that Celsus (*i*) maintained the former to have been borrowed from the fable of the Aloidæ, related by Homer; though Moses was many centuries prior to that poet. Diodorus, Strabo, Tacitus, Pliny and Solinus, relate the fire of Sodom (*k*); and Celsus (*l*) was of opinion, that the punishment inflicted on Sodom and Gomorrah was taken from the history of Phaeton, as related by the poets. Lucian affirms, that there was a very ancient history at Hierapolis of men

(*g*) Eusebii Præp. Evang. Lib. IX. Cap. iii.   (*h*) Ibid.
(*i*) Origenes contra Celsum, Lib. IV.   (*k*) Grotius de Veritate Religionis Christianæ, Lib. I. Sect. 16.
(*l*) Origines contra Celsum, Lib. IV.

and animals preserved in an ark (*m*); and Melo, quoted by Eusebius, assures us, that in three generations after the flood, Abraham was born and had a son Isaac, whom he attempted to sacrifice; but that a ram, having suddenly appeared, was substituted in his place (*n*). Alexander relates the flight of Jacob, to escape the resentment of his brother Esau, and his leaving his father Isaac one hundred and thirty-seven years old; the selling of Joseph into Egypt, his interpretation of the king's dream, and his emancipation and grandeur (*o*). We have the testimony of Eusebius, that in the writings of Theodotus and Artapanus, was to be found the account of Joseph and his brethren, as related by Moses (*p*). The conformity of sacred and profane history, while it confirms the truth of the former, proves that Hebrews and Heathens borrowed from the same source: or, that the latter were indebted to the former, for facts related by each. Moses and Pagan authors might have derived their accounts of the flood, ark, confusion of languages, and fire of Sodom, from tradition; but the latter, probably, received their accounts of Abraham, Isaac, Jacob and Joseph, from an acquaintance with the Mosaic writings, or with the Hebrews themselves.

.(*m*) Grotius ibid.   (*n*) Præp. Evang. Lib. IX. Cap. iv.
(*o*) Ibid.   (*p*) Ibid.

Plato

Plato and other Pagan philosophers probably borrowed from the Mosaic and prophetic writings, refined ideas of God and his attributes: and this sage might have learned these ideas, from some Hebrews who resided in Egypt, when banished from their country. This philosopher asserts, that mankind are without excuse, to whom was manifested the spiritual and eternal nature of God from the creation of the world. The words of Moses, "I am that I am," and "I am, hath sent me unto you," possibly suggested to Plato an idea of the eternity and self-existence of God; and induced him to describe a being, which cannot be said to have existed in time past, nor to exist in future, but only at the present (*q*). The Hebrew lawgiver affirms, that God made man in his likeness; and Plato, as if he had seen the passage, observes, that man can resemble God only in that part which is spiritual (*r*). Moses affirms, that the sun, moon, and stars, were created for signs and seasons; Plato maintains the same opinion; and asserts, that originally God fed men without labour, and that they wore no cloaths; in allusion to the primitive state of man in paradise (*s*). From the Mosaic account of Eve and the serpent we may probably derive Plato's assertion, that they who lived in Saturn's time, conversed not

Plato borrowed from Hebrews.

(*q*) Præp. Evang. Lib. XI. Cap. vi.   (*r*) Ibid.
Cap. xv. and xvi.   (*s*) Ibid. Lib. XII. Cap. viii.

SECT. II. only with men but with beasts (*t*). Moses describes the deluge, and the virtues and crimes of the most famous men before and after it: Plato observes the same order in his writings, and mentions the destruction wrought by the deluge, and the few who had escaped, on the tops of mountains, to people the earth, together with the lives of those who lived after it (*u*). "Give me neither poverty nor riches," says Solomon (*w*); and Plato banishes both these extremes from his republic, as dangerous to communities. The wise man, in his proverbs, enjoins us to call no man happy, before he die; and Plato, in his seventh book of Laws, objects to praising men, before we see an end of their works. Moses prohibited an Israelite to serve an Israelite; and if an Israelite forfeited his liberty, he emancipated him every seventh year: Plato gave a similar prohibition, and forbade children to suffer for the crimes of their parents (*x*). The Hebrew lawgiver ordered a man who stole a beast and killed it, to restore four-fold, and two-fold, if it be found alive but Plato requires in all cases a two-fold restitution. This philosopher divided the citizens of his republic into twelve tribes, and the land into twelve portions (*y*); and required them to build their

(*t*) Præp. Evang. Cap ix.   (*u*) Ibid. Cap. x.
(*w*) Prov. xxx. 8.   (*x*) Præp. Evang. Lib. XII.
Cap. xxiv.   (*y*) Ibid. Cap. xxv.

of Religion on Mankind. 149

metropolis ten miles from the sea, with no other city too near it, lest they should be corrupted by the customs of neighbours or foreigners (z). Plato asserts, that God directs all human affairs, and sees, hears, and knows all things; and whether you descend to the depths of the earth, or fly up into heaven, nothing can escape his wisdom and knowledge: this passage was evidently borrowed from a sublime passage in the psalms, which asserts the providence and omnipresence of God (a). The psalmist affirms, that God is unchangeable, and always the same; and Plato expels from his commonwealth, those who think otherwise (b). Moses affirms, that the earth was originally without form and void; Plato makes unformed matter one of the elements of all things (c); and Ovid (d) assures us, that all, at first, was a rude and undigested heap, until God separated jarring elements, and appointed to each its peculiar function. In some of these instances, Plato does not adhere strictly to the sentiments of the sacred writings; but alters and disguises them, perhaps to conceal his theft, and sometimes perhaps errs, from ignorance of the scriptures. Justin Martyr asks, from whence, except from holy writ, could Plato have learned that Jove was carried in the

(z) Præp. Evang. Cap. xxvii.
(b) Ibid. Lib. XIII. Cap. iv.
(d) Metam. Lib. I.

(a) Ibid. Cap. xxviii.
(c) Ibid. Cap. vii.

L 3   heavens

SECT. II. heavens in his quick chariot? an idea that might have been suggested by the words of the prophet Ezekiel (e); "The glory of the Lord ascended on the cherubims, and the cherubims lifted up their wings, and the wheels beside them, and the glory of the God of Israel was over them."—That Plato borrowed from the Hebrews, appears also from the testimony of Numenius, a Pythagorean, who said of Plato, that he was no other but Moses speaking in the Attic language (f): and from Philoponus (g), who maintains, that he imitates Moses in describing the creation; but without any of the sublimity of the inspired writer.

Orpheus, Homer, Solon and others, borrowed from Hebrews.

We cannot entertain a doubt, that the Greeks were indebted to Hebrews, for certain opinions interspersed in their writings. Orpheus affirms God to be invisible, and known only to one person, a Chaldean, supposed to be Abraham; and entertains ideas of the Deity, that could hardly have been original. "Heaven is my throne, and the earth my footstool," is a remarkable passage; and so is that of "measuring the sea in the hollow of his hand." Orpheus expresses these ideas though in different words: God sits in heaven on a golden seat, and the earth is under his feet, and he reaches his right hand to the remotest extremities of the ocean (h). Such was the paraphrase of Or-

(e) xi. 22.   (f) Marcilius Ficinus de Relig. Christiana, Cap. xxvi.   (g) Joh. Philop. Lib. I. de Mundi Creatione.   (h) Præp. Evang. Lib. XIII. Cap. vii.

pheus

of Religion on Mankind.

SECT. II.

pheus on the words of Scripture, and might have borrowed thefe words from thofe Egyptians, who were in Thrace in the army of Shifhak (*i*). Homer's (*k*) defcription of the gardens of Alcinous, was probably taken from the paradife of Mofes; and the Ate of this poet (*l*) caft down from heaven by Jove, marks the fall of Lucifer mentioned by Ifaiah (*m*). The fable of Prometheus, who made a man of clay, and animated him with celeftial fire, was evidently founded on the Mofaic account of the creation of man (*n*). The equal diftribution of lands in Lacedemon, and the prohibition to alienate them, or marry out of their own family, were Mofaic inftitutions, borrowed by Lycurgus from Cretans and Egyptians, who were ultimately indebted for information to the Hebrews (*o*). Both Mofes and Solon forbid killing a robber in the day; and if a girl's parents died, Solon obliged her neareft relations to marry her according to the law of Mofes, which required perfons to marry in their own tribe (*p*). Hebrews adminiftered bitter waters in the tabernacle and temple, to wives who were fufpected of infidelity to their hufbands: in confequence of which ceremony, the woman and her gallant, if guilty of adultery,

(*i*) Winder, Vol. II. Chap. vii. Sect. 7. (*k*) Odyff. Lib. XVII.   (*l*) Iliad xix. 126.   (*m*) Chap. xiv. (*n*) Aug. Steuchus, Lib. IX. Cap. iv.   (*o*) Craige de Rep. Laced. Lib. III. Tab. iii. Inft. 3.   (*p*) Grotius de Ver. Relig. Chrift. Lib. II. Cap. i. Sect 12.

L 4   fwelled

SECT. II. swelled, languished, rotted and expired (*q*). Heathens imitated this custom, and administered waters and an oath to persons suspected of crimes, and imagined the waters tasted sweet if they swore with truth; if falsely, the whole body was supposed to break out into blisters and imposthumes (*r*). Saxons and other Heathens tried persons suspected of guilt, by different sorts of ordeal, and expected that God would work a miracle to acquit the innocent and punish the guilty, as was usual among the Hebrews. Hence it is evident, that Pagans have stolen from the Jews or their writings, certain tenets; nor can we entertain a doubt, but they blended these tenets with their own inventions, in order to conceal the theft. Plato admits, that the Greeks improved what they received from Eastern nations; that is, altered and embellished them so, that scarce a similitude could be found between them and the originals.

Greeks indebted to them by the testimony of the learned. That the Greeks were indebted to the Hebrews for information, either immediately, or by their intercourse with the Egyptians, will not admit of a doubt, when we shall have examined the opinions of the learned on this subject. Pythagoras, Solon, Plato and other sages, visited nations celebrated for wisdom, where they might have got acquainted with Jews, and the opinions of that people. Josephus (*s*) maintains, that Greeks were

(*q*) Numb. v. 22. (*r*) Selden de jure nat. & gentium, Lib. I. (*s*) Contra Ap. Lib. I. Sect. 22.

indebted for information to the Jews; and Hermippus assures us, that Pythagoras transfused some of the Jewish laws into his philosophy: Aristobulus, an Egyptian Jew, affirms, that this philosopher adopted many Hebrew precepts, and that Plato was acquainted with their laws and institutions (*t*). Numenius, a Pythagorean, accuses Plato of having stolen from the books of Moses, all that he said piously of God and the creation; and Porphyry asserts, that the Chaldeans and Jews possessed true wisdom and piety (*u*). Marcilius Ficinus (*w*) affirms, that one of Plato's disciples admired the theology of the Syrians or Jews, who were known by some under the appellation of Syrians. Justin Martyr and Eusebius, quote an ancient oracle which proves, that the true knowledge of God was peculiar to Jews and Chaldeans;

Soli Chaldæi Sapientiam Sortiti sunt et Hebræi
Pure colentes Deum, regem per se genitum (*x*).

Plato introduces Solon just returned from Egypt telling Critias, that he heard an Egyptian priest say, O Solon, Solon, you Greeks are always children, your doctrines are quite modern, and have no mark of antiquity (*y*). Which of the poets or Sophists, says Tertullian (*z*), that has not drawn from the

(*t*) Selden de jure nat. & gentium juxta disciplinam Hebræorum, Lib. I. Cap. ii.   (*u*) Ibid.   (*w*) De Relig. Christ. Cap. xxvi.   (*x*) Brucker de Phil. Indorum, Lib. II. Cap. ii. Sect. 3.   (*y*) Justin Martyr Cohort. ad Græcos, Cap. xii.   (*z*) Apolog. Cap. xlvii.

pro-

SECT. II. prophets? Hence the philosophers have quenched their thirst: ambitious only of excelling in eloquence, and displaying their subtlety, they altered the opinions which they received, and blended them with their own inventions, so as to render it difficult to discover the truth. From the authority of these ancient writers, we may reasonably conclude, that Pagans introduced into their theology some doctrines of Hebrews: and we find this conclusion maintained by Grotius (a) and Selden (b), two as learned authors as ever wrote in any age or nation. These men, though not ecclesiastics, have adopted the sentiments of the ancients on this subject, and supported their opinions, by the same arguments and authorities which I have produced. The former of these writers (c) asserts, that the Greeks were indebted to the Hebrews, even for their alphabet, and to the laws of Moses for the most ancient laws of Athens, from which the laws of the twelve tables were afterwards taken. The affinity of the sounds of the Hebrew and Greek letters, proves that one was taken from the other; nor can it be doubted, that the Greeks borrowed from the Hebrews, and not the Hebrews from the Greeks. The Greek letters were but marks, while the Hebrew characters were significant, and the name of every letter

(a) De Veritate Religionis Christianæ. (b) De jure nat. & gentium.   (c) De Verit. Relig. Christ. Lib. I. Cap. xv.

of Religion on Mankind.

denotes the figure, which that letter reprefents, according to the language of hieroglyphics. Beth fignifies an houfe, as that letter refembles it; the the gimel or gamel fignifies a camel, as the figure of that letter reprefents its neck; the daleth fignifies a door and is like one; vau fignifies and reprefents a pillar; the zain denotes a fabre, and has the figure of it; fen fignifies teeth, and has the figure of a trident (*d*).

SECT. II.

Greek philofophers and poets derived their theology from Hebrews, Egyptians, and others: Clemens Alexandrinus affirms, that Pythagoras borrowed the doctrines of tranfmigration and the foul's immortality from Egyptians; that Plato was indebted to him for this latter doctrine, and that the Greeks received inftruction from the Brackmans or Gymnofophifts. Steuchus is of opinion that the Egyptians borrowed their theology from the Hebrews, and that the Greeks received theirs from Orpheus, who learned from Egyptians the doctrines of that people. The following confiderations evince, that the moft ancient philofophers were more indebted for refined ideas of God and religion to tradition or revelation, than to the deductions of reafon. Trifmegiftus and Orpheus, according to the theology of Mofes, declared that all things were created, except God, who is without beginning or end (*e*). The latter

Ancient philofophers borrowed their theology.

(*d*) Jewifh Lett. Part I. Sect. 2.   (*e*) Steuchus, Lib. III. Cap. xii. xiii.

SECT. II. of these maintained, that all things were originally produced by Jupiter, who is the first and the last, the beginning and the end; from whom all things derive their origin; he is the primitive father, and immortal virgin, the life, the cause, and the energy of all things; there is but one only power, one only God, and one sole universal king (*f*). Pythagoras, who borrowed from Orpheus and Archytas, was of opinion, that mankind were created by God, made wiser than all animals, and lords of the creation, according to the Mosaic account (*g*). Pythagoras believed God to be invisible, intelligent, the universal spirit, that pervades all things, sees all things; the sole principle, the light of heaven, the author of all virtues, the reason, the life and the motion of all beings; according to this philosopher, there is but one God, who enlightens every thing, animates every thing, and by whom all things were brought from non-existence into being (*h*). Empedocles the disciple of Pythagoras, and interpreter of Orpheus, makes unity the creator of Gods, and maintains, that unity created those things which Moses affirms to have been created by God. Thales, the Milesian, held God to be the most ancient of beings; the author of the universe; the mind which brought the chaos from confusion into order, with-

(*f*) Ramsay's Phil. Principles of Religion, Vol. II. Introd.
(*g*) Steuchus, Lib. IX. Cap. ii.   (*h*) Ramsay, ibid.

out beginning or end; and that night existed before day; an idea possibly suggested by the history of Moses (*i*). Timeus Locrensis affirms, that God created the world out of unformed matter; that before the creation, there were no years, days or changes of seasons; and that after that event, the human body was formed and animated, according to the Mosaic account (*k*). Augustine Steuchus assures us, that Plato transfused into his writings the opinions of Pythagoras, Timeus, Empedocles and Trismegistus; and we find that he entertained, with some slight variations, the ideas of his predecessors (*l*). Plato calls God the architect of the world, who reduced the chaos from confusion into order; the father of the universe; the God over all; the sovereign mind, which orders all things, and penetrates all things, single and self-originated; the maker of heaven and earth, and Gods, and the same in the intellectual world, that the sun is in the visible; one king, one cause, and one providence (*m*). Such were the ideas entertained of God by the most ancient philosophers; but these sublime ideas, being blended with others which were false or unworthy; we may reasonably conclude, that they were not investigated by reason, but were stolen by the Greek philosophers, from those who preceded them.

SECT. II.

(*i*) Ramsay, ibid.   (*k*) Steuchus, Lib. V. Cap. iv.
(*l*) Ibid.   (*m*) Ramsay, ibid.

SECT. II.

Greek philosophers were plagiaries.

No man, who considers the character of the Greek philosophers, will be surprised, that they should borrow knowledge from the Hebrews, without acknowledging the debt; since they pilfered from each other, and disguised what they stole, in order to conceal their plagiarism. Clemens Alexandrinus has exposed the thefts of Greek poets, philosophers, historians and orators; some of which were not ashamed to transcribe entire volumes from other mens works, and publish them as their own: and even to dress up in fables the miracles related in the Old Testament; of which Clemens (*n*) furnishes many instances. Eusebius has proved the dishonesty, ambition, and plagiarism of Pagan authors, who repeatedly accuse each other of pilfering and theft. Porphyry relates a controversy between Caustrius and Maximus, about the merits of Ephorus and Theopompus. Caustrius maintains, that Ephorus wrote nothing of his own, but stole entirely from Damaschus, Calisthenes and Anaximenes; while Apollonius replied, that Theopompus stole a particular oration, word for word, from Isocrates, and even ascribed the actions of one man to another, who never performed them. Nicagoras, quoted by Eusebius, assures us, that Theopompus borrowed a great deal from Xenophon, and altered it for the worse, to conceal his theft. Aristophanes, the Grammarian, compiled six books of the thefts of

(*n*) Stromatum.

Menan-

Menander, and Cecilius convicts him of stealing an entire fable, and transcribing it into his work. Hellanicus borrowed from Herodotus and Damaschus; Herodotus derived great part of his second book from Hecateus the Milesian; and Isocrates and Demosthenes transcribed, almost word for word, particular parts of the works of Iseus. Antimachus borrowed from Homer, and Plato from Protagoras, what he writes against those who maintained there is but one (*o*) being; and Brucker (*p*) affirms, that Aristotle founded a sect on the philosophy of Plato, stole from the ancients, and studied brevity and obscurity, to conceal his theft. Since then the Greeks were such noted plagiaries at home, where they were liable to detection; it might naturally be expected, that such of them as travelled, would more freely indulge their itch for literary theft, where they stole from a people, not equally known to Pagan nations. Plato, though guilty of this crime, candidly acknowledged, that he learned his most valuable dogmas in Egypt, and that a philosopher might be assisted on every side (*q*).

If we examine the theology of philosophers, we shall find it blended with opinions that are false, unworthy of God, and quite inconsistent with those which have already been recited. Py-

Their absurdities prove that they borrowed their theology.

(*o*) Eusebii Præp. Evang. Lib. X. Cap. i. (*p*) De Secta Ionia, Cap. i. Sect. 4. (*q*) Clem. Alex. Strom. Lib. I. Sect. 6.

thagoras,

SECT. II. thagoras, founder of the Italian sect, thought the harmony of numbers was the principle of all things; Thales the Milesian, founder of the Ionic, maintained that water was the principle, and that all things when dissolved reverted to it again. The following were disciples and successors of these two philosophers, in their respective schools, namely, Anaximander, Anaximenes, Heraclitus, Hippasus, Archelaus, Democritus, Epicurus, Empedocles and others; each of which held opinions repugnant to reason, and somewhat different from the rest. Anaximander maintained, that all things were generated from infinity, and terminated in it; Anaximenes derived the origin of all things from air, Heraclitus and Hippasus from fire; Archelaus believed, that air was infinite, and that density and rarity were principles of all things. Democritus and Epicurus affirmed, atoms to be principles; and Empedocles held the four elements, fire, water, air and earth, together with friendship and discord, to be principles of all things (r). Plato and Aristotle differed in some respects from their predecessors, and from each other in their theology and philosophy: the latter pretends, that the Supreme Being exists in some ethereal body; while the former affirms, that he exists in a fiery substance; an idea perhaps borrowed from the appearance of God to Moses, in a flame of fire in a bush. The former held matter and idea to be

(r) Justin. Martyr Cohort. ad Græcos, Cap. iii. iv.

prin-

principles of all things; while the latter denies ideas to be principles at all: the former thinks the foul immoveable and immortal; the latter both moveable and mortal. Some held it to be in us, others about us; some assert it to be fire, some water, others motion, others exhalation, others an influence from the stars (*s*). Plato, who entertained sublime ideas of God, blends them with falshood and human inventions; applauds Socrates for paying his vows to Pallas, and sacrificing a cock to Esculapius; and heaps divine praises on the Demon of Delphi. He has adopted the absurd opinion of the Egyptians, that the souls of men enter into the bodies of different animals, according as they resemble them in their appetites and passions. This philosopher asserts, in one part of his work, that God created the heavens; and in another, that divine honours were to be paid to them: in his Book of Laws, he condemns the fables of poets, and yet falls himself into popular superstitions (*t*). Had his sentiments been original, he could not have contradicted himself in so palpable a manner; the wisdom of philosophers, being blended with vulgar errors, could not be the result of rational disquisition; as men capable of investigating by reason the attributes of God, could not be so inconsistent, nor so frequently degenerate into absurdity and error.

(*s*) Justin Martyr Cohort. ad Græcos, Cap. v. vi. vii.
(*t*) Præp. Evang. Lib. XIII. Cap. vii. and x.

SECT. II. Plato founded the Academic sect, few of his successors sincerely embraced his philosophy, but altered it for the worse. Some of them maintained, that the senses were fallacious; while Sceptics maintained, that nothing was to be comprehended by sense and reason. The Platonics, Epicureans and Stoics, were continually engaged in controversy; while there is a wonderful harmony between Moses and the prophets on theological subjects. The Platonic philosophers considered God as superintending human affairs; the Epicureans believed him regardless about them: the Stoics placed him without the world, and represented him as a potter, governing the universe; while the Platonics placed him within it, like a pilot, steering and directing the whole. Even the citizen of Geneva (*u*) condemns the opinions of philosophers as " vain, dictatorial, and dogmatical even in their pretended scepticism; ignorant of nothing, and yet proving nothing; ridiculing each other, and in this last particular, wherein they were agreed, they seemed to be in the right: affecting to triumph, when they attacked their opponents; they wanted every thing to make them capable of a vigorous defence. If you examine their reasons, you will find them fit only to be refuted; if you number voices, every man is reduced to his own suffrage; they agree in nothing but disputing." Cicero's books, on the Nature of the

(*u*) System of Education, Book IV.

Gods,

Gods, are a melancholy proof of the infufficiency SECT. II.
of reafon to difcover the nature and attributes
of the Deity. This philofopher was learned in
all the wifdom of Greeks and Romans, and faw
thoroughly the abfurdities of others; and yet,
with every advantage of genius and erudition, he
was a Sceptic in religion; and his infufficiency to
devife a pure fyftem of theifm, proves the neceffity of fupernatural affiftance. From the mixture of truth and falfhood in the opinions of philofophers, it is probable that they were indebted
to their own weak reafon for thofe dogmas which
were abfurd, puerile and contradictory;—and to
revelation for rational ideas relative to God. If
they had deduced theological knowledge from
their own refearches, they would probably have
improved in theology, as in arts and fciences;
and men who lived feveral centuries after Pythagoras, would have been better inftructed in facred
knowledge than that philofopher. But hiftory
evinces, that ancient philofophers have entertained the moft fublime ideas of God, and that, as
mankind advanced to maturity, abfurd ones were
the fruits of philofophical inveftigations.

When the advocate of natural religion confiders, Divine at-
how much philofophers have been indebted to re- invefligated
velation for theological information, he will have by reafon.
little reafon to boaft of the powers of unaffifted
reafon, and of the refearches of Plato and other
fagesof antiquity. The gainfayer will perhaps find,

find, that philosophers received pious and moral dogmas from those who learned them from the scriptures, or from those who had an intercourse with that people: that these men were indebted, for almost every sublime idea of God, to Moses, the prophets, and the writings of Solomon; and for their errors and absurdities, to the weakness and insufficiency of unassisted reason. Hence he will perceive the difficulty of proving, that a sense of the being and attributes of God was investigated by reason, independent of revelation. So consonant to reason are the divine attributes, that it would be absurd to deny, that they are capable of such an investigation; but it is impossible to prove, that philosophers actually investigated them, unassisted by revelation. In proving this proposition, the advocate of natural religion should acquaint men, why the modern Chinese, who are a sagacious and learned people, are so ignorant of it; and why, in ancient times, celebrated orators and poets; the subtle inventors of logic and other arts; profound astronomers and investigators of mathematical truths, have been greater strangers to a rational worship, than Jews and Christians, however dull and incapable of invention. To prove that philosophers investigated the attributes of God, unassisted by revelation, the freethinker should point out the time in which an universal and total ignorance prevailed, with respect to these attributes; the periods in which,

which, and the persons by whom they were investigated; and above all, that these persons had no opportunities of borrowing them from the scriptures, either directly or indirectly. On the contrary, it is undeniable, that a knowledge of the divine attributes, and of moral duties, prevailed in the world long before the art of logic, and before sophisters argued on these subjects, *a priori* and *a posteriori*. In the books of Moses, the attributes of God are declared and established by miracles, without a single attempt to deduce them from causes and effects: this is the work of ancient and modern philosophers who stole from the scriptures, and wished to conceal the theft by abstract reasonings, which, in some instances, have been false and inconclusive. These men reason, perhaps, acutely, and their subtlety in arguing on these subjects, has prompted them to arrogate to themselves the whole credit of discoveries made long before. Kepler (w) discovered by calculation, that the periodical times of planets round the same centre are in a sesquiplicate ratio of the distances; Newton (x) afterwards demonstrated the physical necessity of this great law: and we might as reasonably ascribe to this philosopher the honour of Kepler's discovery, as attribute to philosophers the discovery of moral or religious knowledge; because they reasoned on these sub-

(w) Keil's Astronomy, Lect. 4.   (x) Princ. Math.
Lib. I. Prop. 15.

SECT. II. jects from causes or effects: nay more so, since the arguments of the latter have been generally weak, while the reasonings of Newton are solid and incontrovertible. "If," says Hume (*y*), "the arguments for the existence of one God were clear, then polytheism could not have generally prevailed; if abstruse, the knowledge of it must have been confined to few; and therefore polytheism must have been the primary religion of mankind." But does not history acquaint us, that the most ancient nations were not polytheists, but worshippers of the true God? and does not the gainsayer's argument, if valid, prove the divine original of the Mosaic writings? for if the unity of God was discovered by reason, the knowledge of it must have been confined to few, and could not have universally prevailed among the Jews; while Pagan philosophers were grossly ignorant, and Heathen nations were sunk in ignorance and polytheism.

Brucker errs in denying that Heathens borrowed from Hebrews.

Learned authors have denied, that philosophers borrowed any thing from the writings of the Hebrews, or their intercourses with that people; and seem to have been influenced by a spirit of opposition, to combat the opinion which I have endeavoured to establish. The Greeks having traduced both Jews and Christians as ignorant barbarians, destitute of arts and elegance; primitive

(*y*) Essay Nat. Hist. of Religion, Sect. 1.

Christians

Christians retorted on the Greeks, with learning and zeal; and maintained, that they borrowed every thing valuable in their works, from those whom they branded with such opprobrious epithets. Not content with ascribing the best theological tenets of Heathens to Jews, they made them parents of geometry, arithmetic, astronomy, architecture, music, chymistry, and of every art, science and endowment, except eloquence, in which they readily allowed the Greeks to be superior. Other writers, having maintained with equal zeal, that Greeks were not indebted to revelation for any of their dogmas; I have endeavoured to avoid each extreme, by selecting ideas which seem to have been derived by Heathens from Hebrews, and by passing over others not drawn from that source. The learned Brucker having denied that Heathens were indebted to Hebrews for theological knowledge, I cannot pass over unnoticed the opinions of this respectable writer, this critic of philosophers, without attempting to refute them. This author assures us, that Barbarians owed their knowledge more to tradition than investigation; being strangers to the deduction of effects from causes, and to logical subtleties which puzzle and perplex. There were no philosophers among the Hebrews; they did not argue, but assert; their wisdom was not speculative, but political, moral and religious; nor were Moses and the prophets indebted for their laws and precepts to the deduc-

SECT. II. tions of reason, but to tradition and revelation (z). So far I concur with this celebrated author, and even admit the absurdity of supposing the Hebrews furnished with any knowledge except religious in a supernatural way: but I cannot agree with him, that the Greeks received no religious knowledge from the books of the Jews, or from that people, for the reasons produced in a preceding part of this section. Even Brucker deduces the origin of almost all discipline and philosophy, from Barbarians; whilst he maintains, that we are indebted to none but Greeks for logic and the art of philosophising. This writer does not sufficiently distinguish between philosophy and religion: the Greeks, it is admitted, owed but little of the rudiments of philosophy to the Hebrews, though indebted to that people for just ideas of God and religion: and I challenge gainsayers to point out any thing moral or pious in the works of philosophers, which might not be transcribed from the lives of patriarchs, or found in the writings of Moses and the prophets wrote long before. We are not to suppose these men inspired with a knowledge of arts and sciences; the Hebrews were not chosen as repositories of such things; and it would be absurd to imagine them enlightened in a supernatural way with a knowledge of things unnecessary for mens happiness in this world or the next. This author

(z) Bruckeri Hist. Crit. de Philosophia Barbarica, Lib. I. Cap. i. Sect. 3.

affirms,

affirms, that as Moses was learned in all the wisdom of Egypt, Mercury Trismegistus, who was founder of Egyptian wisdom, must have been prior to Moses. But the fallacy of Brucker's argument consists, in supposing Egyptian wisdom to have originated from an individual, and that Hermes was that individual: the gradual progress of knowledge, in every country, proves the former of these suppositions to be false; and even Brucker admits the impossibility of proving the latter; as we may consistently with his opinions form several hypotheses concerning Mercury Trismegistus: some maintained that he was some patriarch; others have doubted or denied his existence; some asserted that he flourished before, and others that he lived after the Hebrew lawgiver. However, none of these accounts can be safely relied on, since, according to this learned writer, the most ancient monuments of Egypt are filled with fables and uncertain traditions; and that country has undergone several changes from inundations, earthquakes and invasions, which dispersed and destroyed the ancient inhabitants, and introduced foreigners with strange customs in their room (*a*). How then can Brucker pretend to say, with any degree of certainty, or even probability, that Mercury was founder of Egyptian wisdom and prior to Moses? How can we, according to

(*a*) De Phil. Ægyptiorum, Lib. II. Cap. vii. Sect. 3 and 4.

his own account, depend upon any thing which has been related of the wifdom or inhabitants of ancient Egypt? His argument tends to prove, that we know nothing of Hermes, and not that he was fenior to Mofes: in this cafe, where we recur to authorities, we muft conclude, that the Hebrew lawgiver was prior to Mercury, as the weight of teftimonies appears on that fide of the queftion.

The fame fubject continued. Brucker doubts, whether Pythagoras ever travelled to the Eaft, though he affirms that he learned in Egypt his averfion to beans, and the doctrine of tranfmigration (*b*): he intimates, that philofophers who differed from each other, did not draw from the Egyptians; though by his own account, it was poffible for them to have derived knowledge from that people, and yet differ among themfelves: fince different provinces differed from each other in their rites and explanations of hieroglyphics; and to this difference he himfelf afcribes the contradictory relations of Herodotus, Diodorus Siculus, and Plutarch (*c*). Brucker denies, that Socrates was indebted to the Hebrews for knowledge, and afcribes his fuperiority over all others to the ftrength of his reafon; but affigns no caufe for his opinion, except that the Jews were not known to him, as he had never travelled (*d*). Socrates was undoubtedly the firft of

(*b*) De Phil. Ægyp. Lib. II. Cap. vii. Sect. 7.

(*c*) Ibid. Cap. vii. Sect. 2.   (*d*) De Schola Socratica, Sect. 7.

the Greek philosophers who reasoned on the virtues and vices of men; and the first who brought philosophy down from heaven, and called off his disciples, from mathematics and physics, to the study of ethics. But no person will affirm, that he was the first who reasoned on the being and attributes of God, or deny, that he might have received theological knowledge from the successors of Thales and Pythagoras, who were parents of Greek philosophy. The former, who founded the Ionic school, was succeeded in it by Anaximander, Anaximenes, Anaxagoras, Diogenes of Apollonia, and Archelaus the teacher of Socrates (*e*). Socrates believed in intermediate spirits, the ministers of God, and directors of human affairs; which opinion was maintained in Greece by Thales and his successors (*f*); and in Italy in the schools of Pythagoras and Empedocles. Since then Socrates was indebted for knowledge to the Ionian and Italian schools, though he had never been in them, why might he not have received information from the Hebrews by tradition, though he had never been in Palestine? especially as a pupil of Archelaus, the lineal successor of Thales, he might have learned from the Egyptians the tenets of the Jews. Brucker affirms, that strangers brought with them into Greece religious and poli-

(*e*) De Schola Socratica, Sect. 7.
(*f*) De Philof. Græcorum Fabulari, Part II. Lib. I. Cap. i. Sect. 7.

tical

SECT. II. tical knowledge; Danaus and Cecrops from Egypt, Cadmus from Phenicia, and Orpheus from Thrace. Cecrops was the first who philofophifed about the Great Jove; Orpheus, after Prometheus and Linus, is confidered as parent of Greek theology; and to the Egyptians, the Greeks were indebted for their theogonies, or fabular philofophy (g). Here we have difcovered another fource from whence Socrates, Plato, and others, might have derived knowledge, which encreafes the difficulty of proving, that they were indebted to reafon for theological information. Brucker maintains, that an handful of Jews, who went to Egypt after the deftruction of Jerufalem, were too infignificant to attract the attention of all Egypt to know their dogmas, and not fo famed for learning, as to invite inquifitive Greeks to defire an intercourfe with them (h). I do not affirm, that the Hebrews were famous for learning or fophiftry; but contend, that curious Greeks who vifited Egypt for information, might have learned religious, moral, and political wifdom from the laws of Mofes, the proverbs of Solomon, and the exhortations of the prophets. Clemens Alexandrinus affures us, that the philofophy of the ancients was delivered in fhort and ftrong fentences, like thefe proverbs; and Plato afferts, that Cretans and Lacedemonians

(g) De Philof. Græcorum Fabulari, Part II. Lib. I. Cap. i. Sect. 7.
(h) De Platone ejufq. Philofophia, Sect. 6.

adopted

adopted this ſtile in their laws and writings. The Egyptians could not be ſtrangers to, or indifferent about the ſingular opinions of men who were conſidered as favourites of heaven; and might have gratified their curioſity from Jeremiah, Baruch, and other Jews, who reſided in Egypt; who, though few in number, might as effectually have inſtructed the inquiſitive, in the dogmas of their religion, as the whole Jewiſh nation. It will readily be admitted, that the bulk of a nation trouble themſelves but little, about any religion except their own; but the curious and learned are never ſatisfied with ſuch knowledge, and deſire to be acquainted with the religious tenets entertained by others. Brucker (*i*) thinks it probable, that Zoroaſter did not borrow his doctrines from the Hebrews; ſince by the diverſity of their laws and rites, they admitted none, except proſelytes, to a participation of their religion. But ſurely theſe proſelytes were likely to propagate the Jewiſh tenets to their Pagan neighbours: and even this writer aſſures us, that different perſons conſidered Zoroaſter as inſtructed by Jeremiah or Daniel, during the Babyloniſh captivity, from his extraordinary knowledge of the Old Teſtament and Pſalms (*k*).

Brucker rejects the authority of Jewiſh and Chriſtian doctors, who aſcribed the wiſdom of

He errs in denying that Plato borrowed from them.

(*i*) De Phil. veterum Arabum, Lib. II. Cap. v.
(*k*) De Phil. Perſarum, Lib. II. Cap. v.

SECT. II. Plato to his journey into Egypt; and thinks they were interested in deducing from Judaism the dogmas of this philosopher (*l*). But besides the doctors who defended this opinion in the early ages of Christianity, on the authority of Pagans; we find it adopted by two modern laymen, as learned and judicious as the objector, and uninterested in supporting the dignity of Jewish institutions against the wisdom of philosophers. Clemens Alexandrinus and Eusebius assure us, on the authority of Aristobulus, that there was in Egypt a Greek version of the Mosaic law which Plato might have read. Brucker objects to his authority, as he does not mention the name, nor occasion of this version; and as it was unknown to all persons who had opportunities of seeing it. But does it follow that this version never was made, because travellers do not mention it? Is their silence sufficient to overthrow the arguments and authorities, which have already been produced? Is it probable that notorious plagiaries, who travelled for information, would, even if they had consulted this translation, published the source from which they derived knowledge, or own themselves indebted for it, to a people whom they hated? He says, that the Jewish nation lived in obscurity, and had no intercourse with foreigners, before the time of Alexander the Great; by this prince the Greek language was introduced into Egypt, and the Jews conceal-

---

(*l*) De Platone ejusq. Philosophia, Sect. 6.

ed

ed their facred books from the Gentiles, fo that he cannot comprehend how fuch a verfion could be made. And yet, this author (*m*) admits that Jews had intercourfe with Egyptians in war and traffic, while they hated each other in matters of religion. If he would infer from the introduction of Greek by Alexander, that a verfion could not have been made before his time, he argues falfely; fince in a learned country like Egypt, the Greek tongue muft have been underftood by many men before Alexander eftablifhed it, and the Mofaic law might have been tranflated for the ufe of fuch men. Brucker (*n*) cannot conceive how fuch a verfion could have been made, as the Jews concealed their facred books from the view of the Gentiles. But let me afk, for what purpofe they would hide from Heathens thofe religious tenets, which they fo freely communicated to profelytes? Were they afhamed to publifh to the world the natural and moral attributes of God, which were fo confonant to reafon, and fo fully eftablifhed by the miracles of their lawgiver? Surely they were not. The Hebrews fhunned intercourfes with foreigners, not from a dread of revealing their knowledge, but left their people fhould be feduced to fuperftition from the worfhip of the true God.

This author admits, in fome cafes, a fimilarity between Platonic and Jewifh dogmas, but afcribes

<small>He errs with refpect to the fimilitude of jewifh and Pagan dogmas.</small>

(*m*) De Platone ejufq. Philofophia, Sect. 6.   (*n*) Ibid.

SECT. II. it to reason and to a law more ancient than the Mosaic, disseminated by tradition, and corrupted in the propagation. He maintains, that a false similarity is often struck out, by men not intimately acquainted with the tenets of Plato, which, if considered as Mosaic, differ essentially from the entire system of this philosopher. I readily agree with this learned writer, that ingenious men often strike out resemblances where perhaps there is none; and partly admit, that where there is a real similarity, it may in some respects be ascribed to reason, and to the Noachian law propagated by tradition to all mankind. But I cannot accede to the opinion, that Plato did not borrow from the Hebrews, nor to the reason on which he founds that opinion, namely, that the Mosaic dogmas differ widely from the entire system of this philosopher. Even Brucker (*o*) allows, that Plato was a plagiary and borrowed his fine feathers from Aristippus, Antisthenes, Epicharmus and Socrates, and adulterated and changed the discipline of Pythagoras. He assures us, that Plato borrowed a great deal of Pythagoras's theology, and attributed it to Socrates (*p*); that he was instructed in the doctrines of Heraclitus and Parmenides, and confounded the systems of different countries and men (*q*). Why then should it be matter of sur-

(*o*) De Platone ejusq. Philosophia, Sect. 6.
(*p*) De Schola Socratica, Sect. 14.
(*q*) De Schola Cyrenaica aliisq. Sect. 1.

prise,

prife, that particular dogmas of Mofes fhould dif- SECT. fer from the entire fyftem of Plato? May we not as reafonably deny that he was indebted to philofophers, becaufe he differs from each, and all of them in fome material refpect? This author thinks it improbable that Plato, who travelled in the difguife of a foreign merchant, fhould receive information in Egypt from cunning priefts, who were hardly prevailed on, by king Amafis, to initiate Pythagoras, though he fubmitted to be circumcifed (r). I readily admit, that juggling priefts might be unwilling to difclofe to ftrangers a knowledge of their own myfteries; but defire to know, from what motive they would conceal the religious tenets of the Hebrews, to which curious priefts could not be ftrangers, and which the Jews themfelves never concealed, but rather boafted of to others?

It has been objected to the mild government of the Jews, and to the wifdom of their policy, that their lawgiver tolerated and even commanded human facrifices. It cannot be denied, that fome offered human facrifices to the gods of the Canaanites; but it is equally undeniable that the Canaanites were cut off for this deteftable practice; and that Mofes exprefsly forbade this worfhip to his people (s). It may as reafonably be objected to the gofpel, that it tolerates fornication

Whether the law allowed of human facrifices.

(r) De Platone ejufq. Philofophia, Sect. 5.
(s) Lev. xx. 2. xxviii. 21.

SECT. II. and adultery, becaufe thefe crimes are committed in Chriftian countries, as object to Judaifm, becaufe fome of its profeffors have been guilty of human facrifices contrary to its fpirit. If God had approved of them, he would not have prevented Abraham from offering his fon; if Mofes had commanded them, he would have determined the perfons to be offered, and on what occafions they were to be facrificed; then pious kings would have offered human victims, and this ceremony would not have been fo reprobated by David (*t*) and Jeremiah (*u*). The Jewifh lawgiver even prohibited his people to imitate the manner in which the Canaanites ferved their gods; " Thou fhalt not do fo unto the Lord thy God; for every abomination unto the Lord have they done unto their gods; even their fons and their daughters have they burned in the fire to their gods (*w*)." To prove that human facrifices have been commanded, fome have urged the facrifice of Jephtha's daughter, and a paffage of Leviticus, which is little to the purpofe. As to the former, it is doubtful, whether fhe was facrificed; and if fhe was, I defire to know whether Jephtha's conduct has been applauded by good men and obfervers of the law (*x*). The mif-tranflation of the following paffage of Leviticus, has occafioned a miftake with refpect to facrifices:—" None devoted, which fhall

(*t*) Pf. cvi. 37.   (*u*) xix. 2.   (*w*) Deut. xlii. 29.
(*x*) Jewifh Lett. Part III. Lett. VI.

be

be devoted of men, shall be redeemed, but shall surely be put to death;" or shall surely die, as the latter part of the verse is more properly translated: then the evident import of the passage is this, No person devoted to the service of God in the tabernacle or temple, as Samuel was, shall be redeemed, but die in that devoted state (*y*). To prove that human sacrifices were tolerated, it is urged that Samuel cut Agag in pieces; it is true he put him to death, but no more sacrificed him, than a man who is slain for rebellion against his sovereign, can be said to be sacrificed unto God (*z*).

Some have judged it inconsistent with the goodness and justice of God, to command the Israelites to extirpate the Canaanites, and seize on lands to which they had no right: such a precedent has been considered dangerous; since it may encourage enthusiasts and impostors, to pretend a commission from heaven, when they wish to possess the estates of their neighbours. But, had not the Governor of the World a right to transfer property, and the Giver of Life to deprive men of it; and to employ the Israelites in punishing those who had forfeited both, by their vices and transgressions? Surely there was no injustice in employing plague, famine, the sword, or fire from heaven, to destroy a wicked people guilty of beastiality, incest, and every impurity, for which So-

How far it was lawful to eject and destroy the Canaanites.

(*y*) Orr's Theory of Religion.
(*z*) Jewish Lett. Part III. Lett. VI.

dom and Gomorrah were deſtroyed, and in uſing the Iſraelites as inſtruments for that purpoſe. The Hebrews were not put into poſſeſſion of the land of Canaan, until its inhabitants had forfeited it for their wickedneſs, and been guilty of crimes puniſhed by the wiſeſt legiſlators, with forfeiture and death. Moſes did not ejeƈt the Canaanites for idolatrous opinions, or errors of the underſtanding; but for deteſtable crimes reſtrained in every well regulated community, as inconſiſtent with the welfare of individuals and ſocieties: to allow ſuch crimes would be impolitic; to call reſtraints on ſuch enormities perſecution, is fooliſh and abſurd. The Iſraelites pretended no claim to thoſe lands except the divine grant; and thought themſelves ſettled in them by the ſame power which delivered them from Egyptian ſervitude. God is the diſpoſer of all property, and daily transfers, or ſuffers it to be transferred from one man to another: if he gave it to the Iſraelites, they could not have held it by a better title; and had they acquired it by the ſword, they had the ſame title, which other nations have, who are indebted to the ſword for all their poſſeſſions. The Canaanites were not maſſacred, but extinguiſhed as a nation; and might have remained in the land unmoleſted, as tributaries of the Iſraelites (*a*). The threat of puniſhing apoſtacy, and cutting off

(*a*) Lowman's Hebrew Government, and Orr's Theory of Religion.

the violators of ritual precepts, was denounced against his own people, and not againſt Heathens and idolaters; Iſraelites or proſelytes of the gate were puniſhed for idolatry, while ſtrangers who lived occaſionally among them were not puniſhed for breaches of the Moſaic laws. Nor does the precedent of deſtroying idolaters, and ſtripping them of their poſſeſſions, expoſe ſociety to the ſmalleſt danger from enthuſiaſts and impoſtors: ſince men who could not clearly prove themſelves divinely commiſſioned, like Moſes, would never pretend to a ſimilar authority; as an attempt to counterfeit miracles, would immediately detect their deſigns, and impoſtures.

SECT. II.

God is no reſpecter of perſons, becauſe under the Jewiſh diſpenſation he choſe the Iſraelites as favourites; and under the Chriſtian, withheld the benefits of the goſpel from a great part of mankind. So far were the Hebrews from having experienced the divine partiality, that ſome have wondered, that their God would ſuffer them to be puniſhed by frequent captivities: nor do objectors conſider, that God had higher objects than the proſperity or adverſity of the Iſraelites, who were inſtruments in producing events of more univerſal importance to mankind, than the happineſs of that people. If God had afforded different degrees of knowledge to individuals and communities, and rewarded them in the direct proportion of that

The election of the Hebrews no argument of divine partiality.

knowledge, then might he juftly be charged with partiality to the Hebrews. But human happinefs or mifery does not depend on ftores of knowledge ; nor was it granted to that people, for their own emolument, but for the benefit of others. They were chofen for the purpofe of preferving and propagating the knowledge of the true God, and not for their own advantage. On the contrary, the abufe of fuperior knowledge deprived them of the divine favour, and expofed them to calamities, which they might have efcaped, had they not been poffeffed of fuperior endowments. Ignorant nations, as well as individuals, may ftand as high in the fight of God as more refined ones, provided they act according to the fmall fhare of knowledge granted them by their Creator; fince to whom much is given, of him fhall much be required. It will appear in the next fection, that the light of the gofpel would be highly ufeful to many, from whom it is withheld; but God does not grant to all focieties the fame conveniences of trade and agriculture; the fame temperature of climate and fertility of foil; nor confer on individuals the fame ftrength of mind or body ; nor has any perfon more reafon to complain, that God has withheld from him the wifdom and talents beftowed on others, than to murmur at not being created with the capacity of an angel. Man is accountable only for the improvement or abufe of his faculties;

culties; and the gospel teaches, that if we employ these properly, we shall have our reward in this world or the next; that God deals equitably with every man; so that " as many as have sinned without law shall also perish without law; and as many as have sinned in the law shall be judged by the law."

SECT. III.

TENDENCY AND EFFECTS OF THE CHRISTIAN RELIGION.

Doctrines and motives of the gospel.—Lord Kaims's idea of universal benevolence.—His opinion of the malignant affections.—Bolingbroke approves of the moral system of Christians.—Gospel motives to obedience preferable to any other.—The practices of barbarous states prove the expediency of the Christian system.—The gospel tends to abolish the evils of revenge among Barbarians.—Cruelty and murder among uncivilized states.—Excellence of the gospel proved from the bad effects of violating its precepts in Peru and other places.—Bad effects of violating it in the English colonies of the West and East Indies.—Effects of violating it in Denmark, Ireland, Poland and Russia.—Effects of modern Paganism prove the excellent tendency of the gospel.—The gospel tends to remove the bad effects of false ideas of futurity.—It tends to abolish austerities and other effects of superstition.—Effects of Paganism at Malabar, Narsinga, and other places.—Effects of Paganism in North and South America.—Some superstitions productive of gentleness among Indians and Peru-

Peruvians.—Frauds in China, Arrakan, and other places.—Frauds in Peru, Congo, Loango, and other places.—Frauds in Whidah, Guinea, and other places.—Frauds in Japan and other places.—Frauds of priests marks of false religion—Difficult to ascertain the actual effects of the gospel.—The gospel abolished divorce and polygamy.—It mitigated the rigours of servitude.—Its teachers preserved justice and checked warriors.—Gospel abolished barbarous practices.—It abolished the fights of gladiators.——It rendered Britons, Scots, Gauls and Irish less barbarous.—It checked cruelty in China and Japan.—It abolished human sacrifices and other cruelties in many places.—Also idolatry and cruelty in Germany, Paraguay, and Canary islands.—It diffused knowledge and abolished some bad effects of superstition.—Its teachers preserved learning.—The example of Christians taught Pagans kindness to the distressed.—Gospel rendered its first proselytes true and honest;—patient, constant and chaste.—Corrected pride and vanity.—Improved the old Roman laws.—Calumnies against Christians and the gospel serviceable to both.—Christians falsely accused of incest and devouring infants.—Of being atheists and authors of public calamities.—Of turbulence.—Of being poor and ignorant.—And useless members of society.—Tertullian and Justin Martyr prove mankind reformed by the gospel.—The same proved by other authors.—Julian and Pliny admit the virtues

tues of Christians.—An assertion of Mr. Gibbon examined.—Animadversions on Dr. Priestley's 56th lecture.

SECT. III.

Doctrines and motives of the gospel.

HAVING, in the preceding sections, pointed out the influence of natural, Pagan and Jewish religions; I proceed to examine the tendency of the doctrines and motives of the gospel, and their actual effects on individuals and communities. We may judge of its excellent tendency, by a recital of its doctrines, and by an history of the pernicious effects of violating its precepts in many nations of the earth. Such an history must tend to vindicate Christianity from the aspersions of weak or designing men, who have imputed to it the wicked acts of its professors; acts perpetrated in direct opposition to its letter and spirit, and which resulted from a want of religion, or from excesses or corruptions of it. A bare recital of the doctrines of Christianity will oblige us to acknowledge, that it has a tendency to promote the happiness of individuals and societies. Private felicity arises from the exercise of love and gratitude towards God, and resignation to his providence; from humanity, justice, and good-will towards man; and from a due government of our appetites and passions. Social happiness proceeds from a disinterested regard for the public welfare; from diligence in our calling; from a strict regard to truth, justice, and charity, in our intercourses

with

with men. The gospel every where enjoins these virtues, and prompts its professors to the exercise of humility, forbearance, self-denial, forgiveness, and beneficence: virtues which tend to moderate the passions, to banish cruelty, and to render men mild, peaceable, benevolent and courteous. Christianity enlarges the mind, inspires us with exalted ideas of the Deity and his attributes, and banishes every idea of him which is unworthy or erroneous. Its ritual observances are few in number, easy to perform, decent, expressive and edifying (*a*). It requires no duties but such as are essential; and prescribes accurate rules for the regulation of mens conduct. It instructs them in their duty, promises the assistance of God's spirit in the discharge of it, and exhibits a striking example of spotless purity, which we may safely imitate. The gospel teaches that worldly afflictions are equally incident to good and bad men; a doctrine highly conducive to the support of virtue. This tenet consoles us in distress, prevents despair, and encourages us to hold fast our integrity, however overwhelmed by trials and afflictions. Christianity represents all men as children of the same God and heirs of the same salvation, and levels all distinctions of rich and poor, as accidental, and insignificant in his sight, who rewards or punishes according to the merits or demerits of his creatures. This doctrine, so friendly to virtue, tends to humble the proud, to

(*a*) Blair's Sermons.

add

SECT. III. add dignity to the lowly; to render princes and inferior magistrates moderate and just, gentle and condescending to their inferiors; subjects resigned and contented with their situation, cheerfully obedient to the laws, and consequently quiet and peaceable citizens. The Christian institution tends to render judges just and impartial in their decisions, and witnesses true and conscientious in their testimonies, as I have already observed. It requires husbands to be affectionate and indulgent to their wives, wives to be faithful and respectful to their husbands, and both to be true and constant to each other. It enjoins masters to be kind and gentle to servants, servants to be sincere and attentive to their masters. If strongly impressed on the minds of men, it must necessarily dispose them to perform their respective duties, in every state and condition, gently, justly, and conscientiously. Were its precepts universally observed, we should see discord banished from societies, individuals would be simple in their manners, sober, industrious and just in their lives; and cheerful and resigned under all the dispensations of providence. The design of the gospel was to teach men to deny ungodliness and worldly lusts; to live soberly and righteously in the present world; to check the influence of pride, vanity and self-love; and to induce them to do kind offices even for their enemies. Such is the purity of the gospel, that it forbids us to harbour impure thoughts, and even to look at a woman to luſt after her. It requires us to abandon our vices, though as dear to us as a right eye or a right hand; and, though wiſe as ſerpents, to be harmleſs as doves. The Chriſtian ſcheme tends to prevent a continuance of immorality, by offering pardon for the paſt, provided offenders return and be obedient for the future. The goſpel aſſures the truly penitent, that their ſins will be forgiven, and the goſpel alone gives this aſſurance. Unaſſiſted reaſon will never tell a man, that his ſins will be forgiven, even on ſincere repentance; we are bound to an uniform obedience through the whole courſe of our lives, and to be obedient for the future, though we had been innocent for the paſt; and therefore that uniform obedience, which was required even from thoſe who had not tranſgreſſed, could never be ſuppoſed to atone for paſt offences (*c*). The goſpel naturally tends to expand the heart and affections, and to inſpire men with charity, univerſal benevolence, and love of their country. Its ſanctions exalt the mind above the paltry purſuits of this world, and tend to render Chriſtians incorruptible by wealth, honours or pleaſures, thoſe general temptations to venality and corruption. Minds impreſſed with the doctrines of the goſpel would ſpurn at a bribe, and not heſitate to ſacrifice every ſelfiſh conſideration, to a regard for the public welfare. The ſincere Chriſtian diſcharges every

(*c*) Conybeare againſt Tindal.

SECT. III. moral and social duty from a love and fear of God, without any regard to temporal interest or the penalties of the law. Not content with fulfilling the duties of justice and honesty, he performs acts of gratitude, charity, and compassion, which, however amiable in themselves, no man can exact. He not only abstains from injustice towards others, but even pardons the injuries of his neighbours against himself, as the indispensable condition of his own forgiveness from God....

Lord Kaims's idea of universal benevolence.

Lord Kaims (*d*) maintains that the social affections are and ought to be narrow, in order to prevent extensive empires, so ill adapted to the happiness of individuals; and that universal benevolence weakens mens attachment to their country, " by dividing their regards for it among so many." But let me ask, how a wish of doing kind offices to every person, with whom we have any intercourse, can weaken our attachment to the public welfare? However extensive the benevolence of individuals, its actual effects must be confined to the small circle in which they move, and cannot operate universally. Could we even suppose it possible, that it should operate effectually, in acts of kindness to every member of a community, yet, even on that supposition, no evil could accrue to any government from such benevolent practices. Men shew their regard for their country by risquing their lives in its defence, by obeying its laws with

(*d*) Book II. Sketch i.

4 cheer-

cheerfulness, and by sacrificing their private interest to the public welfare: and such conduct is more reasonably to be expected from persons of enlarged and benevolent hearts, than from men of contracted sentiments, whose views are confined to themselves, their friends, relations, and neighbours.† Even lord Kaims (*e*) admits, that the Christian religion is most useful in democratic governments; as it renders men less selfish, extends their regards, and tends to check luxury, avarice and ambition, so destructive to republics.

The gospel forbids us to harbour malignant affections, and enjoins us to expel them from the heart as offensive to God, inimical to our happiness, and hurtful to society. Even the author of the Characteristics, who was no friend to religion, maintains that individuals become happy by the strength of the natural affections of love, complacency, good-will and sympathy with the species (*f*); miserable by the intenseness of the selfish passions; and superlatively miserable by the horrid affections of inhumanity, malignity, envy, misanthropy, tyranny, treachery and ingratitude. Lord Kaims also admits, that malice, envy, revenge, treachery, deceit, avarice and ambition, are noxious weeds, which poison society, and threaten a dissolution of government. This he

His opinion of the malignant affections.

(*e*) Book II. Sketch iv.   (*f*) Shaftesbury's Inquiry concerning Virtue, Book II. Part II. Sect. 1.

SECT.
III.
does, in order to prepare his readers for the following paradox; "that the unsocial affections are beneficial to society, and productive of the most elevated virtues." Were these removed, says this writer, all men might be just in their dealings, and their persons and properties secure from thieves and cut-throats; but it could not be expected that theft, robbery, and other evils, should be removed without an extirpation of the unsocial affections. Take away these, and you remove all motives to action, and render man a timid and dastardly being: farewel then to heroism, magnanimity, and every noble virtue; then would the most perfect in those virtues fall a prey to savages, like timid sheep to hungry wolves; an uniform life of peace and security would not long be relished; the golden age of the poets would be more poisonous to man, than Pandora's box; without an object to attain or avoid, the mind sinks into despondence and languor. The inhabitants of Paraguay and of the Torrid Zone, whose wants were easily supplied, were children in understanding. The former were fed out of a public magazine, had particular hours allotted for prayer, sleep, and labour, and were so timid and indifferent as to make no resistance to the Spaniards who destroyed their republic (*i*)." A strange argument to prove the unsocial affections useful to

(*i*) Book II. Sketch i.

mankind! Surely this writer did not confider, that other nations, whofe wants are fupplied by labour and induftry, are not fubject to the languor of this indolent people. I can fee no evil to which fociety would be expofed, were men entirely divefted of the malignant paffions of envy, malice, deceit, avarice and ambition. Were thefe abolifhed, individuals might ftill have fufficient incentives to active virtue from love, hope, fear, gratitude, from the neceffary fupply of their wants, and the gratification of their appetites. The gofpel does not require men to extinguifh the focial affections, but to regulate and direct them to their proper objects: Chriftianity forbids no rational enjoyment, and reftrains no pleafures but thofe that are pernicious; curbing only the excurfions of the licentious, and confining their wanderings within their proper channel; like the banks of a river, which both direct the current and prevent its overflowing, without ftopping its progrefs or retarding its courfe.

Pollio, who fuffered for religion in the year 304, furnifhed an excellent abridgment of Chriftian morality, as taught and practifed by primitive Chriftians. Being accufed, before the governor Probus, of deriding the gods of wood and ftone adored by Heathens, he confeffed himfelf a Chriftian, who, in fpite of tortures, would perfift in fidelity to God, and in obedience to the commands of Jefus Chrift. Probus having then afked, ed, what thofe commands were? Pollio replied in the following manner: "Thofe commands teach us, that there is but one God in heaven; that wood and ftone cannot be called gods; that we muft correct our faults by repentance, and perfevere inviolably in the good we have embraced. Virgins who maintain their purity are exalted to an high rank; and wives are bound to preferve conjugal chaftity, and to make the procreation of children the fole end of the liberties they take with their hufbands. Mafters ought to rule over their fervants with mildnefs, and fervants to difcharge their duty rather from love than fear. We ought to obey kings and the higher powers when what they command us is juft and right. We fhould reverence thofe who gave us life, love our friends, forgive our enemies, bear an affection towards our fellow-citizens, humanity towards ftrangers, pity towards the poor, and charity towards all men. We muft do no injury to any one, and fuffer with patience the wrongs which we receive. We ought to beftow our own goods with liberality, and not covet thofe of others; and believe that he fhall live eternally, who, in defence of his faith, fhall defpife this momentary death, which is the utmoft effort of your power (k)." So fublime is the morality taught by the gofpel, that even lord Bolingbroke fpeaks of it with approbation, in different paffages of his writings.

(k) Broughton's Dictionary, Art. Chriftians.

" No

"No religion ever appeared in the world, says this gainsayer, whose natural tendency was so much directed to promote the peace and happiness of mankind, as the Christian (*l*)."—" The system of religion recorded by the Evangelists is a complete system, to all the purposes of true religion, natural and revealed (*m*)." " The Gospel of Christ is one continued lesson of the strictest morality, of justice, benevolence and universal charity (*n*). Supposing Christianity to have been purely an human invention, it had been the most amiable, and the most useful invention, that was ever imposed on mankind for their good. He even asserts, that " genuine Christianity is the word of God confirmed by miracles, and that it has all those proofs, which the manner in which it was revealed, and the nature of it allowed it to have (*o*)." Such is this writer's testimony of the excellence and truth of the Christian system, though contrary to the general spirit and design of his works!

The Gospel not only points out mens duty, but furnishes motives to the practice of it, far transcending any thing known either to Jews or Gentiles. Its rewards are such as eye hath not seen, nor ear heard, nor hath it entered into the heart of man to conceive; and its penalties are eminently calculated to terrify offenders. The terror

Gospel motives to obedience preferable to any other.

(*l*) Analysis of Bolingbroke, Sect. 12. (*m*) Ibid.
(*n*) Ibid.   (*o*) Ibid.

SECT. III. of punishments is in a proportion compounded of their certainty, duration and intenseness. As to the certainty of a future state, Mr. Gibbon (*q*) admits, that the sagacity of Pagans pointed out but feebly the desire, the hope, or at most the probability of it; and that Sages, who argued for it, could not avoid expressing doubts concerning it: But the Christian revelation has removed all doubt, by such arguments as have hitherto defeated the attacks of artful gainsayers. With respect to the intenseness of future punishments, both Pagans and Christians are equally in the dark; the threats of both being but figurative. The former describe the tortures of hell as inflicted by Furies, Phlegethon, Styx, Cocytus, &c. and the latter by the gnawings of a worm that never dieth, and the burnings of a fire that is never quenched: expressions which are to be considered as types of severe, though undefined punishments. As to the duration of them, unassisted reason is silent; but revelation affirms them to be endless, to the great discouragement of vice and immorality. To restrain from crimes, the evil to be apprehended from the commission of them, should repel more powerfully than the expected pleasure or profit can attract; the discouragement should more than equal the temptation. But future punishments, like other distant objects, would ap-

(*q*) Roman Empire, Chap. xv.

pear but small and inconsiderable, did not the eternity of them reduce the value of temporal advantages, which are of so short a duration. We are not however to conclude, that the Christian religion presents despair to sinners; since it offers pardon, mercy, and endless bliss, upon real repentance and reformation of life; without which they can have no claim to mercy, but are themselves instruments of their own condemnation.

 The detestable practices of unpolished states, unenlightened by the Gospel, and strangers to its motives, prove the excellent tendency of the Christian system to prevent or remove them. I never peruse the history of those states, without regretting their ignorance of Christianity, which is well calculated to abolish those practices, and to compensate, in some degree, for defects of civil establishments. The Christian code would be highly expedient in uncivilized countries, to soften the rugged manners of barbarous tribes, and to remedy imperfections of their political institutions. The Jesuits, without any other laws but those of religion, kept the inhabitants of Paraguay decent, moral, and industrious. In this country, where the government was theocratical, men discharged the several duties of their respective stations, without any regard to civil penalties; uninfluenced by any motive, except future punishments and reversionary compensations. Their obedience was religious, not compulsory; and of-

Sidenote: SECT. III.

Sidenote: Practices of barbarous states prove the expediency of the Christian system.

SECT. III. fenders were often known to confess their faults voluntarily, and even to solicit punishment from the magistrate, to quiet their consciences (r). Such has been the efficacy of the Christian religion, when duly inculcated on the hearts of its professors! I admit that other nations might not be as tractable as the people of Paraguay; but maintain, that the same principle, which kept these in perfect order without the assistance of human laws, might restrain, in some degree, the ferocity of the most savage. Gospel tenets, forcibly impressed on the minds of barbarians, must check cruelty and revenge, and abate, if not entirely abolish, customs incompatible with the doctrines of Christianity.

The Gospel tends to abate the evils of revenge among Barbarians.

The mild and forgiving spirit, inspired by the Gospel, would be highly useful among barbarous tribes, who have no laws to direct them, but such as are imperfect. Among individuals and tribes, unrestrained by law or gospel, the spirit of revenge is implacable; and they observe no moderation in the return of injuries. Revenge is the first maxim instilled into the minds of children, by the natives of America; this destructive principle influences their whole lives, and they wreak their vengeance even on sticks, stones, and other inanimate bodies. In consequence of this passion, injuries are never forgotten, nor expiated among

(r) Refnal's Settlements, Vol. II. Book iv.

the American tribes, but by the death of the of- SECT. III.
fender. Their refentment might be diffembled
or fuppreffed for a time, but never is extinguifh-
ed. Members of religious and well regulated focieties, ufually contend for honour or territory,
and generally terminate their wars, when thofe
ends are obtained, while favages fight to deftroy
their enemies, and are never fatisfied until they
have entirely extirpated them. To appeafe the
fell fpirit of revenge, they devour prifoners taken
in war, and fometimes employ various inftruments
of torture. Some burn the limbs of a captive
with red hot iron; fome mangle his body with
knives, tear his flefh from the bones, pluck out
his nails by the roots, and rend and twift his
finews. When under the dominion of this paf-
fion, fays the hiftorian, man becomes the moft
cruel of animals; he neither pities, nor forgives,
nor fpares (*s*). Had the gofpel been preached to,
and duly inculcated on the minds of barbarous
tribes, the vindictive fpirit would never have become the ruling principle, nor been productive of
fuch direful effects to themfelves or others.

The Chriftian inftitution is well calculated to Cruelty and murder a-
abolifh the various cruelties and murders commit- mong unci-
ted in uncivilized countries. The favages of Bra- vilized ftates.
zil (*t*) in South America, devoured their captives;

(*s*) Robertfon's America, Book iv.
(*t*) Refnel, Vol. II. Book v.

O 4 and

SECT. III. and in Congo parents fold their children, and husbands their wives, for toys and baubles (*v*). The Hottentots, though hospitable to strangers, and affectionate to each other, used to bury children alive, or exposed them to be devoured by beasts of prey; while they left superannuated parents, in the middle of lonely huts, without comfort or assistance, to die of hunger or be devoured by wild beasts (*u*). In New Spain, they kept every 20th day ho'y, and sacrificed men; put children to death on the first appearance of green corn; did the same when it was one foot high; and repeated this barbarous practice, when it was grown to the height of two feet (*w*). In the island of Formosa, priestesses prohibited all women to bring children into the world until they passed the age of thirty-six; in consequence of which custom, infants were frequently murdered in the mother's womb. The inhabitants of this island looked on murder as a trifling offence, and this crime was compounded for, between the murderer and the friends of the murdered, for a few skins or other trifling articles (*x*). Doctor Robertson assures us, that over a great part of South America, they put to death aged parents, for the same reason that other savages do their children, from the

(*v*) Mod. Univ. Hist. VI. folio, Book XXI. Chap. xi.
(*u*) Ibid. Chap. viii.   (*w*) Ibid. Vol. V. folio.
(*x*) Harris's Collection of Voyages, Vol. II. Appendix, p. 40.

difficulty of subsisting them (*y*). "The Caribbees were wont to castrate their children on purpose to fat and eat them; and Garcilasso de la Vega tells of a people in Peru, who were wont to fat and eat the children they got by their female captives, whom they kept as concubines for that purpose; and when past breeding, the mothers likewise were killed and eaten (*z*)." Were the humane tenets of the gospel inculcated in those countries, they would tend to abolish those barbarous practices, supply the want of salutary laws, and remedy defects of political establishments. I have argued for the excellence of the Christian institution from its tendency to check revenge, and abolish barbarous customs repugnant to the spirit and letter of the Gospel. This argument will acquire additional strength, when I shall have proved, that Christianity has actually abolished or abated cruelty, murder, and other crimes, in almost all nations where it has been promulgated. I do not affirm, that it has produced its natural fruits in all cases, in those countries which have embraced its tenets; but maintain, it has done so in numerous instances, and that, where it has been opposed, the violation of its precepts has involved kingdoms and individuals in misery and distress.

(*y*) Hist. of America, Book IV.
(*z*) Locke's Essay, Book I. Chap. iii. Sect. 9.

SECT. III.

Excellence of the gospel proved from the bad effects of violating its precepts in Peru and other places.

If we appeal to the History of all Nations, we shall find that the miseries, which they experienced, arose from actions diametrically opposite to the spirit and letter of the gospel: from avarice, oppression, luxury, and diffoluteness. Every man's reading will furnish instances of revolutions and troubles, arising from abuses of power, and from breaches of the laws of the Christian system. The history of mankind proves, beyond a doubt, that princes who have acted contrary to the genius of the gospel, and the interest of their subjects, were liable to plots and conspiracies, and their kingdoms to civil discord and frequent revolutions. I shall now exhibit the bad effects arising from the cruelty, avarice, and oppression of some professors of the gospel, for the purpose of exposing nominal Christians, and shewing the excellent tendency of that institution, the observance of whose precepts would effectually prevent or remove those inconveniences. When the Spaniards first visited Hispaniola, the natives considered them as beings of a superior order, the noise of their artillery as a sound from heaven, and paid them homage, bordering on adoration. Yet such were the cruelties exercised towards them, in the absence of Columbus, that they were provoked to resistance; and this adventurer, though disposed to humanity, exacted such heavy tribute from them on his return from Spain, that, in order to starve their oppressors, they entered into a resolution

tion of fowing no maize. On inacceffible mountains, to which they fled, they experienced the inconveniences of famine; and our hiftorian (*a*) affures us, that more than a third of this unfortunate people perifhed on this occafion. The Spaniards confidered them born for fervitude, and impofed fuch hard tafks on them, that many funk under the fatigue, while fome ended their days by a violent hand. Nor was the conduct of adventurers lefs cruel, impolitic, or repugnant to the tenets of chriftianity in other parts of America, than it was in Hifpaniola. In Mexico, Cortes put Guatimozin to death, and burned in one province fixty Caziques, and four hundred nobles of that country (*b*). When Pizarro landed at Peru, Valverde his chaplain, required the Inca to embrace chriftianity, and acknowledge the jurifdiction of the Pope, and king of Caftile. The Inca, having heard no arguments to induce him to renounce his religion, flung the breviary, which Valverde reached him, with difdain to the ground. The enraged Monk, a fit chaplain to the bloody Pizarro, cried out, " To arms; the word of God is infulted; avenge the profanation." Thefe words ferved as a fignal for flaughter; Pizarro attacked the Peruvians, feized their Inca or monarch, and killed many of his nobles, who attempted to fave him (*c*). In confequence of

(*a*) Robertfon's America, Book II.   (*b*) Ibid. Book V.
(*c*) Ibid. Book VI.

the

SECT. III. the avarice and cruelty of adventurers, in different parts of America, multitudes fell victims to the difcipline and hardinefs of Spaniards; tafks were impofed on others, to which their ftrength was unequal; many perifhed by famine; and not a few funk under the fatigue of carrying the baggage and provifions of their invaders, in their various expeditions. In fome places, the natives were required to quit the valleys and fruitful plains, and repair to mountains in fearch of mines. The change from fertile to barren foil, hard labour, fcanty or unwholefome food, and the defpondence arifing from their wretchednefs, all contributed to thin thofe countries of their ancient inhabitants (*d*). Planters in thofe countries have felt experimentally the bad effects of violating the gofpel; being obliged annually to import flaves from Africa, at a confiderable expence, to work their mines and cultivate their plantations (*e*). As men naturally hate the religion of their oppreffors, the Indians were averfe from embracing it; and Acofta (*f*), who laboured for fifteen years in converting the Peruvians, confeffed he found no greater obftacle to the progrefs of that work, than the impiety and immorality of nominal Chriftians. Refnel affirms, that avarice

(*d*) Robertfon's America, Book VIII.
(*e*) Refnel's Settlements, Vol. II. Book III.
(*f*) De Procuranda Indorum Salute, Lib. II. Cap. xviii.

was the motive that influenced thofe men: that they were lefs cruel in places where they had no mines; and that many of them were malefactors, and fo ignorant of the gofpel, that they vowed to maffacre twelve of thofe wretches daily in honour of the twelve apoftles. The court of Spain enacted humane laws for the protection of the Indians, and were reprehenfible only for fending criminals from their prifons, to people infant colonies, where fobriety, induftry and juftice, fhould be exhibited to the natives.

A learned and humane prelate (g) affures us, that above four hundred thoufand human creatures are funk in the profoundeft ignorance, in the Britifh colonies of the Weft Indies. In thofe iflands the planter, notwithftanding the endeavours of the fociety for propagating the gofpel, treats his flaves with cruelty, totally regardlefs of the culture of their minds. In confequence of their degraded condition, they are grofsly immoral, ftrangers to truth, honefty and fidelity; in conftant need of the lafh, and frequently confpire againft their inhuman tafk-mafters. This prelate, and other learned Englifh divines, have maintained, that thefe men, if indulged with a moderate fhare of liberty, might have become honeft, faithful and cheerful labourers, inftead of being vicious, treacherous and dangerous flaves. The Portuguefe, on the contrary, have treated their

Bad effects of violating the gofpel in the Weft and Eaft Indies.

(g) Porteus, Serm. XVII.

SECT. III. American subjects with humanity, and even indulged the Brazilians with civil liberty; an example worthy the imitation of other nations in Europe (*h*). The French and Spaniards also treat their negroes with tenderness, instruct them in religion, and have enacted humane laws for the protection of their slaves. In consequence of this gentle treatment, the negroes in the French and Spanish colonies are more decent, honest and industrious, than those of the English; who are treated with severity, and untutored in the gospel. The slaves in the English West-India islands hate their haughty masters, who rarely smile upon, or speak to them familiarly; while they love the French, who are less haughty and severe (*i*). Such are the effects of irreligion and inhumanity, that the inhabitants of St. Domingo, at the arrival of Drake, in the harbour of that town, formed the desperate resolution of having no intercourse with their wives, in order to prevent their having children subject to oppression (*k*). In consequence of the cruelties exercised by Europeans in general, on the ancient inhabitants of the Caribbee islands, the natives were almost extirpated, and planters are obliged to purchase slaves from Guinea and the slave coast. The separation of those wretches from their friends renders them indolent and

(*h*) Refnal, Vol. II. Book V.   (*i*) Ibid. Vol. III. Book II.   (*k*) Ibid. Vol. II. Book IV.

despond-

desponding; and the hardships they endure in the plantations, exhaust their health, and shorten their lives. The hard labour required of negroe women procures abortions, or prompts them, from compassion or revenge, to sacrifice their children, to save them from the cruelty of oppressive masters (*l*). English planters have, in many instances, been punished for their cruelty to their West-India slaves, with rebellion and massacre. The negroes of Jamaica, grown desperate by hardships, sometimes murdered their masters, set fire to their plantations, fled to inaccessible mountains to escape their cruelty, and have been known to elude their oppression by a voluntary death (*m*). When the enemies of England landed at St. Kitt's, during the war with America, the negroes of that island refused their assistance; whereas, if treated with humanity, they would have cultivated the plantations with cheerfulness, not have harassed their masters by revolts and insurrections, and have assisted in repelling hostile invaders. Hence it appears to be the interest as well as duty of princes to practise mildness and moderation towards their subjects, and of planters, in the islands, to treat their slaves with gentleness and humanity. Did planters practise the gentle precepts of the gospel, they would have had sufficient hands to cultivate the soil; but by violating its tenets, they have

(*l*) Resnal, Vol. III. Book II.   (*m*) Ibid. Vol. III, Book V.

SECT. III. almoſt deſtroyed the ancient inhabitants, and deprived their mother country and themſelves of the fruit of their labour. Such were the effects of cruelty on the natives and ſlaves in the Engliſh colonies, that when miſſionaries attempted to convert them, from a view of the happineſs offered by the goſpel, thoſe wretches have made a natural obſervation, that they cannot be perſuaded we wiſh them a place in heaven, when we refuſe them either peace or happineſs on earth (*n*). In the Eaſt Indies, extortion and rapacity have rendered the Engliſh government odious to the peaceable Gentoos, armed the Indian tribes againſt it, and makes them averſe from the reception of their religion. In the Britiſh houſe of commons, in the year 1783, it was generally agreed on, by thoſe who oppoſed and ſupported Mr. Fox's bill, that the Indians were treated with cruelty, and robbed and murdered by the ſervants of the company. In the upper houſe alſo, ſeveral lords maintained the neceſſity of reſtraining the rapacity and delinquency of men, who committed acts diſgraceful to the Engliſh name, and even to humanity. It is much to be lamented, that the Britiſh parliament, ſo eminent for wiſdom, have not hitherto exerted themſelves, in defence of their injured fellow-creatures; oppreſſed by adventurers, generally deſtitute of religion and virtue.

(*n*) Account of the Society for propagating the goſpel.

Reſnal

Refnal (o) assures us, that these men purchase their employments, in order to make the most of them; and as they hold them only for a few years, their impatience to acquire wealth totally over-rules every other principle. The conduct of these plunderers furnishes a striking example of the bad effects of irreligion and anarchy; and proves the expediency of both divine and human laws to restrain the passions of cruelty and avarice. Here I must observe, that these men act contrary to the spirit of the British constitution, and the common feelings of humanity; nor have we any more right to condemn the established religion of England, because it does not restrain their avarice and cruelty, than to inveigh against the constitution of that country and the feelings of humanity, because some are so depraved as not to be influenced by either.

We find, even in countries professing christianity, the evils arising from breaches of its laws, and from a corruption or perversion of the doctrines which it enjoins. In Denmark, where they exercised oppression over the farmers, and even bought and sold them with the lands which they cultivated, the country was poor, agriculture little improved, and nine parts of its inhabitants were wretched and miserable (*p*). Sir John Davis as-

Effects of violating the gospel in Denmark, Ireland, Poland, and Russia.

(*o*) Vol. IV. Book I. Northern Kingdoms.

(*p*) Williams's History of

SECT. LI.

sures us, that in consequence of the oppressions formerly exercised on the peasantry of Ireland, by the chieftains of that country, the natives were extremely addicted to idleness, being reluctant to labour for those possessions, of which they might be d prived by the rapacity of others. In other countr'es there are many inconveniences resulting from acts contrary to the genius of the gospel. In consequence of oppression, and a corruption of christianity in Poland, the inhabitants are kept in a constant state of servitude and bigotry. Their devotion consists in repeating prayers, by rote, to the Virgin Mary; and in hearing masses, one word of which they do not understand. Oppression has rendered them as lazy and stupid as the negroes in the West Indies; and Williams affirms, that two millions of freemen accomplish more work than six millions of slavish Poles, who want spirit and inclination to exert themselves in labour. Such are the bad effects of oppression and want of the humane spirit inspired by the gospel! This historian ascribes those evils to Romish ecclesiastics, who, in order to obtain property and privileges for themselves, inculcated passive obedience, and taught that kings are accountable to God alone for their conduct in the administration of public affairs. I shall not enquire whether this charge against the clergy is founded in truth; but maintain, that the crimes of the professors of christianity are not to be imputed

of Religion on Mankind.

puted to this useful institution, but to the passions of men, or to ignorance, excesses, or corruptions of religion. Soon after the introduction of christianity into Poland, an act was passed, that all the teeth of those, who eat flesh in Lent, should be extracted, unless they paid for that indulgence (*q*). This act fully proves, that the Christian religion was deplorably corrupted when introduced into that country, and was afterwards employed to the purposes of avarice and extortion. In Russia, the peasants are slaves, subject to the absolute will of their lords; and experience evinces, that oppression, which is exercised in that empire, is as impolitic as it is adverse to the spirit of the gospel. Russian slaves sleep away all the time they can spare, after finishing their master's business, and providing themselves with food, fuel, and other absolute necessaries (*r*). Nor is oppression confined to the lower orders of the people: no person of any rank can quit the Russian empire without a passport, or send money or goods into foreign countries, without obtaining permission. In consequence of those restraints, no stranger wishes to settle in a country, where he may be deprived of his liberty and possessions, at the will of a tyrant; no merchant will give credit to those whose estates may be confiscated; and no man, whose spirits are sunk by oppression, will make

(*q*) Williams, Folio. (*r*) Mod. Univ. Hist. Vol. XIII.

SECT. III. any vigorous effort in the arts, or exhibit any work of taste or genius. It is not any particular precept of christianity, but the gentle and humane spirit of it, which is so adverse to oppression, and tends to inspire men with sentiments of tenderness. I admit that the Christian religion is professed in Russia by the Greek church: but the following facts fully prove, that it is deplorably corrupted, or misunderstood in that country. Russians deem it criminal to eat pigeons, as the Holy Ghost is painted in the shape of a dove: and a learned compiler (s) acquaints us, that they put into the hands of the deceased letters of recommendation to St. Nicholas, whom they consider as their chief mediator and intercessor with God. In this country, persons of quality are not buried for eight or ten days; during which time, the priest daily sprinkles the body with holy water; and at the grave puts into the hands of the deceased a certificate, recommending him for admission into heaven. The principal ecclesiastic of the place, and the confessor, sign this passport; and certify, that he died in the true faith, and acquitted himself to his confessor (t). These facts forcibly prove the people's ignorance of the gospel, and the necessity of true religion, to prevent the inconveniences of superstition, and the

(s) Ross's Religions, Sect. 14. Vol. XIII. Folio.

(t) Mod. Univ. Hist.

frauds

frauds practiced by Ruffian ecclefiaftics, on the inhabitants of that empire.

Among uncivilized tribes, ftrangers to political wifdom, the Chriftian code would be particularly ufeful in fupplying defects of civil eftablifhments, and abolifhing the religious fyftem of Barbarians; which is more cruel, more fraudulent, and upon the whole, more deformed and defective than in polifhed focieties. That the precepts of the gofpel would effectually remove the dreadful effects of Paganifm, will appear from a view of Heathen practices totally repugnant to the tenets of chriftianity. Some of thefe practices will, doubtlefs, appear incredible to men who are ftrangers to the fruits of fuperftition; but the connexion of effects, with the caufes which produced them, and the fimilarity of cuftoms of divers nations, related by different writers, reafonably add weight to their feveral authorities. Even polifhed Heathen focieties offered human victims to their gods; and were, on particular occafions, guilty of every abomination imputed to the uncivilized, except devouring their children. The people of Bagota (*u*) offered human victims to their deities; while the natives of Biafra worfhipped the devil, and facrificed children in honour of him (*w*). The inhabitants of Madagafcar, who were addicted

---

(*u*) Robertfon's America, Book IV.   (*w*) Mod. Univ. Hift. Vol. VI. Folio. Book XXI. Ch. xiv.

SECT. III. to astrology, distinguished between lucky and unlucky days, and put to death all children born on the latter (*x*); while in Camdu, they prostituted their wives and daughters, in honour of their idols (*y*). The Giagas were taught by priests, that their tutelar gods were the spirits of bloodthirsty heroes or princes, who required blood from their votaries on account of the torments which they endured, in the next world, for want of it. This people imputed plague, disease, and every calamity, to the deities which they neglected; and hoped to avert their anger by hecatombs of victims. They ascribed the noise of winds, or the howling of wild beasts, to the thirst of the gods for blood; and butchered their fellow-creatures to avoid the disasters with which they thought themselves threatened. The actions of this people were cruel; as might naturally be expected from the deformity of their religious system, and their ignorance of the true God. In consequence of these doctrines, their conjurors sacrificed men and children, and educated men to arms, for the purpose of providing plunder and captives, and preventing the extinction of the human race. They fed on their captives; nay, devoured their own children, for want of food; and young persons were killed, every day, for the tables of grandees.

(*x*) Resnal's Settl. Vol. I. Book III. Historical Dictionary, Art. Tartars.   (*y*) Great

One of their queens, from a savage policy, enacted **SECT. III.** a law, that they should pound their children alive in mortars, besmear their bodies with the ointment, and bring up captives in their room: and this people, though extremely respectful to the memories of departed friends, yet had a total disregard for the sick, whom they suffered to languish without pity or assistance (z). Such were the effects of false ideas of God, and the want of that humane spirit inspired by the gospel, which might remedy those inconveniences, and supply defects of political institutions!

Pagan nations, involved in superstition, formed such absurd opinions of a future state, as led them to self-murder, and to other acts hurtful to individuals, and their respective communities. An idea generally prevailed, among ignorant tribes, that all who died required many necessaries in the other world for their comfort and accommodation. In consequence of this opinion, when a king or great man died at Guonia, the inhabitants buried wine and food for his subsistence; and his wives and slaves were slain to attend him. Besides this, one person offered a servant, another his wife, a third a son or daughter; and all these were put to death, and their bloody carcasses were interred together for the service of the king (a).

The gospel tends to remove the bad effects of false ideas of futurity.

(z) Mod. Univ. Hist. Vol. VI. Folio. Book XXI. Ch. xiv.
(a) Ross, Sect. 3.

SECT. III. At Casta, women got themselves buried, and in other places burned alive, with their deceased husbands (*b*). In New Spain, the officers and domestics of a great man were buried with him; and two hundred were sacrificed for the purpose of serving a departed prince (*c*). The fifty wives of the king of Java stabbed themselves, in five days after his death, as a mark of affection (*d*): and when the prince of Marava died, in the beginning of the eighteenth century, his forty-seven wives flung themselves upon the pile on which his corpse was burned, and were consumed by the flames (*e*). In the kingdom of Benin, they sacrificed several to the manes of a departed prince (*f*); and the inhabitants of the Grain Coast, though a civilized and commercial people, used to burn widows alive in the graves of their departed husbands (*g*). The widows of Bramins were obliged, by the laws, to burn themselves on the death of their husbands; those of other men did so, of their own accord, when they had no children (*h*). Even the Brachmans, or Indian philosophers, required multitudes of women to burn themselves alive with the bodies of their deceased

(*b*) Ross, Sect. 2. (*c*) Mod. Univ. Hist. Vol. V. Folio, p. 72. (*d*) Ibid. (*e*) Martin's Lett. to de Villette, quoted by Millar, on Propagation of Christianity, Ch. vii. (*f*) Mod. Univ. Hist. Vol. VI. Folio. Book XXI. Ch. xv. (*g*) Ibid. Vol. VII. Book XXI. Ch. xvi. (*h*) Resnal's Settl. Vol. I.

husbands.

of Religion on Mankind.

SECT. III.

husbands (*i*). In some provinces of South America, a cazique or chief was interred with certain wives, favourites and slaves, to administer to his pleasures, or attend him in the next world (*k*). The Japanese worshipped an image with three faces, representing the sun, moon, and elementary world; and were persuaded, that there existed different paradises, to one of which each god carried the votaries who adored him. This persuasion induced some to drown themselves; others, to cut their throats, or fling themselves from precipices, to the emolument of priests, whose interest was solicited, to admit their favourites into paradise (*l*). From these and many similar instances, we may judge, that the gospel doctrine of a future state would, if duly inculcated on the minds of Pagans, remove the bad effects of opinions which are false, and contrary to its spirit.

The Banians have an idol, called Quiay-Paragray, which is carried in solemn procession in a triumphal chariot, attended by ninety priests, dressed in yellow sattin. Some devotees prostrate themselves on the ground, that his chariot wheels may run over them; while others throw themselves upon sharp iron spikes, fastened on purpose to the car; esteeming it an happiness to be

It tends to abolish austerities, and other effects of superstition.

(*i*) Hornbeck de Conversione Indorum, Lib. I. Cap. v. p. 32, quoted by Millar, ibid.   (*k*) Robertson's America, Book IV.   (*l*) Ross, Sect. 2.

mangled

SECT. III. mangled and wounded, in honour of their god (*m*). In Japan, Amida and Xaca, the two ancient deities of the Xinto sect, are supposed to have led lives of mortification and austerity; and, being weary of this life, to have dispatched themselves here, in order to be deified hereafter. This doctrine has a considerable influence on the conduct of the Japanese, who frequently imitate their example, and voluntarily embrace death from discontent, or the ambition of being canonized (*n*). In Japan, they have a sect called Icoxus, whose founder, though a vicious person, gained such a reputation of sanctity, that his superstitious admirers annually celebrated a festival in honour of him; and came to his temple in crowds, early in the morning, from a persuasion, that he who first entered it was entitled to particular blessings. When the doors were opened, every person was so eager to be foremost, that several, in squeezing forward, were pressed to death in the crowd: some were even so zealous, as to prostrate themselves in the entrance, that they might be trampled on by the multitude (*o*). The East Indian Bramins have an idol called Ganga Gramma, in honour of which pagodas are erected, and festivals celebrated. At particular seasons, the idol is carried about in a chariot, and some devotees volun-

(*m*) Broughton, Art. Quiay-Paragrav. Univ. Hist. Vol. IV. Folio, Book XVII. Art. Icoxus.

(*n*) Mod.
(*o*) Broughton,

tarily

tarily undergo whipping; while others endure pains shocking to relate. Two hooks are fixed to the skin of their backs, and by these they are lifted up into the air, where they act many apish tricks, though in exquisite torture. Others suffer a packthread to be drawn through their flesh in honour of Ganga; and some are so infatuated with zeal, as to prostrate themselves before her chariot, in order to be run over (*p*). The Fakirs, or Indian monks, exercise the greatest austerities; some have vowed to continue their whole lives in a standing posture, and have kept the vow; others never lie down, but continue standing, supported only by a stick or rope; some mangle their bodies with knives and scourges, on pretence of conquering their passions, and triumphing over the world (*q*). These men, like some nominal Christians, do not consider, that they were sent into the world for the purpose of discharging social duties, and not to live in idleness and self-torment, on the industry of others. According to the gospel institution, men are no more entitled to heaven, for negative virtues, than sticks or stones; and have no claim to future rewards, unless they imitate the example of Christ, who went about doing good; leaving us an example, that we should follow his steps.

(*p*) Broughton, Art. Ganga Gramma.   (*q*) Broughton, Art. Fakirs.

SECT.
III.

Effects of Paganism at Malabar, Narsinga, and other places.

There were several other bad effects of Paganism, which the gospel would have abolished, if established in the countries where they prevailed. At Malabar they imagined, that God resigned to Satan the charge of all worldly affairs, thinking the trouble too great for himself. They had an image of the devil, which they worshipped; and celebrated a jubilee every twelfth year in honour of it. At this solemnity, the king first cut off his nose, ears and lips; and after that hideous operation, closed the scene by cutting his throat, in honour of the idol (*r*). The people of the two great cities of Bisnagar and Narsinga, had an idol which they worshipped, and maintained by the gold, silver and jewels presented to its temple. They carried it in procession every year; and pilgrims and other devotees wished to be crushed to death by his chariot: some stabbed themselves; others tore their flesh in honour of the idol; and women prostituted themselves to get money for his maintenance (*s*). At Panama they had an idol called Dabaiba, to which they sacrificed slaves; and the inhabitants of Tunja, near Panama, had another, called Chiappen, who was their god of war. Before an engagement, the votaries of this god sacrificed slaves and prisoners to his idol; and besmeared its body with the blood of victims (*t*). The inhabitants of Tibet adored a

(*r*) Ross, Sect. 2.   (*s*) Ibid.   (*t*) Broughton, Art. Chiappen, Appendix.

ruddy

ruddy youth, called the Grand Lama, who eat, drank, and refided in a temple crofs-legged, without fpeaking a word. The Grand Lama appoints the king his firft deputy, and nominates feveral other deputies, and inferior Lamas, to the adminiftration of the kingdom, it being beneath his dignity to be concerned about it. The government is a pretended theocracy; and all the dictates of the king are afcribed to the idol, who, doubtlefs, is but an inftrument in the hands of the prince. The Grand Lama is purchafed, when a child, from fome peafant, and educated privately in the duties of his office. When grown old, and incapable of acting his part, he is difpatched, and another is fubftituted in his room, more fit for the employment. He is fo honoured by Tartars that they mix their medicines with his excrements; and grandees hang about their necks, in a box of gold, a particle of his dried excrements, to prefervethem from difafters (*u*). The Mexicans had an idol, called Quitzalcoult, which was worfhipped by all perfons concerned in traffic; and they exhibited a fcene of cruelty that bore fome refemblance to that practifed at Tibet. Forty days before his feaft, the merchants purchafed a beautiful flave, who, during that time, reprefented the deity, and was obliged to put on an appearance of mirth, and to dance and rejoice, while devotees

(*n*) Atlas, and Guthrie's Geog. of Tartary.
(*w*) Broughton, Art. Quitzalcoult.

SECT. III. worshipped him. On the feast day, after adoring him for forty days, they sacrificed him, offered his heart to the moon, and then laid it before the idol. This idol was worshipped in a different manner at Cholula, where his devotees thought they pleased him, by fasting and drawing blood from their tongues and ears; and sacrificed to him five boys and five girls, before they engaged in any martial expedition. Such were the effects of ignorance of the gospel, and of the spirit which it inspires!

Effects of Paganism in North and South America. The chief gods worshipped in North America, before the introduction of christianity, were the sun and moon, which the inhabitants honoured by singing, dancing, howling, feasting, and cutting their flesh. Different tribes differed from each other in their worship; the Canadians adored the devil; the people of Virginia and Florida the devil and a multitude of idols: they sometimes sacrificed children to him; and when he complained of thirst, quenched it with human blood (*x*). The inhabitants of New Spain worshipped the sun and idols, offered them the hearts of men for sacrifices, and drowned boys and girls in a lake, to keep company with its idol (*y*): but these bloody practices were abolished in those places when the gospel was promulgated among them. The South Americans generally worshipped the

(*x*) Ross, Sect. 3.   (*y*) Ibid.

sun,

sun, moon, and idols; and the devil in various shapes. In some places it was considered a mark of devotion to offer their daughters to be defloured by priests: in Paria and Guiana, they sacrificed men to the devil, and to idols; and afterwards devoured them (z). The Mexicans exhibited their deities in temples, under the figures of serpents, tygers, and other fierce and destructive animals, which inspired the mind with gloomy and terrible ideas. They sprinkled their altars with human blood; sacrificed, in the temples, every captive taken in war, and employed various other means to appease the vengeance of their angry deities. Those exhibitions produced the natural effects on the minds of this people: they were incessantly engaged in war, hardened against every tender sentiment, and adhered to their superstitions, after they were advanced in policy and arts, and when their minds were enlarged in other respects (a). Every emperor, at his accession to the throne of Mexico, was obliged to make war for the purpose of obtaining captives to offer to the gods: the priests feasted on part of the sacrifices, sent part to the emperor and nobles, and complained, that the gods were perishing with hunger after a long peace (b). The people in general devoured the flesh of captives with a barbarous joy, nor suffered one of them to be

(z) Ross, Sect. 3.   (a) Robertson's America, Book VII.   (b) Resnal's Settl. Vol. II. Book II.

spared

SECT. III. spared or ransomed. When an emperor or great man died, they put to death a certain number of his attendants, and buried them along with him, to attend him in the next world (c). Unhappy fruits of false religion, and of ignorance of the doctrines enjoined by the gospel! Barbarous tribes, it must be admitted, are free from several vices quite common in Christian countries; but their innocence arises from their condition, and their crimes from defective policies, from false religion, or ignorance of the true. The vices of the professors of the gospel arise from a civilized state; and no Christian can commit them, without acting contrary to his principles: while Pagans might perpetrate the greatest crimes, without remorse, and even in compliance with the will of their gods.

Some superstitions productive of gentleness among Indians and Peruvians.

We shall now perceive, that as the Mexicans were cruel and vindictive on superstitious principles, so the Indians and Peruvians were gentle and humane, from the tenets which they professed. The doctrine of transmigration, believed by the Indians, inspired that people with such tenderness, that they would not shed the blood of man or beast, as it might contain the soul of some departed friend (d). The inhabitants of Cambaia, who entertained this doctrine, dreaded to kill a gnat or worm, and redeemed condemned

(c) Robertson's America, Book VII.
(d) Resnal's Settl. Vol. II. Book I.

male-

malefactors and fold them for flaves; nay, fome redeemed even birds or beafts, appointed to be flain, and carried them to hofpitals, if they were fick or hurt (*c*). The Peruvians adored the fun, as the fource of various bleffings, and a fit emblem of divine beneficence: goodnefs was the object of their worfhip, and therefore the fpirit of their fuperftition was beneficent; nor did their principles allow them to perform any rites, but fuch as were gentle and humane. They offered to the fun fruits matured by his heat, facrificed animals nourifhed by his influence, but condemned human facrifices, believing they could not be acceptable to that beneficent being. Manco Capac and his wife, obferving the veneration of the Peruvians for the fun, pretended to be his children, and delivered their laws in his name: in confequence of this pretence, the Inca, or Peruvian monarch, appeared not only as a legiflator, but as a meffenger from heaven; his fons were reverenced, as children of that luminary, and his precepts were received as the mandates of the deity. To fubmit implicitly to his authority, was the neceffary confequence of a belief of his divinity; to oppofe his commands, was confidered as an act of impiety, as well as rebellion. Subjects cheerfully obeyed a being, fuppofed to be invefted with divine power; and fovereigns kept up the opinion of their heavenly defcent, by an imitation of the beneficent

(*c*) Rofs, Sect. 2.

SECT. III. being, which they were supposed to represent; nor is there a single instance of a tyrant or rebel in Peru, during the reigns of twelve successive monarchs. The Peruvians did not fight to destroy, or to satisfy blood-thirsty divinities with human sacrifices; but to reclaim the vanquished, and to communicate their arts, and privileges to them: they did not torture, nor insult their captives; but instructed them in their own tenets, that they might add to the number of votaries of the sun (*f*). Such were the happy fruits of gentleness and humani y! The Peruvians, however, who were so gentle and humane in their general conduct, yet inconsistently retained a practice which prevailed among the savage tribes of America. They sacrificed men and children for the health and prosperity of the emperor, or for success in war; offered children to the ghosts of departed friends; and if a father was sick, the son was slain, and death was solicited, to accept of the child instead of the father (*g*). When the Inca, or other person of quality died, many of his attendants were put to death, and buried in the same grave, that he might appear in proper dignity and splendour in the next world: on the death of Huano Capac, one of their monarchs, a thousand human victims were sacrificed and interred with him in the tomb (*h*).

(*f*) Robertson, Book vii. (*g*) Ross, Sect. 3.
(*h*) Robertson's America, Book vii.

Heathen

of Religion on Mankind.

SECT. III.

Heathen superstitions were productive, not only of cruel rites and bloody practices, but of frauds and juggles of priests and impostors. All history, both ancient and modern, furnishes numerous instances of the credulity of the vulgar, who have so frequently been the dupes of knaves and impostors. The Pagan East Indians have an idol, called Quenavady (*i*), seated on a throne, behind a curtain; and draw back this curtain, when devotees come to worship him. The Indian doctors represent him as insatiable, and greedily devouring every thing that is set before him; and say, he dwells in a sea of sugars: to gratify this idol, he is constantly attended by two women, who are incessantly throwing sugar down his throat, with very large spoons. Artificers of all kinds invoke his assistance; some offer him the first fruits of their works, and all his worshippers think they must serve him thirty-six years, before they can obtain their petitions. In the kingdom of Arrakan, the inhabitants are superstitious, and their temples abound with idols, which they feed every day, and clothe in winter (*k*). In the kingdoms of Cochin-China and Tonquin, the kings, grandees, nobles, mandarins and literati, hold the doctrines of Confucius; while the common people devote themselves to the stupid worship of Fo, and allow themselves to be duped by their Bon-

Frauds in China, Arrakan, and other places.

(*i*) Broughton, Art. Quenavady. Hist. Vol. III. folio, Book xv. Cap. iii.

(*k*) Mod. Univ.

zas,

SECT. III. zas, who subsist chiefly, on their ignorance and credulity (*l*). These impostors have recourse to several tricks, to excite pity, and extort money from their bigotted followers; and, when the common arts of address fail, try what public acts of penance will do. Some sit on the highway, knocking their heads against flint stones; others set fire to particular drugs on their heads; and father Le Compte tells of a penitent Bonza (*m*), in a country town, who stood erect, in a chair thick set with long sharp nails; so that he could not lean any one way without tearing his flesh. As this Bonza was carried from house to house by two men, he besought the people to pity his condition; said, he sat in that chair, for the benefit of mens souls, and was determined never to stir out of it, until he sold all the nails, consisting of two thousand: each of these, said he, is valued at ten-pence, but there is an innate virtue in them, which renders them worth their weight in gold. The Chinese empire abounds with temples, monasteries and idols; and the Bonzas or priests feed those idols with the smoak of meat, wisely reserving the substance for themselves (*n*). The Bonzas require devotees to build monasteries for themselves, to erect temples to Fo, and to offer donations to these temples; and threaten to transform the souls of those, who refuse to comply, into rats,

(*l*) Mod. Univ. Hist. Vol. III. folio, Cap. xv. and xvi.
(*m*) Broughton, Art. Bonzas.   (*n*) Ross, Sect. 2.

mules,

mules, and other animals. They offer marks of indignity to their idols, if they reject their petitions; but restore them to favour, when they have obtained the object of their prayer (*o*).

<small>SECT. III.</small>

The Peruvians believed, that the souls of the departed wander up and down in cold, hunger, and thirst; and put gold and silver in their mouths in order to supply them with meat, drink, apparel, and other necessaries (*p*). In Loango and other parts bordering on Congo, they worshipped idols, by various kinds of offerings and donations: the husbandman presented his idol with corn, the weaver with cloth, and every man offered such presents as belonged to his occupation (*q*). The idolaters of New Spain were lavish of gold, silver and jewels, in adorning their idols; and these ornaments, together with the money paid for the redemption of persons appointed for sacrifice, added considerably to the revenues of the priests (*r*). The Congoese acknowledge one supreme being, and a multitude of subordinate deities, who preside over winds, rain, drought, heat, cold, fish, fowls, animals, vegetables and other things, which tend to the happiness or misery of man. Their Gangas, or priests, place the exterior worship of them in genuflexions, prostrations, fumigations, and other superstitious rites; but chiefly in donations of food and apparel, which

<small>Frauds in Peru, Congo, Loango, and other places.</small>

(*o*) Mod. Univ. Hist. Vol. III. folio. Sect. 3.   (*q*) Ibid.   (*r*) Ibid.   (*p*) Ross,

SECT. III. constitute their revenue. As these men are supposed to have a considerable influence with those deities, they are solicited to derive blessings upon the nation, to avert judgments, to cure difases, and to undo witchcraft. In all these cases, they fell the favour of the gods to the laity at an exorbitant price; and pretend, that all calamities proceed from the anger of the Gods against apostacy, and those who encourage it. This was the chief stratagem by which they were enabled to keep their flocks from straying; and to fleece and tyrannize over them, in opposition to the princes, who wished to introduce Christianity, as a means of abolishing idolatry, and the authority of the priests: for the Shalone, or chief priest, had such an influence in the state, that the civil magistrate could not enter on any momentous business of war or peace, without courting him by presents (s).

Frauds in Whidah, Guinea, and other places. In the kingdom of Whidah, knavish priests persuade the people, that from the time corn is sowed, until it is grown up, the snake, which is one of their Fetiches or inferior deities, seizes on young virgins and renders them delirious. To prevent this mischief, parents commit their daughters to the direction of the priests, during that time, at a considerable expence. The king and priests share the profits; and the former sends his

(s) Mod. Univ. Hist. Vol. VI. folio. Book xxi. Cap. i.

own

own daughter to the hofpitals, in order to carry on the impofture (*t*). The Negroes of this place were fo fuperftitioufly attached to their idols, that they maffacred the Englifh who ignorantly killed one of them, and flaughtered all their hogs, becaufe one of thefe animals devoured a fnake (*u*). At Guinea, if medicines fail in recovering the fick, the Negroes have recourfe to fuperftition to remove the difeafe; and the phyfician, who is a prieft, tells the patient that he has no chance of recovery, except by offerings to the Fetiches (*w*). Thefe Negroes will not undertake any important bufinefs, without confulting their Gods; and the priefts anfwers are ufually fuch, as are moft acceptable to the enquirer, and moft likely to impofe on the credulity of the fimple. If his predictions are fulfilled, he is extolled, and receives liberal prefents; if they are not verified by the event, the laity are induftrious to find apologies for him; nor does the prieft himfelf ever want an excufe to juftify his failure (*x*). At Guinea, they held trees in great veneration, confulted them as oracles, and daily fed the tops of mountains with meat and drink (*y*). Negroes efteemed certain trees guardian Gods, affembled round them on feftivals, facrificed at the foot of them, and fpent the reft of the day in dancing round them, to the found of

(*t*) Mod. Univ. Hift. Vol. VI. folio, Book xxi. Cap. i.
(*u*) Ibid. Cap. xv. (*w*) Ibid. (*x*) Ibid. Cap. xvi.
(*y*) Rofs, Sect. 3.

SECT. III. music. The priest offered sacrifice to the Fetiches near a kind of altar, dipped a wisp of straw into a pot of a certain liquor, and sprinkled the people with this holy water (z). At Angola, they new clothed their dead, and buried with them meat, drink, and some part of their goods. They worshipped wooden idols, imputed sickness or other calamity to their displeasure, and imagined, that they appeased them by presents of wine (a). The Brachmans, or Indian philosophers, persuaded the simple, that the pagods or temples eat as men do; made their idols of a gigantic size, and furnished them with monstrous bellies, in order to induce men to make large offerings. If these offerings should be found insufficient for them, and their families, they assured the people, that the offended pagods threatened the country with some dreadful calamity, or that the gods would forsake them, because they suffered them to die of hunger (b).

Frauds in Japan and other places. The Japanese priests inculcate very forcibly future rewards and punishments, the latter particularly: within and without their temples, they paint multitudes of devils, in the most horrid shapes and frightful attitudes, tormenting the souls of guilty mortals. Priests persuade the people that Amidas and Xaca exercised austerities, for

(z) Broughton, Art. Fetiches.   (a) Ross, Sect. 3.
(b) Bahour's Life of Xavier, Book II. Appendix to Religion and Learning of the Malabarians, by Danish Missionaries, p. 64, quoted by Millar, Cap. vii. p. 138.

the

the purpose of delivering their votaries from those torments, by their voluntary sufferings; and these impostors, by prayers, mortification, and performing works of supererogation, pretended an interest with those Gods, which they sell to the laity at a moderate price (*c*). Jemma, judge of hell, according to the theology of the Japanese, sees the most secret transactions of men in a large looking glass, and is considered as inexorable; and yet it is believed, that if priests intercede for sinners to the God Amidas, and the relations of the deceased make liberal offerings to his temple, Jemma will be prevailed on to mitigate the punishment. In conformity to this opinion, the pagod is crowded with multitudes, from all quarters, with oblations in their hands, to redeem the souls of their friends from the torments of hell (*d*). The Japanese Mendicant friars practise the following ceremony, for the purification of souls; they write the names of persons, whose souls they purify, on chips, rub them with the branch of a certain tree, repeat a certain form of words, in a low voice, during the action; and are rewarded for the trouble of performing this ceremony (*e*). The Japanese have an idol, called Abbuto, which is famous for curing inveterate distempers, and procuring a favourable wind and quick passage by sea. To secure the good will of this idol, sailors

(*c*) Mod. Univ. Hist. Vol. III. on Japan.   (*d*) Broughton, Art. Jemma.   (*e*) Ibid. Art. Siegaki.

and

SECT. III. and passengers usually tie small pieces of coin to a bit of wood, and throw it into the sea, as an offering to the God. The priests assure his devotees, that these offerings never fail to come safe to shore; however, the idol himself comes out, in fine weather, in a small boat, to demand tribute of all ships and boats that pass (*f*) by. These are inconveniences experienced in no country in which the Gospel is inculcated in its purity; though similar ones are exhibited, by those who have adulterated it, from motives of lucre. The Japanese have some obscene as well as fraudulent practices: to a brazen idol, hollow within, called Dabis, they annually offer a spotless virgin, who is instructed to ask of it some particular questions: a Bonza, inclosed within the idol, is the sacred interpreter of the deity, returns answers to the virgin, and usually debauches her. Egyptian priests formerly practised a similar imposture; by telling the male devotees, who visited the temple, that the deity required an interview with their wives; among which, the amorous priest chose the handsomest for his favourite (*g*). In Japan they have an order of Mendicant nuns, called Bikunis, who are generally beautiful, and allure passengers to their embraces in direct terms, or by lascivious gestures, as they travel through the country (*h*). Such were the effects of Pagan su-

(*f*) Broughton, Art. Abbuto. (*g*) Ibid. Art. Dabis.
(*h*) Ibid. Art. Bikunis.

perstitions

perstitions and ignorance of the gospel! Some, doubtless, will think it unfair, to judge of the influence of Paganism, from the conduct of men as ignorant of political wisdom, as of the precepts of true religion: but we have considered only those actions of Pagans which originated from superstition, and have argued from these, concerning the tendency of the gospel to prevent or abolish them. It should likewise be considered, that Mexicans, Peruvians, and others, whose superstitions have been described, do not deserve the name of savages; as they had cities, rulers, laws, subordination, and arts somewhat matured, though inferior to Europeans in all these respects (*i*).

The history of mankind acquaints us, that Pagan priests have generally taken advantage of the ignorance of a superstitious people, to fleece and defraud them; and one grand effect of the Christian code is, that it enables any person, who studies it with attention, to detect fraud, and to judge with certainty, whether any religion is false, from the tendency of its doctrines. That system, whose tenets are calculated for the emolument of priests, and whose chief object is to gratify the avarice or ambition of any class of men, at the expence of the rest, is naturally to be suspected of falshood and fraud; while that institution, whose primary end is the good of mankind, in this world and the

SECT. III.

Frauds of priests marks of false religion.

(*i*) Robertson's America, Book VII.

next,

next, might possibly be dictated by God, for the benefit of his creatures. This is the test whereby we can distinguish true from false systems of religion; this is an argument, which the plainest understanding can comprehend, as well as the most subtle and refined. The gospel of him, whose kingdom was not of this world, and whose doctrines are not calculated to advance the fraudulent designs of ecclesiastics, assists in discovering false religion, and tends to prevent or remove its pernicious influence: and though the Christian institution has not, in all cases, operated according to its tendency, yet has it done so in numberless instances, as will presently appear. The frauds of priests, arising not from true religion, but from the want of it, prove the utility of that institution, which is free from them, and which enables us to detect them. Gainsayers might as reasonably attribute the fraudulent practices of mountebanks and pettifoggers to the useful professions of physic and law, as impute the frauds of Pagan priests, or nominal Christians, to the gospel of Christ. In Hispaniola, and other parts of America, professors of physic were conjurers and diviners, who imposed by their tricks on the credulity of the people; these men ascribed diseases to supernatural influence, and performed incantations, sorcery, and several kinds of imposture, to cure their disorders (k). In the island of Madagascar, Ombi-

(k) Robertson's America, Book IV.

asses, who were priests, physicians and soothsayers, sell talismans, and other charms, to the rich, to preserve them from disasters (*l*). The Hottentots are of opinion, that all disorders are brought on patients by magic, and cured by magic; and have conjurers and wizards, who cherish the ignorance of this silly people, while they cheat and defraud them. They lay a diseased person on his face, beat him all over, and at last exhibit a bone which, they say, was conjured into him, and extracted by them, from his nose, ears, or other parts of his body. If a patient is not cured by a single operation of this kind, he undergoes several of them; and should he die under it, his friends only lament, that he was bewitched beyond the power of any one to relieve him, and that some more powerful magician, a foe to the deceased, had brought this misfortune upon him (*m*). However, we need not go as far as Hispaniola, or the Cape of Good Hope, to discover the bad effects of the frauds of quacks and empyrics; every country abounds with mountebanks, and it would be unfair to impute these bad effects to the medical art, but to ignorance or want of skill in that useful profession.

SECT. III.

Having pointed out the good effects that would naturally result from an observance of the gospel, and the evils which have arisen from superstition

Difficult to ascertain the actual effects of the gospel.

(*l*) Broughton, Art. Ombiasses.
(*m*) Sparman's Voyages, Vol. I. Chap. v.

and

SECT. III. and breaches of Christianity, let us enquire how far its doctrines and motives have actually operated on its professors; and whether its fruits have been such as might reasonably be expected. In order to this, we should carefully examine its influence, in its primitive state, before it was adulterated and blended with human inventions; lest we should judge of it from its corruptions, and confound real with nominal Christians. It is difficult, if not impossible, to do justice to Christianity in the discussion of this subject; as its genuine fruits are gentleness, patience, benevolence, justice, temperance and purity of manners; virtues which are generally exerted in private, without noise or ostentation. The Man of Ross, celebrated by Mr. Pope, was a private character, which is likely to live to the latest posterity; and yet the name of this man, though possessed of many virtues, would be sunk in oblivion, was it not for the able pen of that elegant poet (*a*), who thus expresses himself, after describing those virtues:

> And what? no monument, inscription, stone?
> His race, his form, his name almost unknown?

Individuals in private life seldom engage the attention of the historian; his object is to record the actions of princes, warriors and statesmen, whose conduct has an immediate influence on the welfare of states. Were there no persecutions in

(*a*) Pope's Epist. III. verse 250.

the early ages of Chriſtianity, and no accuſations againſt its profeſſors, we ſhould be ſtrangers to the names and virtues of ſaints and martyrs, and to the learning and endowments of the firſt apologiſts for Chriſtianity. It ſhall therefore be the chief object of the remainder of this ſection, to point out the effects of the Chriſtian ſyſtem in improving mens morals in civilized ſtates; and in aboliſhing barbarous practices in unpoliſhed ſocieties. How far it has anſwered theſe purpoſes will appear, by comparing mens moral condition before and after it was promulgated, and by taking a view of the errors and crimes which it was inſtrumental in aboliſhing, in different parts of the earth.

SECT. III.

The Chriſtian inſtitution has had conſiderable influence on domeſtic happineſs, in many countries, where its tenets were embraced. The goſpel aboliſhed polygamy, a practice repugnant to the intention of our Creator, who at firſt created one male and one female for ſocial comfort, and the propagation of the ſpecies. A learned writer (*b*) maintains, that polygamy muſt, in a courſe of time, leſſen inſtead of encreaſe population; and calculation evinces, that if one man has many wives, many men can have no wives, from the equality of males and females born into the world (*c*). In conſequence of polygamy, perpe-

The goſpel aboliſhed polygamy and divorce.

(*b*) Doddridge's Lectures, Part III. Prop. 59.
(*c*) Derham's Phyſico-theology, Book IV. Cap. x.

tual

SECT. III. tual jealousies would subsist between the wives and children of one man; and partialities, which are unavoidable, must be a constant source of strife and discontent. For these, and perhaps weightier reasons, the gospel prohibited polygamy; and the first Christians, who understood the spirit of their religion, better than the author of the Thelyphthora, condemned a practice so destructive of the happiness of individuals of both sexes. Montesquieu (d) allows, that the climate of some Asiatic countries seems favourable to polygamy; while he censures the practice as an inlet to unnatural crimes, and unserviceable to parents, children, or human kind. Moses permitted divorces to the Israelites in some cases on account of the hardness of their hearts; and the Jews, in process of time, solicited and obtained them on the most trifling occasions (e). This abuse was grown so insupportable, at Christ's appearance in the world, that he absolutely forbade them, except for the cause of adultery. Pagan lawgivers (f) also allowed divorces on the most frivolous pretences, though with few bad effects, while rigid morals lasted in their republics: but when luxury had corrupted mens morals, the inconveniences of this practice were sensibly felt. Where separations were easily obtained, neither husband nor wife were solicitous to please each other; nor could parents, who were

(d) Spirit of Laws, Book XVI. Ch. ii. and vi.
(e) Broughton, Art. Divorce.   (f) Ibid.

likely to separate, unite cordially in the education of their children. According to the system of oppression, which generally prevailed, when the gospel was promulgated, the husband, instead of being the friend and protector of his wife, was tyrant over her; and the wife, as must naturally be expected, obeyed from a principle of fear, rather than of love, gratitude, or a sense of duty (*g*).

Before the promulgation of the gospel, the Roman customs and laws relative to slaves were cruel and severe; masters used to put aged, sick or infirm slaves into an island in the Tyber, and suffered them to perish without pity or assistance (*h*). At Christ's appearance, the majority of subjects, in the freest republics, groaned under oppression; and were doomed to drag out a wretched existence in hard labour, and to be transferred, like beasts, from one master to another. Slaves were not so severely treated until despotism was established in the Roman empire; before that period, several expedients were employed to mitigate the rigours of servitude, and lighten the burden. Some wise regulations of the Roman republic were a powerful restraint on oppression, while they were strictly observed; but when they were violated by contending parties, and liberty was subverted by the tyranny of emperors, then was the Christian religion ushered into the world, and the hardships

It mitigated the rigours of servitude.

(*g*) Robertson's Sermon on the Propagation of the Gospel.
(*h*) Leland's Christ. Revel. Part II. Ch. iv.

SECT. III. of servitude were eased, not by any particular precept, but by the gentle and humane spirit infused by the gospel. I admit, that Christians carry on the slave trade, and that adventurers and planters enslave and oppress in the islands and colonies of the East and West-Indies. But is not the conduct of these men reprobated in Christendom? And have not many efforts been made to abolish the slave trade, so contrary to the genius of the Christian religion? The evils arising from violating the gospel prove its excellent tendency, and oblige us to lament that many of its professors are not real, but nominal Christians. The spirit of the Christian code condemns despotism, and all sorts of oppression; and no genuine Christian could be guilty of either. A writer, acquainted with the history of all nations, asserts, that moderate government is most agreeable to the gospel, and despotic to the koran; and appeals to experience, whether the former has not operated in a striking manner in restraining tyranny, and mitigating the rigours of servitude, in all countries in which it has been established. "The mildness so frequently recommended in the gospel, says Montesquieu, is incompatible with the despotic rage with which a prince punishes his subjects, and exercises himself in cruelty. It is the Christian religion which, in spite of the extent of empire and influence of climate, has hindered despotic power from being established in Ethiopia, and carried into Africa

the

the manners of Europe. The heir to the empire of Ethiopia enjoys a principality, and gives to other subjects an example of love and obedience. Not far from hence, may be seen the Mahometan shutting up the children of the king of Sennar, at whose death, the council sends to murder them, in favour of the prince, who ascends the throne."

—" Let us, continues this writer, set before our eyes, on one hand, the continual massacres of the kings and generals of the Greeks and Romans; and, on the other, the destruction of people and cities by the famous conquerors Timur Beg and Jenghir Khan, who ravaged Asia; and we shall perceive, that we owe to Christianity, in government, a certain political law, and in war, a certain law of nations, which allows to the conquered the great advantages of liberty, laws, wealth, and always religion, when the conqueror is not blind to his own interest (*i*)."

SECT. III.

During the ignorance and barbarism which prevailed in Europe from the 5th to the end of the 11th century, in consequence of the irruption of Goths and Vandals, we find that the Christian religion, though adulterated by its teachers, and insufficient to abolish all the evils of the feudal system, was capable of abating them. In all states of Europe, during that period, governments degenerated into systems of oppression; subjects were

Its teachers preserved justice and checked warriors.

(*i*) Spirit of Laws, Book XXIV. Ch. iii.

slaves

SECT. III. slaves to aristocratic power; perpetual wars subsisted between the barons; and at length all adopted the manners of their barbarous invaders. To check the martial spirit, so prevalent in those days, ecclesiastics interposed their own authority, and that of religion; councils prohibited hostilities, on pain of excommunication, and warriors were required to sheath their swords, in compliance with the gospel. The threats and exhortations of these men had some influence in restraining the violence of war, and absolutely suspended hostilities on certain days, and seasons consecrated to solemn acts of devotion (*k*). Mosheim assures us, that Christian princes exerted themselves in the 10th century in converting nations, whose fierceness they had experienced, in order to soften and render them more gentle (*l*). The Danes, who were originally a fierce nation, were rendered more blood thirsty by the doctrines of Woden; but we have the testimony of Resnal (*m*), that they were less cruel and fierce when Christianity was introduced into the northern kingdoms. History acquaints us, that modern warriors are less vindictive, and more humane to vanquished enemies than ancient heroes unenlightened by the gospel. The spirit of this humane institution has corrected the fierceness of war, and checked the rage of

(*k*) Robertson's View of the State of Europe, Sect. 1.
(*l*) Eccl. Hist. Cent. X.
(*m*) Settlements, Vol. II.

this barbarous practice. As the vanquished were sometimes condemned to servitude, men fought on both sides with that rage and ferocity, inspired by despair, and the apprehension of a defeat: whereas in Christian countries, where servitude is unknown, they have no reason to apprehend such consequences; nor are modern battles so bloody or obstinate as those among the ancients, from the gentle spirit inspired by the gospel. The British and Irish senates, in the year 1783, unanimously voted thanks to one of their commanders for his distinguished humanity, in saving the lives of the officers and soldiers of the enemy at Gibraltar. And as religion and its teachers checked the fierceness of warriors, so, during barbarous ages, the spiritual courts were more just in their decisions than civil tribunals. Civil courts, instead of restraining acts of violence, allowed of combats, as arbiters of right and wrong, of truth and falshood; and judges required little more knowledge than a recollection of few customs relative to duels. The clergy remonstrated against the dreadful effects of trial by combat as unjust and adverse to the genius of the gospel; in their courts they appealed to maxims of equity and to the testimony of witnesses, and sometimes from one court to superior tribunals; while the determinations in the civil courts, however erroneous or unjust, were absolutely irrevocable. A celebrated historian affirms, that men were induced by the equity observed in spiritual

SECT. III. ritual courts, to reform or abolish martial tribunals; and that many excellent regulations were borrowed from the practice of ecclesiastical courts (*n*).

The gospel abolished barbarous practices.

If we consult the history of nations we cannot entertain a doubt, that men, who embraced the gospel, became reformed from several vices and criminal practices, common among Heathens, before it was introduced. Bardesanes, the famous Syrian heretic, observed, that the Christian code has been extremely useful in a moral and political view; since Christians of all nations have retained the virtues, and rejected the vices of the different countries, where it was promulgated. In Parthia, where polygamy prevailed, they are not polygamists; in Persia, they do not marry their own daughters; in Bactria and Gaul, they do not violate the marriage bed; nor do they, wheresoever they reside, yield to the influence of corrupt laws and wicked customs, familiar to others (*o*). By the laws of Zoroaster the Persians committed incest until they embraced the gospel; after which period they abstained from that crime, and observed that temperance and chastity, enjoined by its precepts. This people exposed the bodies of the deceased to be devoured by birds or beasts of prey, but abstained from this custom, and decently interred them after it was promulgated. Eusebius has

(*n*) Robertson's View of the State of Europe, Sect. 1.
(*o*) White's Sermons.

furnished

furnished a catalogue of abominable customs, some of which have been abolished by the gospel; and proves its professors to be free from several crimes, not even condemned in the Pagan world. Christianity was useful not only in its positive precepts, and the genius which it inspired, but also in delivering men from detestable practices, perfectly repugnant to the feelings of Christians. This learned writer assures us, that proselytes to Christianity no longer married their own mothers in Persia; nor in Scythia did they as usual eat human flesh, and sacrifice their children, prompted by superstition. The Massagetæ used to sacrifice their relations, and eat their flesh, when worn out with age; the Tibareni were wont to fling them down precipices; the Hyrcani and Caspians exposed them to be devoured by birds and dogs. These and such like cruel and inhuman customs prevailed not only among barbarous nations, but even among the Greeks, who were polished and refined. In Salamis a man was sacrificed to the daughter of Cecrops; and another at Chios was cruelly torn to pieces and sacrificed to Bacchus: three were daily sacrificed to Juno; and a man was dragged thrice round the altar in Diomede's temple, struck by the priest with a spear, and sacrificed to Diomede. The Greeks in general, before they went out to war, sacrificed a human victim; Aristomenes sacrificed three hundred together to Jove on that occasion; the Celtæ and Car-

SECT. III. Carthaginians ufed human facrifices; and Italy was faid to have been vifited by calamities becaufe the tenth part of the men was not facrificed to the gods. In Laodicea a virgin was flain in honour of the Syrian Pallas; in Lefbos they facrificed to Bacchus, in Phocis to Diana, and the Taurofcythæ offered up, at the fhrine of the fame goddefs, as many as were driven to their coafts by winds or waves (*p*). It is unneceffary to multiply inftances of cruelty among Pagan nations; ancient hiftory abounds with them; and the fecond fection of this work has already furnifhed many of this kind. It is admitted that human victims ceafed in fome of thofe places before Chrift's appearance, and that animal facrifices were fubftituted in their room: but thefe and other abominable cuftoms were exploded, in many countries which embraced the gofpel, as will prefently appear.

It abolifhed the fights of gladiators.   The Romans, though a polifhed people, were cruel and blood thirfty before the promulgation of the gofpel, and its eftablifhment in the empire. The breaking of a glafs, or fome fuch trifling offence, was fufficient to provoke Vidius Pollio to caft his flaves into fifh-ponds, to be devoured by lampreys. The effufion of human blood was their frequent entertainment; fome of their fellow-creature were fet to fight with beafts, others to be devoured by them, and fome to fight againft

(*p*) Eufebii Præp. Evang. Lib. IV. Cap. vii.

each

each other (*q*). Lipſius aſſures us, that no wars ever made ſuch havock on mankind, as thoſe games of pleaſure, which ſometimes deprived Europe of twenty thouſand lives in one month (*r*). From the deteſtable practice of killing perſons at the funerals of great men, aroſe another cuſtom equally cruel and ſhocking to humanity, the fights of gladiators. The Romans, as if aſhamed of human ſacrifices, trained up perſons to engage in voluntary combat, and to fight until they killed each other at the tombs of the deceaſed. This was the origin of thoſe bloody ſhows afterwards ſo delightful to the people of Rome: theſe were the amuſements, with which the principal magiſtrates of Rome, and afterwards the emperors, entertained the citizens, and by which they acquired popularity among the people of that city. Julius Cæſar preſented three hundred and twenty pair of gladiators; even the worthy Titus exhibited a ſhow of gladiators, and Trajan, though not cruel in other reſpects, furniſhed another diſplay, where one thouſand pair of gladiators were exhibited on a theatre, for the entertainment of the ſpectators (*s*). In all thoſe ſpectacles, every pair of combatants was matched and pitted againſt each other, and obliged to maim and murder, in cold blood, thoſe who never had offended them. The paſſion for

(*q*) Hackwell's Apology, Book IV. Ch. iv. Sect. 7.
(*r*) Ibid. Sect. 8.
(*s*) Kennet's Antiq. Book V. Part II. Chap. iv.

theſe

SECT. III. these bloody encounters rose to such an height, that senators and knights turned gladiators; and even women engaged in them, under Nero and Domitian. These champions became formidable by their numbers; and one of them had the boldness to proclaim war against the Roman state. In sword-fights, the spectators did not so much praise skill in defence, as undauntedness in inflicting or receiving wounds; were displeased with the fencers, unless one of them was presently slain, were impatient of delays, as if they thirsted for blood; and carefully examined those who lay weltering in blood, lest they should deceive by a feigned death (*t*). Christian divines soon exercised their pens against these practices; Constantine the Great restrained them by edicts, and the emperor Honorius entirely abolished them (*v*).

It rendered Britons, Scots, Gauls and Irish less barbarous.

The following instances may evince the utility of Christianity in banishing idolatry, and barbarous practices from some countries, where it did not immediately produce virtue, among converts to the gospel. The Gauls and ancient Saxons employed various absurd methods of discovering, whether persons suspected of any crime were innocent or guilty. Sometimes the person accused was obliged to engage in single combat, to prove his innocence; and both priests and people prayed in silence, during the combat, that the inno-

(*t*) Hackwell, Book IV. Chap. iv. Sect. 9.
(*v*) Ibid. Sect. 10.

cent

cent might be victorious. Sometimes he was forced to the disagreeable alternative of grasping red hot iron, or acknowledging himself guilty; sometimes, to walk blind-folded and bare footed over red hot ploughshares, placed at certain distances; and sometimes, to thrust his arm into boiling water. In all these cases, he was judged innocent or guilty, according to the effects which these trials produced. In some instances, a person was flung into a river with a rope about his arms; if he staid at the bottom, until he was drawn up, he was looked on as innocent; but if he floated, he was considered as criminal. These four sorts of ordeal lasted for a considerable time, after the introduction of Christianity, but were abolished by a decree of pope Stephen II. as impious and unjust, and frequently exposing the innocent to manifest hazard (*u*). It is generally admitted, that the Irish were extremely fierce and barbarous, before the time of St. Patrick, and that their ferocity was somewhat abated after that primitive Christian preached the gospel among them. St. Jerome tells us, that the Scots adopted Plato's community of wives, and had their appetites no better regulated than those of beasts; that the Attacotti, a people of Britain, eat human flesh, and reckoned the haunch of a shepherd or the

(*u*) Hackwell, Book IV. Chap. ii. Sect. 5.

breast

SECT. III. breast of a woman, a delicious repast (*w*). Whether the Attacotti were a people of Scotland or not, let antiquarians determime; my object is only to prove, that some nations of Britain were extremely barbarous, before the Christian code, that softener of manners, was published among them. Gildas (*x*) the Wise affirms, that Britons, before they were civilized by the gospel, were rude, barbarous, and impure in their manners, sacrificed human victims, and that their idols were more numerous than the idols of Egypt. Collier is of opinion, that the inhabitants of Great Britain were extremely cruel, before the introduction of Christianity, and founds his opinion on the following facts. In Gaul, before that period, the druids managed the sacrifices, interpreted omens, and directed all matters relative to their superstitions. In times of public distress, they offered animal sacrifices, and in case of sickness or other calamity, which befel individuals, they required human victims to appease their deities. Their idols were hollow and capacious, and in them they placed wretched victims, and burned them to death. They generally sacrificed thieves, robbers, or other criminals; but where they were not supplied with a sufficient number of these, they sacri-

(*w*) Hieronymus adversus Jovinienum, Lib. II. Edit. Paris, 1706, p. 201.
(*x*) De excidio Britanniæ.

ficed

ficed the innocent. Cefar (*y*) gives this account of the Gallic druids, and acquaints us, that thefe borrowed their fuperftitions from thofe of Britain; whence the ecclefiaftical hiftorian fairly concludes, that the Britons were as fuperftitious in their worfhip, and as barbarous in their manners, as the Gauls; and ftrengthens his conclufion by the authority of Tacitus, who affirms, that in the ifle of Anglefea druids ufed to facrifice prifoners taken in war, and put perfons of both fexes to death, for the purpofe of infpecting their entrails, and prying into futurity (*z*). This rough people were foftened in their manners, and human facrifices exploded in Great Britain, Gaul, and other places, by the promulgation of a code, whofe fpirit is fo adverfe to cruelty and bloodfhed.

We are furnifhed with additional proofs of the real efficacy of the gofpel, in removing the evils experienced from falfe religion, and the paffions of mankind. The practice of expofing infants, and putting them to death, was fo common among the ancients, that it is remarked, as an extraordinary thing, that the Egyptians brought up all their children (*a*). Puffendorf (*b*) affirms, that even in China the poorer fort fell and frequently put female children to death, with impunity; and

It checked cruelty in China and Japan.

(*y*) De Bello Gallico, Lib. VI.
(*z*) Collier's Eccl. Hift. Cent. I.
(*a*) Strabo, Lib. XVII. and Diod. Siculus, Lib. I. Cap. viii.
(*b*) De jure Nat, & Gentium, Lib. VI. Cap. ii. Sect. 9.

Potter

SECT. III. Potter (c) proves from ancient authorities, that among the Greeks even a poor man will not expose a son, and that a rich man will scarce preserve a daughter. This crime is prohibited in all countries, where Christianity is established, and men, impressed with its humane spirit, cannot think without horror on the execrable custom. Mr. Gibbon sometimes compliments the Christian institution, and its professors, when it answers his general design of subverting its foundation. In order to account for the increase of Christians and the progress of the gospel, by means merely human; he affirms, that pious Christians rescued multitudes of infants, who were exposed by their parents; baptized and maintained them, out of the public funds of that society. And yet these are the men whom he traduces, whose indiscretions he magnifies, and whose virtues he suppresses or endeavours to vilify! The historian (d) of the Roman empire admits, that above three thousand new-born infants are annually exposed in the streets of Pekin, of which number many have been preserved by the humanity of Christian missionaries. Mosheim (e) assures us, that the Japanese were easily prevailed on to embrace the gospel from the cruelty exercised by the Bonzas or priests towards the afflicted, compared to the benevolence and humanity of Romish missionaries.

(c) Antiq. Chap. xiv. (d) Hist. Chap. xv.
(e) Eccl. Hist. Cent. XVII.

of Religion on Mankind.

SECT. III.

The Bonzas maintained, that the sick and needy are odious to the gods, and thus prevented the relief of them by the affluent; while missionaries proved, that the good things of this world are often a curse, instead of a blessing, to the possessors; and that the favourites of heaven are often afflicted in this life, and compensated in the next. By such doctrines they, no doubt, inspired their new converts with benevolence; and prevailed on them to relieve the wretched and necessitous.

In the reign of the emperor Heraclius, Amandus Gallus converted the people of Ghent to the gospel; and destroyed the altars, on which they offered human sacrifices (*f*). In the province of Virginia, in North America, the inhabitants, who were idolaters, sometimes sacrificed children to the devil, before the Christian religion was published among them (*g*). In Mexico, their king Ahuitzol sacrificed sixty-four thousand and eighty men in the year 1486, at the consecration of a temple; and though human sacrifices be banished from those cities, converted by Spaniards, yet do the Indians perpetrate such abominable deeds in the mountains to this day (*h*). At Cholula, on the decease of a king a man was sacrificed, and in-

It abolished human sacrifices and other cruelties in many places.

(*f*) Alstedius de conversione populorum, quoted by Millar, History of the Propagation of Christianity, Chap. vi.

(*g*) Harris's Collection of Travels, Vol. I. p. 815 to 848.

(*h*) Acosta's Hist. of Indies, Book V. Chap. ix. quoted by Millar.

SECT. III. ferior priests held the legs, arms and head of the victim, while the chief priest laid open his breast and pulled out his heart, to offer to the sun and idol: five or six thousand children were annually sacrificed to the numerous idols of this place, before the introduction of the Romish religion by the Spaniards (*i*). In Mexico they kept every twentieth day, which was the last of their month, holy, and offered human sacrifices; and on a certain festival drowned a boy and girl to accompany the idol of a lake. These abominable customs were exploded by the introduction of the gospel, and the spirit which it inspired. The Herulians, a people near the Danube, who were converted to Christianity in the sixth century, by the emperor Justinian, appeased their gods by human sacrifices; put to death the aged and infirm; and required the wife of an Herulian, who would be thought virtuous, to kill herself at the tomb of her deceased husband (*k*). The Abasgi, an idolatrous people of Scythia, were barbarously used by their princes, before their conversion to Christianity: these tyrants forced from parents such of their children as were beautiful, made them eunuchs, sold them to the Romans, and killed the parents themselves, lest they should revenge the injuries offered to their children. The emperor Justinian prohibited this custom, and appointed

(*i*) Acosta's Hist. of Indies, Book V. Chap. xx.
(*k*) Evagrius, Lib. IV. Cap. xix.

priests

priests to instruct this people in the doctrines of
Christianity, and to wean them from the idolatrous
and criminal practices so usual among Heathens (*l*).
In Congo, before the king became a convert to the
Romish religion, a multitude of his concubines
and court ladies attended his corpse to the grave,
and twelve of them were buried alive with him,
while many more solicited that honour (*m*). In
the kingdom of Metamba, subject to Congo, they
used to put sick persons to death, on pretence of
friendship, and shortening the continuance of their
pain; and some idolatrous provinces of Angola
fed on human flesh, and sacrificed a number of
victims at funerals, until the Christian religion was
introduced by the Portugueze (*n*). The Lithuanians, who were the last people in Europe converted to Christianity, celebrated a solemn sacrifice every October, in honour of their gods, and
burned the spoils taken in war, together with one
of the prisoners. This odious custom was entirely
abolished, when Lithuania was annexed to the
dominions of Poland; for when Uladislaus, great
duke of that territory, married the Polish king's
daughter, in the year 1386, and was baptised, he,
assisted by the clergy, propagated and established
Christianity in that country, on the ruins of idolatry (*o*).

(*l*) Evagrius, Lib. IV. Cap. xxi.
(*m*) Mod. Univ. Hist. Vol. VI. folio, Book XXI. Ch. 11.
(*n*) Ibid.   (*o*) Hottinger Hist. Eccl. Seculum 14. p. 867.

SECT. III.

It also restrained idolatry and cruelty in Germany, Paraguay, and Canary Islands.

Before the introduction of the gospel into Germany, its inhabitants offered human victims to Mercury on certain days; but refrained from this odious practice, when the Christian religion was published among them. Here it is worthy of observation, that this warlike people were induced to embrace Christianity from an opinion, that a religion is excellent, whose professors were victorious and successful in war. These men mistook the tendency of the Christian code, which was not calculated for extending conquests by war and violence, like the Pagan and Mahometan religions, but to render men happy and satisfied with their condition. Even some moderns have objected against Christianity, that the Roman empire was subverted after it was introduced; but let me ask, whether any wise man would wish for the continuance of an empire, founded on violence and supported by despotism? Whether extent of empire constitutes the happiness of a people? And whether the Roman empire was not prepared for a fall, by the vices and corruptions of emperors, senate, and mass of the people? But to return to the influence of the gospel, in abolishing the idolatries and cruelties of Pagan nations. The dean of Gloucester has, from Muratori, furnished a striking contrast between the manners of the unconverted and converted inhabitants of Paraguay. Before these Indians embraced the Christian institution, they were cruel and vindictive, had but little

little feeling for the diftreffes of one of their own tribe, and not a fpark of benevolence for the diftreffed members of any other. The miffionaries not only civilized this people, and taught them the arts of induftry, but even converted them into the moft humane and benevolent of all inhabitants of the earth (*q*). The inhabitants of the Canary iflands were grofs idolaters, before the beginning of the fifteenth century; and killed and butchered ftrangers, and even each other, without mercy or compaffion. Some flung themfelves from precipices in honour of a deity which they worfhipped; being perfuaded that they fhould enjoy all forts of happinefs, after fo noble a death (*r*). Chriftianity, when introduced into thofe iflands by the Spaniards, extirpated thefe practices; though it was adulterated by its teachers, and blended with the lucrative inventions of interefted men. The Romifh religion, though a corrupt fubftitute for the Chriftian fyftem, is averfe from cruelty and bloodfhed; inculcates that benevolence and humanity taught by the gofpel, and has abolifhed many favage cuftoms of idolatrous nations. Popifh miffionaries have been induftrious in propagating their religion and making profelytes in Pagan countries: and it is but juft to afcribe many good effects of the Chriftian code, to the endea-

---

(*q*) Tucker's Treatife on Government, Part II. Chap. ii.

(*r*) Millar's Hift. of the Propagation of Chriftianity, Ch. vi. p. 132.

SECT. III.

It diffused knowledge and abolish- ed some bad effects of su- perstition.

vours of men, zealous in extirpating abominable customs, while they held some maxims, which distinguished them from Protestants, whose influence shall be pointed out in the course of this work.

Besides the advantage of abolishing cruel practices in many places, the Christian religion has laid a foundation, for distributing religious and moral instruction; and been instrumental in kindling and preserving a spirit of erudition in many countries, where it has been established. The apostles were commissioned to preach to all nations, however remote in situation or different in language. Paul, who was peculiarly appointed for the instruction of the Gentiles, nominated Timothy and Titus for the same purpose; and authorized them to nominate subordinate ministers, as the gospel extended, and congregations grew numerous. If we compare this mode of propagating religious and moral instruction, with the limited operations of Pagan philosophers, and Jewish prophets and synagogues, we shall readily be convinced of the superior excellence of the gospel, in disseminating knowledge. The gospel, at its first appearance in the world, produced a group of apologists, whose works abound with various kinds of literature, which must have enlightened the minds of Pagans, and filled them with more rational ideas of God and virtue than they entertained before. Even philosophers, who did not embrace Christianity, could not avoid being improved

improved by those learned works, and by the spirit of the gospel, which was then read to gratify curiosity, or for the purpose of refuting it. It is for this reason, perhaps, that the works of Seneca, Epictetus, Arrian, Plutarch, Hierocles, Simplicius, Plotinus, and other Pagans who wrote in the early ages of christianity, abound with more useful moral instruction than is to be found in the writings of more ancient philosophers. The Christian religion, by enlarging the mind, contributed to banish superstition, and abolish Heathen oracles, which were a system of fraud, and a considerable expence to the Gentile world. These oracles were so numerous, that Hermippus filled five volumes with descriptions of them; Vandale furnishes a catalogue of near three hundred; and affirms, that they amounted to near one thousand (*s*). This learned writer denies that their silence is to be ascribed entirely to Christ's appearance, as Eusebius and other Christian writers were inclined to imagine (*t*). He admits, at the same time, that the gospel was the chief cause which enabled men to perceive their vanity, and the fraudulent practices which were the fruits of them.

As mens minds were enlarged and enlightened by the gospel, they were also preserved by its teachers from relapsing into ignorance. When a

Its teachers preserved & advanced learning.

(*s*) Vandale, Dissert. II. de Oraculorum Ethnicorum duratione et interitu, Cap. vii.

(*t*) Dissert. I. de Oraculorum Origine & Authoribus, Cap. xv.

SECT. III. love of science was succeeded by a love of arms, few had inducements to study arts and sciences, except men educated for the clerical profession: nor would erudition of various kinds have been propagated so universally, nor transmitted to our times through so many dark ages of war and violence, had it not been necessary for a knowledge of theology, and the works of the fathers. History acquaints us, that churchmen possessed all the learning of those times, handed it down in succession, and collected and preserved books, which must have inevitably perished, when a taste for literature was almost extinct, and the passion of the laity turned towards arms (*u*). The studies of men educated for the ministry have been of some importance to the literary world, and the foundation of their proficiency in solid and polite learning, in the subsequent part of their lives. The course of erudition, absolutely necessary for obtaining degrees in our universities, and for preparing young men for the sacerdotal function, is sufficient to introduce them to a moderate acquaintance with different branches of literature, and to try to which of them their capacities are adapted. We may appeal to experience, whether mankind are not indebted to learned ecclesiastics for new discoveries in arts and sciences, or for improvements on the discoveries of those who went before them. In the priesthood there have

(*u*) Minute Philosopher, Dial. 5.

been

been so many able writers on useful subjects, that it would require extensive learning to recite their names, and the advantages to literature derived from that order. These however are not the necessary but accidental effects of christianity, and not to be ascribed to the Christian code but to ecclesiastical establishments for the support and maintenance of the teachers of the gospel. The clerical order are an appendage of the Christian system, and absolutely necessary to maintain its purity, to confute gainsayers by their learning, and to prevent the bad effects arising from ignorance and perversion of the scriptures. Learning is the general consequence of a competent provision for the priesthood, and ignorance, among both clergy and laity, the natural and unavoidable effect of the want of regular or legal establishments. Were there no ecclesiastical establishments, teachers would soon degenerate; as few would sacrifice time and expence to study in colleges, on the bare prospect of being assistants to, or even masters of schools. If instructors of youth grow ignorant, a proportionable ignorance must soon prevail among their pupils; and we may easily judge of the consequences that might ensue. Were an ignorant laity freely to indulge their fancies on religious subjects, unassisted and uncontroled by the learned, a nation might soon be stocked with fanatics and rebels; if they submit implicitly to ignorant teachers, without enquiry, they

SECT. III. they might become dupes and slaves to impostors and tyrants.

The charity of Christians taught Pagans kindness to the distressed.

Juvenal, Tacitus, Sallust, and other Pagan writers, furnish abundant proofs of the corruption of manners which prevailed in Rome and other places when the Christian religion was published to the world; nor can it reasonably be denied, that it had a considerable influence on the hearts of its professors. The affection of Christians for each other was proverbial; and even Heathens used to say of them, how those Christians love one another! Epiphanius, bishop of Salamis, spent his whole fortune in relieving the distressed, especially those who were shipwrecked on the coast (*w*). Cyprian sold his estate to relieve mens wants; and, while he laments the degeneracy of Christians, acknowledges that they surpassed Heathens in the practice of virtue (*x*). In the city of Alexandria, so many persons were appointed to take care of the sick, that Theodosius was under a necessity of limiting the number to six hundred; as appears from a law extant in his codes. Instances of the charity of primitive Christians, in redeeming captives, and founding hospitals for the poor, are too numerous to be recounted; nor can it be denied, that to the genius of the gospel, christendom is indebted for many pious and charitable establishments, little known

(*w*) Cave on Primitive Christianity, Part III. Ch. ii.
(*x*) Cyprian de Lapsis.

to the Gentile world. In cases where tenderness and loving kindness were necessary, Christians did not confine their bounty to those of their own sect, but were kind to all men, even to their enemies: for all men, as Tertullian observes, love their friends, but it is peculiar to Christians to love their enemies, to return kindness for hatred, and to pray that their enemies might obtain mercy from God (*y*). Lucian bears testimony of their kindness to Peregrinus, a Pagan philosopher, and makes a panegyric upon them where he intended a satire. "Their legislator, says this humourist, has made them believe, that they are all brethren; they worship a crucified impostor, live according to his laws, and have all things common (*z*)." Another enemy to christianity admits, that its professors were more virtuous than Pagans; and that some, who did not embrace its tenets, were much improved by the example of Christians. The emperor Julian, in a letter to an Heathen pontiff, desires him to turn his eyes to the means by which the superstition of Christians was propagated: by kindness to strangers, by sanctity of life, and by the attention which they paid to the burial of the dead. He recommends an imitation of their virtues, exhorts him to prevail on the priests of Galatia to be attentive to the worship of their gods, and desires him to strip them of

(*y*) Lampridii, Alexander Severus.   (*z*) Lucian de Morte Peregrini, Paris Edit. 1615, p. 996.

SECT. III.

the sacerdotal function, unless they obliged their wives, children and servants to do the same. He also enjoins works of beneficence, desires him to relieve the distressed, to build houses for the accommodation of strangers of whatever religion; and says, it is a disgrace to Pagans to disregard those of their own religion; while Christians do kind offices to strangers and enemies. Whence it is evident, that Christians were improved in their morals by the gospel, and even Pagans improved by the example of Christians (*a*).

Gospel renders its first proselytes true and honest.

Primitive Christians were upright in their dealings, religiously observed oaths and promises, and observed the rule of doing unto others, whatsoever they would, that men should do unto them: a rule so excellent, that the Pagan emperor Alexander Severus ordered it to be proclaimed by a public crier, and written on the walls of all public buildings (*b*). "We deny not, says Tertullian, any pledge left with us; we defile no man's marriage bed; we piously educate orphans, relieve the necessities of the indigent, and render to no man evil for evil." They allowed or practised no acts of deceit or dishonesty; or if any were convicted of such crimes, the whole body of Christians protested against them. The following narrative proves the excellence of the Christian religion,

(*a*) Juliani Imperatoris Epistola 49, ad Arsacium Pontificem Galatiæ.   (*b*) Hist. Augustæ Scriptores, Edit. Paris, 1610, p. 132.

and

and the bad effects of the Pagan, on the actions of its professors. In the sixth century, Al Nooman, king of Hira, in a drunken frolic, ordered two of his intoxicated companions to be burned alive. When sober, he repented of his crime; and, in order to expiate the offence, set apart two days every year in honour of them, and resolved to sacrifice, on one of these days, the first person he met; and dismiss him whom he met on the other, with magnificent presents. On one of those unfortunate days, the king was met by an Arab, who had once entertained him when fatigued with hunting, and separated from his companions. In gratitude for this favour, the prince granted him a year's respite, provided he could find security for his returning from a distant province to suffer death at the expiration of the year. One of the prince's court, in compassion, offered himself as his surety, and the Arab was released. When the Arab appeared on the appointed day, the king asked him, why he would offer himself to death when he might have escaped it by the death of his security? He replied, that he was taught to do so by the religion which he professed: the king, having enquired about his religion, and finding him a Christian, desired an explanation of the doctrines of christianity, embraced the gospel, pardoned the Arab, and totally abolished the barbarous custom (c). Hence it is evident, that these

(c) Sale's Preliminary Discourse, Sect. i.

doctrines

SECT. III. doctrines had excellent effects in banishing inhumanity; and that the virtues of Christians were not confined to the first ages of christianity, but were practised by individuals, even in a country in which its precepts were deplorably corrupted.

It rendered them patient, constant, and chaste.

No dangers could terrify, nor threats, nor torments engage primitive Christians to desert their profession: they neither repined, nor railed at their enemies, but bore their sufferings with invincible meekness. Is it not, says the Heathen in Minucius Fælix, a strange folly, and incredible boldness, to despise present torments, and yet fear those that are future and uncertain? So foolishly do they flatter themselves, and lull their fears by a deceitful hope of some unknown comforts that shall arise to them hereafter! Tertullian ascribes the propagation of the faith, in some degree, to the patience of Christians: this apologist tells Scapula, that every person who beheld such eminent patience, could not but enquire into the cause, and when informed of the truth immediately embraced it (*d*). Collier furnishes a strong instance of the steadiness and inflexibility of Christians in the reign of the emperor Constantius. That emperor, to try the principles of his courtiers, and whether they were sincere or nominal Christians, pretended an aversion for the Christian religion, and commanded them to sacrifice to the gods, on pain of being dismissed. They, who

(*d*) Tertullian ad Scapulam, Cap. v.

were sincerely attached to the gospel, said they must resign their employments, and incur his displeasure rather than the divine, while others contented to offer sacrifice to the deities of the Pagans. The emperor, having made the wished-for discovery, applauded the former for their constancy and integrity, and admitted them to a share in the administration of the state, but disbanded the latter from his court, and severely reprimanded them, saying, they never could be true to their prince who were so false to their God (*e*). Even Mr. Gibbon (*f*) affirms, that " a caliph of the house of Abbas was heard to declare, that the Christians were most worthy of trust in the administration of Persia;" and that when the gospel was corrupted by its professors. Such was the constancy of primitive Christians, that Arnobius assures us, servants will rather suffer torments by their masters, wives sooner part from their husbands, and children prefer being disinherited by parents, rather than abandon the faith of Christ. The historian of the Roman empire bears testimony to the rigid morals of primitive Christians; and admits, that the most atrocious criminals became, after baptism, the most eminent saints, whose faults, or rather errors, were an excess of virtue (*g*). They could not be allured by promises, nor terrified by

(*e*) Collier Eccl. Hist. Book I. (*f*) Hist. Rom. Emp. Ch. li. p. 390. (*g*) Adversus Gentes, Lib. I.

SECT. III. threats to violate their chastity; and Cave gives instances of persons of both sexes who endured dangers and death rather than be guilty of an unchaste compliance (*h*). When you prefer condemning women to the stews to casting them to the lions, says Tertullian to the Pagans, you acknowledge that we look on the violation of chastity as an heavier penalty than any you can inflict. Some Christians ran into excesses in their ideas of chastity, and even made vows of perpetual continence from an excessive zeal, and from a mistake of the genius of the Christian institution.

It corrected pride and vanity;   Pagans were vain, arrogant, and strangers to modesty and Christian humility, commended their own personal abilities, and grosly flattered their emperors, who received, with pleasure, the most blasphemous titles. Ovid, at the conclusion of his Metamorphoses, boasts that he finished a work that shall last for ever; Horace vaunts that he accomplished one more lasting than brass; Cicero asserts, with the most undisguised vanity, that it was happy for Rome he had been consul: and instances of the self-sufficiency of Stoics, and other sects, are too numerous to be recited. The sacred writers, on the contrary, modestly publish to the world their own infirmities, and those of their party; and Christian authors speak humbly of themselves, while Pagan writers were arrogant

(*h*) Cave, Part II. Ch. v.

and

and vain-glorious to a shameful degree. So efficacious was christianity in repressing vanity, and humbling its professors, that several of them rejected the crown of martyrdom, and would not suffer men to call them martyrs. Dioclesian admitted none to greater familiarity than kissing his toe: Domitian published his edicts with this preamble, " Our Lord and God so commands it;" and required these titles when men wrote or spoke of him. Caligula built a temple to himself, erected a golden statue, and instituted sacrifices and priests to officiate in the service (k): and other emperors claimed and obtained the honours paid to the gods. Virgil divides the empire between Jupiter and Augustus; and Lucian declares, that all the outrages committed in the civil wars were advantageous, considered as preparatory to Nero's accession to the throne. The emperors, in their rescripts, were not ashamed to confer divine attributes upon themselves: Augustus was worshipped as a god in the provinces, and temples were erected in honour of him (l). If we compare the conduct of these Pagans with that of some Christians, the contrast is so striking as to appear at first view. Dr. Cave (m) points out several instances of Christian humility in an empress, and in other personages at the court of Rome, where blasphemous titles were formerly

(k) Hackwell's Apology, Book IV. Ch. x. Sect. 1.
(l) Ibid. Sect. 2.   (m) Part II. Ch. vii.

SECT. III.

and improved on the old Roman laws.

conferred, which at present would shock the vainest monarch in christendom. We cannot entertain a doubt but inferiors, in all parts of the empire, exhibited humility and condescension, unknown to them before, in imitation of their superiors, and in compliance with the precept and example of their Lord and master.

A person sufficiently acquainted with the Roman laws, before and after the establishment of christianity, might, doubtless, perceive, that they were considerably improved by the precepts of the gospel. We may well suppose, that the spirit of that system, which had such powerful influence on the hearts and manners of its professors, must have had some effect on the Christian emperors, and on the laws which they enacted. It is impossible but a change in the spirit of lawgivers should be perceptible in their edicts. They who prescribed creeds, and entered deeply into theological matters, could not have omitted blending Christian morality with their civil institutes, and transcribing into the civil code, the humanity and benevolence inspired by the gospel. A learned Civilian acquaints us, that the emperor Justinian, finding the Digest defective, supplied its defects by employing the first book of his code in treating on religion. This emperor, besides the care and superintendence of charitable institutions, empowered bishops to interpose their authority where the civil magistrate was absent, or voluntarily

tarily delayed judgment; and to perform the double part of civil judges and overseers of their flocks (*n*). The former of these powers was the foundation of ecclesiastical courts, afterwards so useful as I have already observed. Hence it appears, that christianity was productive of salutary effects in the execution of justice; in relieving distress of every kind; in mitigating the cruelty of Heathens, and disposing their hearts to pity and beneficence. The Justinian law, besides these advantages, restrained libertinism, by enacting that bawds, once warned to relinquish their wicked profession, and persisting in it, shall be put to death; that any person who lets an house to a bawd, knowing the infamy of his character, shall be fined in a large sum to the prince, and his house exposed to the danger of confiscation (*o*).

Nothing can more strongly evince the moral virtues of the first Christians than the apologies which have been published by some of that order against the accusations of gainsayers. Had not christianity and its professors been attacked at a time that its evidence, and the actions of these men might have been scrutinized, there might appear a suspicion of fraud in the contrivance of the Christian system; and many virtues of primitive Christians would, perhaps, have been unno-

Calumnies against Christians, and the gospel serviceable to both.

(*n*) Sir Th. Ridley's View of Civil and Eccl. Law, Part I. Ch. ii. Sect. 2.   (*o*) Ibid. Ch. iii. Sect. 4. Collation 3d.

T ticed,

SECT. III. ticed, were it not for the crimes imputed to them by their adversaries. The enemies of the gospel first attempted to stop its progress by open assaults; but finding such attempts fruitless, they endeavoured to hinder its reception, by reviling its professors, and loading them with calumnies. For this reason the first converts to christianity admitted none to their communion, except such as would not disgrace their profession; and required proselytes to give security that they would strictly observe the tenets of their religion. This precaution had a tendency to exclude unworthy members from the church, and was the foundation of sponsorship at baptism, as Mosheim assures us (*p*). Yet Christians were branded with the opprobrious name of Atheists for their aversion to the Pagan gods; and some declaimed against them as magicians, on account of the miracles wrought by Christ and his followers. They were accused of worshipping the sun and the head of an ass, of endeavouring to subvert the Roman government, of killing and eating children in celebrating their mysteries, and of most shocking incests in their feasts of charity (*q*). These and other calumnies propagated by their enemies, and especially the Jews, operated so powerfully on the minds of Pagans, that they were condemned unheard, and exposed to several persecutions

(*p*) Eccl. Hist. (*q*) Broughton Art. Christians.

during

during the firft three centuries, though other caufes contributed to them befides the malice of enemies: but the lives of Chriftians were fufficient to refute thofe accufations, and furnifhed apologifts with opportunities of difplaying their learning in defence of innocence, and of exhibiting virtues which might perhaps have lain in obfcurity, had it not been for the malignity of virulent opponents.

"There is an infamous report, fays an Athenian philofopher (r) and profelyte to the gofpel, that we are guilty of Thyeftean feafts, or feeding on murdered infants, of inceftuous copulations, and impiety towards the gods." In anfwer to fuch accufations, Chriftians appealed to their actions, and confented to undergo the fevereft penalties, if convicted of the crimes they were accufed of by their enemies. "If any man, fays this apologift, convicts us of a greater or leffer crime, we feek not to efcape punifhment; nay, we willingly fuffer the crueleft that you can inflict upon us."—" If thefe be true, fpare no age, no fex; punifh us with our wives and children; extirpate us out of the world; but if thefe are forged and fcandalous calumnies of wicked men, from malice, mark them as fuch; enquire into our lives, opinions, obedience to authority, and our concern for your perfon and government; allow us but the common

Chriftians falfely accufed of inceft and devouring infants.

(r) Athenagoras Legatio pro Chriftianis.

SECT. III. justice you grant your enemies; we ask no more, and are assured of victory." He thus proceeds in his defence against such aspersions; "How can we be suspected of breach of chastity, who think that to look with concupiscence is to commit adultery, and believe we shall be judged for our very thoughts? How can we, who think it our duty to exclude all impure thoughts, be supposed guilty of actions which we dare not think of? We marry for procreation, and that but once; many remain all their lives single; and some have carried the idea of chastity so far as to emasculate themselves. Do they, who keep a fair for sodomy, and all manner of lewdness, accuse us of the crimes which they are themselves guilty of, and which they ascribe to their gods as laudable actions? Adulterers and sodomites accuse us who marry but once, or make eunuchs of ourselves for the kingdom of heaven's sake, that we may have a nearer union with God. None of our servants, from whom it is impossible to conceal our actions, have seen us eat human flesh, or even falsely accused us of any such crime. How could we, who charge women with murder that cause abortion, be supposed to kill children born into the world? Or we, who think it criminal to expose our children, be capable of murdering them? How could we, who abstain from all sights of the combats of gladiators with each other, and with beasts, as contrary to our feelings, embrue our hands in the blood

blood of innocents (*s*)?" The learned Watson (*t*) thinks it probable, that the clandestine manner in which Christians were obliged to celebrate the Eucharist, for fear of Jews and Pagans, and the words eating the body, and drinking the blood of Christ, made use of in that solemnity, together with the custom of imparting a kiss of charity to each other, and calling each other brothers and sisters, gave occasion to the malicious tale of their feasting on murdered infants, and of incestuous intercourses at the meetings of Christians.

Dion Cassius acquaints us, that the emperor Domitian put to death multitudes of Christians, and confiscated their estates, on pretence of Atheism, and because they embraced the religion of the Jews, who were often confounded with Christians, because Christ and his apostles were born in Judea. It must be admitted, that, according to the ideas of Heathens, Christians were Atheists; since they worshipped but one God, and not a single deity of the thirty thousand, adored by Pagans, as a learned apologist judiciously observes. Christians were also accused of being authors of public calamities; an accusation, to which the world is indebted for learned treatises, written for the purpose of wiping off that aspersion. " If, says Tertullian (*u*), the city is besieged, if any thing happen in the fields, in the garrisons, in the

SECT. III.

Of being Atheists and authors of public calamities.

(*s*) Athenagoras Legatio pro Chriſtianis.   (*t*) Anſwer to Gibbon.   (*u*) Apolog. Cap. xl.

islands,

SECT. III. islands, they presently cry out, it is because of the Christians. Our enemies conspire the ruin of good men, and cloak their hatred with this vain pretence, that Christians are the causes of all public calamities. If the Tyber overflows its banks, and the Nile does not overflow the fields; if there be an earthquake, famine, or plague, they instantly cry out, Away with the Christians to the lions." We may reasonably suppose other accusations against Christians to be as groundless as this, and as destitute of foundation. Augustine wrote his famous work, De Civitate Dei, for a refutation of this charge; Arnobius (*w*) enumerates the disasters experienced by mankind before the appearance of Christ; and Orosius wrote his history to prove, that, in all ages preceding the introduction of christianity, men had felt calamities similar to those falsely ascribed to the religion of the gospel. Cyprian (*x*) maintains, that their cruelty to Christians was one of the sins which provoked God to inflict severe judgments upon them; that " they were punished less than they deserved, who were proud, covetous, cruel in anger, extravagant in game, drunk with wine, full of envy, debauched with lust, or mad with cruelty. Why, says he, do you wonder, that the flames of divine anger rise higher, when the sins of men call daily

(*w*) Adversus Gentes, Lib. I. Edit. Paris, 1605, p. 5, & seq.   (*x*) Adversus Demetrianum, Edit. Paris, 1726, p. 219.

for it." I might cite many other instances, in which apologists displayed great learning in refuting this futile charge; and I have dwelt on it for the purpose of proving how little credit is due to the other accusations of men so bigotted and absurd.

{SECT. III.}

Christians were not disturbers of the peace, and enemies of the civil government, but honoured magistrates, revered their power, paid tribute, obeyed the laws, where they were not evidently contrary to the laws of Christ; and, where they refused to observe them, submitted quietly to the severest penalties. When a tax was demanded of Christ, he refused not to pay it; when arraigned before Pilate, he acknowledged his authority, and submitted to his sentence. The apostles, though unjustly accused before the council, went away rejoicing, and we may well suppose, that the same spirit of piety and submission was displayed in succeeding ages by the genuine followers of Christ, who imitated these and other virtues even to a fault. I admit that they refused to swear by the emperor's genius, which, according to Tertullian, was to pay divine honours to devils; or to celebrate their festivals, which were scenes of vanity, luxury, debauchery and other vices (*y*): so far they were disobedient, and were punished for their disobedience, by cruel persecutions, horrid to re-

Of turbulence.

(*y*) Cave, Part III. Cap. iv.

T 4 late!

SECT. III.

late! The Greeks and Romans had laws against meetings, and desired to have them executed against Christians, who were accused of seditiously holding unlawful assemblies. Their defence clearly proves them innocent of the charge; they desired to distinguish between their own meetings, and those against which the law was directed, and maintained, that the prohibition did not relate to them, and that the law was not applicable to such meetings as theirs (z). Here we are enabled to overturn that false and dangerous assertion of Cardinal Bellarmin, that it is lawful to depose and murder heretical princes; and that primitive Christians only wanted means to attempt it on Nero, Dioclesian and Julian, who cruelly persecuted them. The Cardinal did not consider, that resolute men, who showed a contempt of life in other instances, might easily have assassinated them, if their consciences permitted them. If it was agreeable to the spirit of the gospel to put heretical princes to death, St. Paul would not have advised the Romans to obey Nero, but to murder and depose him. It is dangerous to teach, that any man may lawfully rebel against his sovereign, where he thinks his own religion preferable to that of the prince: and since it was not attempted by zealous Christians on the vilest tyrants, as well as on the most cruel persecutors, we may be assured,

(z) Cave, Part III. Cap. iv.

that such conduct is perfectly repugnant to the genius of the gospel (*a*).

Of being poor and ignorant,

In order to asperse Christianity, the Heathen in Minucius Fælix represents its professors as poor and ignorant, mute in public; and talkative in private, to women, children and mechanics. Celsus (*b*) alleges, that the learned were excluded from the mysteries of Christianity, and none admitted but fools, slaves, women and children, all which accusations are denied by Apologists. Octavius (*c*) affirms, that where they eclined to preach in open day, it was from a dread of persecutions, which frequently threatened them. " Christians, says Origen (*d*), do not readily admit men to hear them, until they have pre-examined their dispositions, and found them resolved to lead a pious life. It is false that we address our discourses to women and children only, and that in corners; since we openly promise eternal happiness to those who observe the laws of the gospel, and explain the sublime mysteries of religion to the wise and learned; while we adapt our discourses to the capacities of the weak, who stand more in need of milk, than strong meats." Doctor Watson (*e*) denies that " they preached in single houses, or obscure villages, or impure brothels, but in the synagogues and temples, in the

(*a*) Cave, Part III. Cap. iv. (*b*) Origen contra Celsum. Lib. III. (*c*) Minucius Fælix, Sect. 31.
(*d*) Lib. III. (*e*) Lett. IV. to Gibbon.

streets

streets and market places of the great cities of the Roman provinces, in Jerusalem, Corinth, in Antioch, in Athens, in Ephesus and in Rome." The erudition of apologists may convince us that Christianity was embraced by men of learning and abilities. Arnobius (*f*) observes, that orators, grammarians, rhetoricians, lawyers, physicians, and philosophers, men of great genius, love our religion, despising those things wherein they before trusted. We should not be surprised, if men of low birth, and humble fortunes, accustomed to self-denial, should more readily embrace the gospel, than the opulent, whose passions were inflamed by sinful indulgence. Besides, the truth of a religious system does not depend on the estates of its professors: and if it depended on such circumstances, we are furnished with an argument in its defence, supported as it was by persons of distinguished rank, and in course of time, by princes and potentates. In Domitian's time, Flavius Clemens, that Emperor's nephew, and Acilius Glabrio, who had been consuls, embraced the gospel; and many of the greatest birth and fortune became converts in the reign of Commodus; among whom was Apollonius a senator, a philosopher, and man of refinement, who pleaded his cause before the Roman senate (*g*). Tertullian remonstrates with the Roman governors, and maintains, that by persecut-

---

(*f*) Adversus Gentes, Lib. I.   (*g*) Cave, Part I. Cap. iii.

ing Christians, they will depopulate their respective countries, and banish the best citizens in all places and departments in the state; in cities, islands, castles, corporations, councils, armies, palace, senate and courts of judicature. This author entreats Scapula, deputy governor of Africa, to consider, how many thousand men and women of every rank and condition, would readily offer themselves, if he persisted in persecuting them. He asks, " What fires and swords must he have to dispatch them? Carthage itself must be decimated, his own friends and persons of his acquaintance, the principal men and matrons of the city will suffer; if you spare not us, spare yourself, spare Carthage, have pity on the province (*h*)."

The enemies of Christians, among other charges, accused them of being useless members of society, instead of being serviceable to communities. To this charge Tertullian (*i*) replied with his usual eloquence, and strength of reasoning: " How can this be, when we have the same diet, habit and manner of life? We are no Brachmans, nor Indian Gymnosophists, who live in woods secluded from the world; we are sensible of our obligations to our Creator, and despise none of the good things which he bestows, though careful to use them with temperance and sobriety. We make use of your markets, shambles, baths, taverns,

and useless members of society.

(*h*) Tertullian ad Scapulam, Cap. v.   (*i*) Apolog. Cap. xlii.

shops,

SECT. III. shops, fairs, and other places of social intercourse. We go to sea, cultivate and improve the ground, employ ourselves in merchandise, exercise mechanic arts, and sell our manufactures like other men: how then are we unserviceable to your affairs with whom we live? None have reasonable cause to complain that we are unprofitable, except bawds, panders, bullies, ruffians, sellers of poison, magicians, soothsayers, wizards and astrologers, the lucre of which men must be hurtful to the state." Other apologists maintained, that Christians were of advantage to commonwealths, by restraining vices, which were detrimental to society, by precept and example. " Enquire, says Origen (k), into the lives of some of us; compare our former and present mode of life; and you will perceive in what impurities and impieties men were involved, before they embraced our doctrines. But since they embraced them, how just, grave, moderate, and constant, are they become? Yea, some are so inflamed with the love of purity and goodness, as to abstain even from lawful enjoyments: the church abounds with such men, wherever the doctrines of Christianity have prevailed. How is it possible they can be pestilent members of society, who have converted many from the sink of vice, to the study of virtue and a life of temperance, conformable to the dic-

(k) Contra Celsum, Lib. I.

tates

tates of right reason?—We reclaim women from immodesty, quarrelling, or parting from their husbands; men, from the wild extravagance of the sports and theatres, and restrain youth, who are prone to vice and luxury, by not only painting the vileness of lust, but the punishment reserved for the vicious and dissolute."

From the testimonies of Tertullian and Justin Martyr it appears, that mankind were improved in their manners by the gospel, notwithstanding the prejudices entertained against it by Jews and Gentiles. "The husband, says the former of these writers, now cured of his former jealousy, by his wife's conversion, turns her and her new modesty out of doors together. The father, so tender of his undutiful son whilst an Heathen, disinherits him, when he becomes a Christian and obedient to his will. The master, hitherto so kind to a faithless slave, disbands him now, upon his religion and fidelity. So much is the name of Christian hated, notwithstanding the advantages of the Gospel, that a husband prefers a false wife; the father a rebellious son; the master a knavish servant, to having them good and virtuous Christians (*l*)." The following passage proves, that a considerable alteration has been wrought in the manners of those, who embraced the gospel, especially of Jews and Gentiles in their behaviour

Tertullian and Justin Martyr prove mankind reformed by the gospel.

(*l*) Tertull. Apolog. Cap. iii.

towards

SECT. III. towards each other. Juſtin Martyr, who had been a Platonic philoſopher, ſpeaks of this happy change in the following words. " We, who formerly delighted in adultery, now obſerve the ſtricteſt chaſtity; we, who uſed the charms of magic, have devoted ourſelves to the true God; we, who valued money and gain above all things, do now caſt what we have in common, and diſtribute to every man according to his neceſſities; we, who hated each other and refuſed to aſſociate with thoſe of a different tribe, now familiarly converſe together, ſince Chriſt's coming, and pray for the converſion of thoſe who unjuſtly hate us (*m*)." The Jews were extremely illiberal, reproached the Gentiles as the vileſt of mankind, and loaded them with the ſcurrilous epithets of dogs and outcaſts; while Heathens hated and deſpiſed the Jews, who declined ſocial intercourſe with other nations. In conſequence of the mutual hatred which ſubſiſted between them, Pagans oppreſſed them every where, and at laſt the Romans came and took away both their place and nation. Chriſt, by his gentle doctrines, and by the manners of his followers, broke down the partition which ſeparated Heathens and Hebrews; leſſened their prejudices, and rendered them more liberal, in their conduct to each other (*n*).

(*m*) Juſtin Martyr, Apol. II.
(*n*) Cave, Part III. Cap. iii.

Other

Other apologists appealed to the lives of Christians for a refutation of calumnies, and a proof of improvement in morals. "Among us, says Athenagoras (o), the meanest labourers and old women, though unable to discourse, and dispute for the usefulness of their profession, yet demonstrate it by their lives and good works. They do not indeed critically weigh their words, and recite elegant orations; but manifest honest and virtuous actions. Being buffetted, they strike not again, nor sue those at law, who spoil and plunder them; they give liberally to those who ask, and love their neighbours as themselves." Clement the Roman commends the many virtues of Corinthians in his epistle to that people; "who, faith he, did ever live among you, that did not admire your sober and moderate piety, and declare the greatness of your hospitality? You do all things without respect of persons, walking in God's statutes, subject to those who rule you, giving due honour to your elders. You command men to live honestly and soberly; women, to live chastly and holily, loving their husbands, and managing their houshold affairs with all sobriety. You are humble, not proud; content with the daily bread which God supplies; hearing diligently his word, and enlarged in charity." From the following passage it appears, that Christians excelled the

SECT. III.

The same proved by other authors.

(o) Legatio pro Christianis.

most refined Pagans in moral virtues; "if we should be compared with you, says Minucius Fælix to the Heathen, though our discipline should seem, in some degree, inferior, yet shall we ourselves be found far superior to you. You prohibit adultery and practise it; we continue faithful to our wives; you punish wickedness when committed; we think it sinful to indulge a wicked thought.— It is with your party that prisons are crowded, but not a single Christian is there, except it be a confessor or apostate."—He tells his adversary how much Christians surpassed the best philosophers, who were notoriously wicked, adulterers, tyrannical and eloquent, to declaim against the vices, of which they were most guilty." Lactantius (*p*) boldly affirms, that Christians were free from several detestable crimes, common among Heathens: "They are not Christians, says this writer, but Gentiles who rob by land and turn pirates by sea; who prepare poisons and dispatch their wives for their dowries, or their husbands, that they might marry their adulterers: who strangle or expose their infants, commit incest with their daughters, sisters, mothers or vestals; who prostitute their bodies to unnatural lusts, seek heaven by witchcraft, and commit several other crimes odious to relate."

(*p*) Lib. V. Cap. ix.

Having

of Religion on Mankind.

SECT. III.
Julian and Pliny admit the virtues of Christians.

Having produced the testimonies of Christians to prove the virtues of that people, and the calumnies against them; it may be thought necessary to adduce some drawn from Heathens, and enemies of the gospel. For this purpose, I have selected two, that are more remarkable than the rest; the first is, a letter of the emperor Julian to Arsacius, in which he requires that pontiff to recommend the virtues of Christians to the imitation of Heathens: the second is an epistle of Pliny (*q*) the younger, proconsul in Bithynia under Trajan, to that emperor in Rome. "The governor of that province asks his master, whether Christians are to be punished for the name, though innocent in other respects: tells him, that he repeatedly asked persons brought before him, whether they were Christians, and persevered in the profession of the gospel; that he threatened to correct those who persisted, and enforced those threats; as they deserved to be chastised, at least for their obstinacy. Some, says he, were accused of being Christians, who, as a proof of their innocence, offered incense to the Gods, uttered imprecations against Christ, and made libations to your image, which I commanded to be brought out with the images of the Gods. Others who were charged by an informer, with professing Christianity, acknowledged they had formerly

(*q*) Lib. X. Epist. 97. ad Trajanum.

SECT. III. been Christians, but had renounced their error: these also worshipped your image and the images of the Gods, and vented imprecations against Christ. These latter affirmed, that the great crime of Christians consisted in assembling on a certain day, before light, to sing hymns to Christ; binding themselves by an oath, to be guilty of no crime, not to steal, rob, commit adultery, or break faith. After this they usually departed, and met again to take an innocent repast and eat promiscuously: I tried to find the truth by torture of two women, who were present at their worship; but found nothing, except an obstinate kind of superstition, carried to excess." Tertullian complains, that the mere name of Christian was a crime, and that Christians were not fairly tried like other malefactors: " Christians only, saith he, are denied this privilege; no such favour is shewn unto us; we are condemned unheard; to be a Christian is thought a sufficient proof of murder, sacrilege, incest or sedition, without enquiring into the fact, time, place, and persons of the delinquents (r)." Serennius Gracchus, proconsul of Asia, represented to Adrian the injustice of putting Christians to death when no crime was proved against them (s). Antoninus Pius, Adrian's successor, acquainted the commons of Asia, that they slandered Christians, and accused them of crimes

(r) Tertullian Apolog. Cap. i.
(s) Eusebii Hist. Eccl. Lib. IV. Cap. ix.

which they could not prove (*t*). This Pagan emperor exculpates them from being the cause of earthquakes which happened in that country; and reminds the states of Asia, that "they themselves were always discouraged and sunk under such disasters; whereas Christians never discovered more cheerfulness and confidence in God, than on such occasions."—That " they pay no regard to religion, and neglect the worship of the eternal: and, because Christians honour and adore him, are jealous of them, and persecute them even unto death."—" Many persons have consulted me relative to Christians, and I have returned the same answer to them all; namely, that if any one accuse a Christian, merely on account of his religion, the accused person shall be acquitted, and the accuser himself punished (*u*)." Could the adversaries of Christianity have proved the crimes, imputed to its professors, they would not have condemned them unheard, nor fabricated lies, to inflame both princes and populace against them. Could they have been convicted of any crime in the reign of Nero, that tyrant would not have set fire to the city of Rome, nor charged it to Christians, that he might have a pretext for persecuting them. All accusations were in time completely silenced, by the lives of Christians, which were exemplary, and austere even to an extreme.

(*t*) Justin Martyr, Apol. II. and Euseb. ibid. Lib. IV, Cap. xiii.   (*u*) Broughton, Art. Christians.

SECT. III. Eusebius (w) assures us, that the Christian religion had, by the gravity, modesty, and virtues of its professors, silenced every cavil; so that no person dare asperse the gospel, or charge it with any of the calumnies formerly fastened on it by its enemies.

An assertion of Mr. Gibbon examined.

Had the historian of the Roman empire reasoned fairly, or duly considered the effects of the Christian code on the morals of individuals, and the welfare of communities; he could not have asserted, that monastic institutions have produced evils, which counterbalanced the advantages of the gospel; nor have ascribed these evils to the Christian system. Celibacy and monastic institutions owed their rise to excesses of religion and virtue in the primitive Christians, who were extremely austere: but it would be as absurd to impute these excesses to the gospel, as to ascribe the errors of men, and the abuses of reason, to the rational faculty duly cultivated and improved. Had Mr. Gibbon considered that the gospel tends to prevent or remove the bad effects of Pagan and Mahometan religions; and that it actually abolished paganism and several of its bad effects, in many countries, where it was established; he could not have compared the benefits of Christianity, with the disadvantages which have arisen from abuses of it. The Christian institution not only encou-

(w) Eccl. Hist.

rages

rages morality, but has removed the mischiefs of false systems of religion; and not only produced certain benefits to individuals and communities, but tends to prevent the bad effects generally resulting from sects, which are false and erroneous. True religion not only has removed political inconveniences in countries, where it was formerly introduced; but is well calculated to prevent in Christian countries, the evils arising from excesses of religion, or corruptions of it by its professors. These evils shall be pointed out in the subsequent parts of this work, that men may not impute to the gospel disadvantages, arising from irreligion, superstition and enthusiasm; and that rulers might see the necessity of properly supporting a rational establishment, capable of doing much good, and preventing much mischief in their respective governments.

Dr. Priestley, in his lecture on the influence of religion on civil society, treats the subject with little candour, and still less information. Amidst the numerous bad effects of paganism, he mentions none except cruelty, austerity, and human sacrifices, and treats of these but slightly and superficially; and while he hints at some trivial advantages of heathenism, he passes over those which were most striking and essential. In speaking of the superstitions of the Jews, he affirms, that in the beginning of their wars under the Maccabees, their strictness in keeping the sabbath was nearly

Animadversions on Dr. Priestley's 56th Lecture.

fatal

SECT. III. fatal to them; but is totally silent with respect to the various benefits which have arisen from judaism. According to this author, mahometanism has rendered the Saracens brave and obedient, he should have said servile, to princes; while he passes over in silence its other effects. He affirms, that religion has been detrimental to society, " comprehending, under that term, enthusiasm, superstition, and every species of false religion as well as true;" and thus raises a prejudice against true religion, which tends to remove or prevent the inconveniences of false. He dwells more on the few advantages arising from excesses or corruptions of the gospel, than on its genuine effects, which were more numerous and permanent. To excesses he attributes the liberty of Britain; to the extensive power of the popes, the easy intercourse of different nations, and the union of them when the Roman empire was disjointed; to the pomp of popish worship the preservation of the fine arts during barbarous ages; and to popery itself the check on despotism in Spain, Portugal, and other places. Thus he expatiates on the advantages which have arisen from those excesses or abuses, while he mentions but a single advantage of it, namely, the abolition of servitude in the western world; and overbalances this advantage, by the excesses of German Anabaptists and English Levellers, and by the cruel persecutions

secutions of the bloody Mary and Philips of Spain. "Those evils," says this writer, "and particularly these arising from persecution, ought certainly to be taken into the account, when we make an estimate of the benefits accruing to the world from Christianity." Had this author wished his readers to make a fair estimate of the benefits of Christianity, he would have enumerated many happy effects accruing from it, in different parts of the globe; and would not unjustly have imputed to it the evils of persecution. He himself admits, that persecutions subsisted in the world, before the promulgation of the gospel; and it would be easy to prove, that the persecutions which prevailed since that period, have arisen from a diametrical opposition to its spirit and letter. Let me ask then, why the evils of persecution should be taken into account, in estimating the benefits which have accrued from Christianity? The 9th and 10th sections of this work will evince, that the cruelties of persecutors, and the excesses of fanatics, have originated from avarice, ambition, or mistaken policy; or from ignorance, corruption, or perversion of the gospel; and that those persecutions and excesses, far from originating from Christianity, prove the excellence of that institution, by an observance of whose laws all the evils of fanaticism and persecution must vanish and disappear. The author might insist

SECT. III. more largely on the happy effects of the Christian code; but as his answer to gainsayers will supply ideas which have been omitted in this section, he now passes them over in silence, lest he should tire his readers by needless repetitions, in a subsequent part of this treatise.

SECTION IV.

ON THE ORIGIN, PROGRESS, AND EFFECTS OF MAHOMETANISM.

Enquiry into the origin of Mahometanism, useful and curious.—State of religion in Arabia, and the disputes of Christian churches favoured Mahomet's designs.—Imbecility of neighbouring nations, and the political state of Arabia contributed to his success.—Means employed in propagating his religion. —The same subject continued.—Parts of the Koran designed to extricate him from some difficulty or gratify some passion.—Character of Mahomet.— He abolished some superstitious and barbarous practices of Pagan Arabs.—Many of his doctrines borrowed, and inferior to those in the originals.—His unborrowed opinions false, contradictory and ridiculous.—His paradise and hell.—Paradise and other doctrines contributed to his successes.—Death of Mahomet, and establishment of the Caliphat.— Mahometanism assisted Caled in reducing Persia and other places.—It assisted him in reducing Damascus.—It assisted Obeidah in reducing Hems, Jerusalem, and other places.—All Syria, Egypt, and part of Persia, submit to the Saracens in the Caliphat of Omar.—Other places submitted to them in his Caliphat.—Other causes concurred with Mahometanism in promoting the conquests of the Sara-

Saracens.—Comparison of Christianity and Mahometanism in the tendency and effects of their doctrines.—Comparison of the lives and doctrines of Christ and Mahomet.—Difficulty of making apostates from Mahometanism.—Despotism an effect of the conquests of the Saracens.—The Koran secures private property to individuals.—Ignorance an effect of Mahometanism.—Revenge, illiberality, and extortion effects of it.—Effects of the doctrine of Predestination.—Effects of Mahometan devotions on individuals and communities.—Effects of Mahometanism prove the excellent tendency of Christianity.

SECT. IV.

Enquiry into the origin of Mahometanism, useful and curious.

BY Mahometanism I mean that system of doctrines and rites enjoined by the Koran, and which distinguish it from the Hebrew and Christian revelations. As Mahomet was acquainted with the law and the gospel, many of his doctrines are derived from these sources; while he adopted others, which differ from them essentially, and had a considerable influence on the state of societies. Hence we may ascribe the chief advantages, produced by the Koran, to the Jewish and Christian institutions, and all the evils, which resulted from Mahometanism, to deviations from the gospel. The prophet of Arabia has been indebted for his useful tenets, chiefly to the Mosaic and evangelical writings; and for his absurdities and contradictions to the weakness of unassisted reason, and to a compliance with the superstitions of his illiterate countrymen. It would not be difficult to point out the sources, from whence he derived, and the originals, from whence he transcribed most of the doctrines and rites which he enjoins. Such a disquisition would prove, beyond a doubt, that the Koran has not the smallest pretension to an original revelation, but is a medley of Jewish, Pagan, Christian, and Arian tenets, blended with the trifling, absurd, and contradictory notions of the prophet himself. Mahomet, in order to make as many proselytes as possible, held the unity of God, allowed by all sects, adopted tenets maintained by each of them, and indulged his followers with sensual gratifications. But to judge of the effects of Mahometanism, it will be necessary to consider its rise and progress, the doctrines which it inculcates, and the duties which it enjoins. Some of my readers may possibly desire to know the steps, by which a people, once so despicable, erected so formidable an empire; the means by which a private man was enabled to raise himself to be a prince and a pontiff, and the several causes which concurred to favour his designs. An enquiry into the doctrines and effects of the Mahometan code, is extremely useful to the cause of true religion, as it displays the superior excellence of the Christian institution, whether we judge of those two systems from the lives of their respective authors, the doctrines they

con-

SECT. IV. contain, or the effects they produced on the state of society. As truth never appears so amiable as when contrasted to error, men should be acquainted with false, as well as true opinions. The doctrines of the Koran should be exhibited to the rational Christian, to render him enamoured of the gospel; just as Spartans exposed drunken slaves to their youth, for the purpose of attaching them to sobriety, and creating an abhorrence for so beastly a vice. By reading the religious tenets of different countries, and by observing the erroneous opinions of men in all ages and nations, we learn to tolerate those who are in error, and become grateful to God for the superior excellence of the religion we profess. Nor is an enquiry into the effects of Mahometanism less curious than it is useful; since they make a considerable figure in the annals of oriental history, and exhibit scenes in which the welfare of nations and individuals was so much concerned. We shall see, in the course of this section, that the Mahometan religion was instrumental " in subduing whole nations, altering ancient governments, and introducing a new face of affairs into the world," as Ockley (a) expresses it.

State of religion in Arabia, favoured Mahomet's designs.

Several circumstances concurred to assist Mahomet in reforming his countrymen, and advancing his designs. The religious state of Arabia,

(a) History of the Saracens, Preface.

at that juncture, was such, as might have induced a good man to wish for a reformation, and encouraged a wise man to undertake it from a prospect of success. The Arabs at this time believed in one supreme being, creator, and lord of the universe; while they worshipped inferior deities and idols, whose intercession they implored as mediators with God. They had a multitude of those idols; and Mahomet, while he retained some superstitious rites of his countrymen, totally abolished this idolatrous worship. Some of the tribes embraced the religion of the Magi; others that of the Jews and Christians; some denied a resurrection, some asserted it, while others believed the doctrine of transmigration. To prove the ignorance and superstitions of others, it may suffice to observe, that they left camels to perish at the graves of the deceased, that their friends might not go on foot at the resurrection, which was considered as disgraceful (*b*). Arabia abounded with heresies, owing perhaps to the liberty and independency of the tribes. Some of them worshipped the Virgin Mary as God; and, at the Nicene council, some believed her divinity, and said there were two Gods, besides the Father, namely, Christ, and the Virgin Mary. Others imagined her exempted from humanity, and the completion of the Trinity, as if it was imperfect

(*b*) Sale's Preliminary Discourse, Sect. 1.

without

SECT. IV. without her: which abfurd idea induced Mahomet to queftion the doctrine of the Trinity itfelf (c).

State of the eaftern and weftern churches favoured Mahomet.

The ftate of the eaftern and weftern churches, in Mahomet's time, alfo affifted him in accomplifhing the reformation which he had concerted. The weftern was divided into fects, who hated and perfecuted each other; and the eaftern was become degenerate and corrupt, no longer endued with that union, and purity of doctrine, which diftinguifhed the primitive Chriftians. The clergy were ambitious, and fond of controverfy; and deftroyed that peace and love enjoined by the gofpel. After the Nicene council, the eaftern church was rent by the difputes of Arians, Sabellians, Neftorians and Eutychians: and in the weftern church two candidates for the epifcopal chair carried their contefts fo high at Rome, that feveral were murdered on the occafion. Thofe diffenfions were fomented by the emperors, and particularly Conftantius, who, inftead of reconciling differences, confounded the pure religion of the gofpel with intricate queftions, and vulgar fuperftitions. When princes and ecclefiaftics had arrived at fuch a degree of corruption in doctrine and morals, we might naturally expect that a general depravity of the people would be the neceffary confequence. At this period Mahomet appeared in the world, perhaps as a fcourge to chaftife the eaftern churches,

(c) Sale's preliminary Difcourfe, Sect. 1.

who

who were continually employed in religious diffen-sion, inftead of practifing the love and harmony required by the gofpel. Men fond of controverfy, and who difregarded the peace, enjoined by their religion, were indulged with a fyftem that encouraged war, were abfolutely prohibited to difpute, and obliged to fwallow the groffeft abfurdities, without daring to murmur.

Not only the diftracted ftate of religion was favourable to Mahomet, but alfo the imbecility of the Romans and Perfians, who would readily have crufhed him, had they flourifhed as formerly (*d*). His fucceffes againft thefe powers, once fo formidable, made many converts, and induced men to believe him affifted from heaven. His divifion of the fpoil with new profciytes, and the pretended interpofition of the angel Gabriel, and other celeftial auxiliaries, contributed to advance his reputation and conquefts; while the fublimity of the Koran, in fome paffages, perfuaded his illiterate countrymen, that he was infpired by the Almighty. After Conftantine the Great, the Roman empire rapidly declined; as his fucceffors were, in general, remarkable for cowardice, cruelty, and other bad qualities. At Mahomet's appearance in the fixth century, the weftern part of the empire was overrun by Goths, and the eaftern fo reduced by Huns on one fide, and by Perfians on the other, that it was incapable of ftemming the violence of a

Imbecility of neighbouring nations and the political ftate of Arabia contributed to his fuccefs.

(*d*) Sale's preliminary Difcourfe, Sect. 1.

powerful

SECT. IV. powerful invasion. Though the emperor Heraclius was a prince of courage, and drove the Persians out of his dominions, yet the vitals of the empire had received a mortal wound when Mahomet appeared. The Greeks also were degenerate at this period, and the Persians on the decline, on account of the intestine dissensions which prevailed among this people. As those empires were weak and declining, so Arabia was in a strong and flourishing condition, when Mahomet began the work of reformation. Many fled thither, as to an asylum, from the persecutions, which raged in the Grecian empire; and the Arabs were inured to hardships, and lived in a frugal manner, strangers to the luxuries of the Greeks and Romans. The tribes were divided and independent on each other in religion and government; a circumstance very important, nay absolutely necessary to the propagation of his religion. Had all the tribes been united under one government, the impostor would soon have been obliged to yield to superior power, and been punished as a disturber of the public tranquility. Had they all one established religion, universally received, he never could have thought it safe to attempt to subvert it. In Arabia several tribes and princes embraced the Jewish religion, when the Jews fled thither from the destruction of Jerusalem. Mahomet adopted many of their opinions and rites, in order to seduce them to his party, and encrease his followers; but finding them

them inflexibly averfe from his doctrines, he repeatedly inveighs againſt them in his Koran, as his bittereſt enemies, and employed various means to accompliſh his defigns.

<small>SECT. IV.</small>

Many caufes concurred to promote the plan devifed by this impoſtor: when young he was employed in Syria, Egypt, and Paleſtine as a factor to a rich merchant, and had an opportunity of being acquainted with the religion and manners of different countries (*f*). After the death of this merchant, Mahomet conducted mercantile affairs for the widow, and acquitted himſelf fo much to her fatisfaction, that ſhe put him in poſſeſſion of her perfon and property. He then formed the project of reforming religion, and purging it from the corruptions introduced into it by Jews and Chriſtians. For this purpofe he retired to a cave, after the example of the Perfian reformer (*g*); aſſumed great gravity in his deportment; was diligent in his devotions, and liberal in his charities, that he might acquire a character of fanctity and virtue. In order to prepare mens minds for his intended reformation, he employed a famous aſtrologer to report, that a mighty prophet ſhould eſtabliſh a new religion, and make great changes in the condition of mankind (*h*). Mahomet began with making converts in his own family, before

<small>Means employed in propagating his religion.</small>

(*f*) Guthrie's Geography, Art. Arabia.
(*g*) Bruckerus de Philofophia Perfarum, Lib. II. Cap. iii. Sect. 2.   (*h*) Bayle's Obfervations.

SECT. IV. his attempts upon strangers: finding himself successful among these, he resolved to try what he could do by persuasion among persons of his acquaintance, and had the address to gain over some of the principal men at Mecca to his interest, in the course of three years. Being encouraged by his success, he no longer made his mission a secret, but proclaimed to every person, that he was commissioned by God to admonish his near relations (*i*), and fixed a day for the purpose; when many, who were invited to hear his admonitions, became proselytes to his opinions (*k*). He accommodated his discourses to the sentiments of his hearers: told the Arians, that as the endeavours of other prophets proved ineffectual, God sent him with a more ample commission than Moses or Christ, to establish an earthly kingdom for the propagation of religion, and the extirpation of those who refused to be converted (*l*). He did not deny that Moses and Christ were prophets, but maintained, that, as the Mosaic and Christian writings were corrupted by Jews and Christians, he came to purge them from errors. He did not object to the truth or divinity of the Jewish and Christian revelations; but maintained that they were defective, while he pretended his own to be the final and complete declaration of God's will to mankind; so that men were not to expect any

(*i*) Koran, Chap. lxxiv.   (*k*) Guthrie.   (*l*) Ibid.

other

other revelation. His opponents defired to fee fome miracle, fimilar to thofe wrought by Mofes and Chrift, as a proof of his divine commiffion. He refufed to comply with this requifition, alledging, as an excufe, the fuggeftion of the angel Gabriel, that if he fhould work miracles, and his followers did not believe, they muft be utterly deftroyed (*m*). Sometimes he told them, that Mahomet was a prophet, fent to preach the rewards of paradife, and the pains of hell; that their anceftors defpifed the miracles of other prophets, and he would work none: at other times he faid that they, who were ordained to believe, fhould do fo without miracles, according to the doctrine of predeftination (*n*). The Arabian impoftor, in order to encreafe his followers, proclaimed liberty to all; fo that multitudes of flaves and fugitives crowded to his ftandard. He fometimes enjoins forgivenefs, that he may not offend Chriftians; but fo frequently inculcates revenge, by precept and example, that it becomes the prevailing doctrine of the Koran. He promifed falvation and a fenfual paradife to thofe of his own fect, however vicious and diffolute; and denounced damnation againft infidels, without regard to their actions. According to the prophet, infidels alone fhall be eternally damned, while Moflems, though guilty of the moft heinous offences, fhall be delivered,

(*m*) Broughton, Art. Aiat.   (*n*) Koran, Chap. xvii.

SECT. IV. when they shall have expiated them by their sufferings. No unbeliever or idolater shall ever be released, nor any believer damned to eternity. Moslems shall be punished in hell according to their crimes, but shall be delivered when purged of their sins by Abraham, or some other prophet (*o*).

The same subject continued. His refusal to work miracles having created dissatisfaction in the minds of some of his adherents, a powerful party was formed against him at Mecca; where the magistrates, dreading the troubles which usually attend on innovations in religion, declared themselves his enemies. He preached in public, and was heard with pleasure and patience, until he upbraided them and their fathers with idolatry and corruption: then, indeed, the Koreshites joined the magistrates in banishing him from the city. He retired to Medina with few friends, but was soon joined by a multitude of devotees, to whom he proposed the scheme of establishing his religion by force of arms. In his first expedition he could not boast of success; but in the second, he defeated a caravan of one thousand Koreshites, with three hundred and nineteen men; obtained considerable booty for himself and his adherents, and lost but fourteen men, whose names he enrolled in his catalogue of martyrs. We see that this persecution advanced rather than obstructed the propagation of his religion; had he not been forced

(*o*) Koran, Chap. ii.

to take up arms in his own defence, he might, perhaps for ever, have continued a private perſon in the capacity of a preacher. But having got at the head of a ſmall army, ambition then probably prompted him to form ſchemes, before unthought of. Before his flight to Medina, the ſucceſs of his religion was owing to perſuaſion and not to compulſion; at firſt he declared himſelf only a prophet, ſent by God to admoniſh men, but without any authority to compel them to embrace his religion; and even pretended to bear with patience injuries, which were offered him, while he was unable reſiſt (*p*). Having encreaſed the number of his followers, he told them that God allowed them to defend themſelves againſt enemies; and as he gathered ſtrength he pretended to a divine permiſſion even of attacking, for the purpoſe of aboliſhing idolatry, and corruptions of religion. When he came to Medina, ſupported by an army, he told thoſe, who deſired to ſee his miracles, that God ſent Moſes and Chriſt to reform mankind by perſuaſion and miracles: that, when thoſe methods proved ineffectual, he was commiſſioned by God to compel men by the ſword to do his will (*q*). At firſt he preached, and exhorted men to embrace his doctrines; but as ſoon as his party was encreaſed, we find the preacher transformed into a warrior, and offering death or converſion as the

(*p*) Sale, Sect. 2.   (*q*) Koran, Chap. ii. iii. iv.

SECT. IV. only alternative to the vanquished. He told his disciples that the Koran was an abstract of the great book, in which the divine decrees were registered: that the angel Gabriel transcribed from thence faithfully, verse by verse, and chapter by chapter, and delivered them to him, as it was necessary to promulge them. He did not publish his Koran together; for then numerous objections might have been raised against it, which it would be impossible for him to answer. By bringing down the Koran by chapters, he was prepared to refute objections made to preceding chapters, to extricate himself from embarrassments, to quiet discontents among his followers, and to indulge or justify some criminal passions (*r*).

Parts of the Koran designed to extricate him from some difficulty or gratify some passions.

Great part of the Koran was invented occasionally, to solve some difficulty, or gratify his ruling passions of lust or ambition. Being defeated at Ohud, the prophet was ashamed, and said, that God suffered it on account of the transgressions of some of his followers, and to distinguish true from false believers. To silence the clamours of those, who lost their friends in the engagement, he invented the doctrine of fate, and maintained, that all events have been irrevocably fixed from eternity; that God had accurately predetermined the good or bad fortune of every person; his faith or infidelity, his obedience or disobedience:

(*r*) Bayle's Life of Mahomet.

that

that life cannot be protracted by any human means, beyond the destined period; that a man must die somewhere at the appointed time; and that it is more desirable to die martyrs in the cause of God, than at home in their beds. We shall presently see that, in consequence of this maxim, Mahometants rushed dauntless into the jaws of danger and of death, and " esteemed their bodies as dirt and rubbish to fill up the enemies trenches, for their brethren to pass over," as Sir Paul Ricaut (s) strongly expresses it. Nor is it extraordinary, that this doctrine produced this effect; since nothing renders men so regardless of life, or induces them to fight so desperately, as a persuasion, that no caution could avert any evil which threatened them, or protract life a moment beyond the destined period (t). He prevailed on Zeyd to put away his wife, married her himself, and pretended this crime was dispensed with from heaven. He published the thirty-third chapter of his Koran in vindication of himself, and introduces God approving of this marriage, and rebuking him for abstaining so long from her, though he had his permission. In this instance he was guilty of adultery in marrying another man's wife, and of blasphemy, in making God the author of this crime. To satisfy two of his jealous wives, who took him in the act of adultery with a servant, he swears against

(s) Maxims of Turkish Polity, Book II. Chap. viii.
(t) Koran, Chap. iii.

SECT. IV. similar offences for the future; but commits this crime in violation of his oath, and publishes the sixty-sixth chapter of the Koran, which permits the prophet to lie with a maid servant, and allows Moslems to violate their oaths. The Arabian impostor limited the number of wives and concubines of each person to four, but reserved to himself the privilege of marrying as many as he pleased (*v*). He obliged others, who had two, three, or four wives, to treat them in the same manner; but retained the liberty of using his own wives, according to his discretion. He prohibited his disciples to marry near relations; but, in the thirty-third chapter, introduces God, exempting him from that prohibition, and allowing him to marry whomsoever he pleased, without any regard to degrees of consanguinity. Mahomet, being repulsed at the siege of Mecca, made a league with the inhabitants; but next year violated the treaty, by surprising that city; and, to justify his perfidy, allowed his followers to disregard promises or leagues, made with infidels (*u*). In consequence of this doctrine, and the example of the prophet, Ricaut mentions several instances of perfidy among the Turks, who assume it as a maxim, that they should not keep faith with unbelievers, where the breach contributes to the propagation of religion (*w*). But besides these, we find several

(*v*) Koran, Chap. iv. and xxxiii.   (*u*) Ricaut's Maxims, Book I. Chap. xxii.   (*w*) Ibid.

other

other occasional precepts and prohibitions of the Koran: Mahomet prohibited wine and other inebriating liquors, of which some of his principal officers having drank to excess, excited much riot and confusion in the camp. This prohibition was extremely neceffary in sultry climates, where the fumes of liquor inflame to the highest degree, and render men frantic. The prophet also forbade cards, dice, tables, and other games of chance, as the frequent occasion of quarrels and disturbances. The gospel does not absolutely prohibit the moderate use of wine, nor any innocent amusement; but forbids its professors to drink to excess, or to covet other mens goods, which is the usual foundation of the passion for gaming, and renders that vice so criminal and destructive to societies.

<small>SECT. IV.</small>

Writers have differed widely with respect to the character of Mahomet, and the motives which influenced him to a reformation of religion. Some think him actuated by enthusiasm, others by ambition: some have represented him as a monster destitute of abilities and of every virtue; while others confider him as endowed with all the virtues. However, most authors have in one respect or other mistaken the character and motives of the Arabian impostor. The laudable ambition of restoring religion to its purity, and abrogating the superstitious rites, and idolatrous practices, then prevalent in his country, might possibly have been the first motive, that influenced him to attempt a refor-

<small>Character of Mahomet.</small>

SECT. IV. reformation. He could not at first have foreseen the successes which attended him; he could not have aspired to the power, to which he afterwards arrived; nor expected to gratify any ambition, except that of reforming his countrymen from ignorance and superstition. The Pagan Arabs were in a deplorable state before his time, and he might have thought it a meritorious work to bring them to the knowledge of the true God from idolatry and corruption. Though guilty of many crimes he must have carefully concealed them, and at least have observed some exterior decorum in his actions. Adultery, perjury, blasphemy, and other offences, must have blasted his reputation as a prophet, if known to the world. These crimes he must have hid, until he got at the head of an army, and acquired the reputation of generosity, charity, bravery and other virtues, which captivate mankind. The prophet of Arabia doubtless possessed many splendid virtues, tarnished and blended with many enormous crimes, arising from his predominant passions of lust and ambition. He, at first, directed the latter to the laudable purpose of reforming his countrymen in religion and morals; but afterwards, to the destruction of mankind for the acquisition of power. He recommended virtues which he did not practise; inveighed against many vices which he himself committed; and left convincing proofs that he was actuated by a love of fame, and not by a sincere regard

regard for religion and virtue. The impostor borrowed his ideas of fasting, almsgiving, and other virtues, from the gospels, though he but feebly imitates those great originals. He requires and enforces those duties on narrow principles; confines the exercise of them to those of his own sect; and does not extend them to all mankind indiscriminately, with that large, and benevolent spirit, enjoined by the gospel. Were he a teacher sent from God, he would have furnished the world, if possible, with a more perfect system of religion than the Christian; and improved on former systems, instead of debasing them, just as Christianity was an improvement on the law.

The author of the Koran was, notwithstanding his crimes, serviceable to his country in some instances, by restoring the worship of the true God, abolishing idolatry, and forbidding his countrymen to steal, commit fornication, forge calumnies, or kill children, as the Pagan Arabs were accustomed to do (*x*). His knowledge of the gospel assisted him in reforming the doctrines and manners of the Arabs. The Mahometan system contained many tenets of the Christian institution, and so far was productive of salutary effects, and preferable to the monstrous idolatry that prevailed in Arabia. He prohibited the use of the three arrows, which were employed in divination, and deposited in the temple of Mecca, with a blank on one,

He abolished some barbarous and superstitious practices of the Pagan Arabs.

(*x*) Koran, Chap. vi.

and

SECT. IV. and the following inscriptions on the two others, "My Lord hath commanded; my Lord hath forbidden." Before they engaged in marriage, undertook a journey, or any momentous business, they generally consulted those arrows. If the second was drawn, it was looked on as an assent of God; if the third, as a mark of disapprobation; if the blank was drawn, they mixed them up, until a decisive answer was given by one of the others. The prophet abolished several other superstitious customs relative to camels, sheep, and other animals, which the Pagan Arabs turned loose, and exempted from labour, in honour of their idols (*y*). This people refused to widows and orphans any share in the properties of their husbands or fathers, on pretence that they only should inherit, who are able to fight (*z*). They considered the birth of a daughter as a misfortune, and the death of one a blessing; frequently buried daughters alive, and even put males to death to fulfil a vow that, if they had a certain number of sons, they would offer one of them in sacrifice (*a*). The Arabian reformer abrogated these and other barbarous practices which were common among that people, before his appearance in the world.

Many doctrines of Mahomet borrowed, and inferior to those in the originals.

Having considered the character of Mahomet, the causes that contributed to his successes, and some of the means which he employed in propa-

(*y*) Koran, Chap. v. and vi.   (*z*) Koran, Chap. iv.
(*a*) Sale, Sect. 5.

gating

gating his religion, let us take a view of the Koran; shew whence he derived many of its precepts; and point out their effects on the welfare of society. Mahomet, like almost all reformers, accommodated his religion, in some degree, to the prejudices of his converts; and laboured to unite, into one system, their discordant opinions. He was no stranger to the law and the gospel, as I have already observed; from these he selected several tenets, and blended them with the popular traditions and superstitions of his countrymen. The Koran is a strange compound of heterogeneous opinions, and contains excellent moral precepts, and sublime descriptions of God, interspersed with contradictions, blasphemies, and ridiculous falshoods. According to the Mahometan (*b*) creed, there is one God, and Mahomet is his prophet; mens actions are registered; and at the resurrection and judgment, they shall be summoned to give an account of their conduct; and rewarded or punished according to their works. All faithful Mussulmen shall be transported into a state of glory; while the excuses of others will not be admitted. Their actions are weighed in a balance, and they, whose good works outweigh the bad, enter into paradise; if the bad preponderate, they are cast into hell: if the scales are equally poised they are sent into an intermediate state and excluded from the happiness enjoyed by the righteous.

(*b*) Mahometanism explained by Mahomet Baradan.

SECT.
IV.
ous. If a man slander his neighbour, some good action shall be taken out of the slanderer's balance, and added to that of the person slandered; and if the slanderer have no good works, God will diminish the punishment of the person slandered, and augment that of the slanderer: so that if we injure our neighbour, in fortune or reputation, such a subtraction shall be made from our good works, or such an addition to our punishment, as will fully manifest the divine justice. This was an useful doctrine, but did not originate with the prophet, being entertained long before his time, by the ancient Persians (*c*). The Koran prohibits adultery, false witness, avarice, usury, oppression, lying, gaming, swine's flesh, wine, eating blood, whatever died of itself, was killed by a blow, or by another beast: all which prohibitions, and many others, contain little more than was already suggested by the practice of Jews and Christians, or by the spirit or letter of the sacred writings (*d*). The Koran permits of polygamy and divorce; repeatedly enjoins pilgrimages to Mecca; and promises paradise and pardon to those, who perform them (*e*). It requires a perjurer to feed and clothe ten poor of his religion, or to emancipate a Mahometan slave, to atone for his crime (*f*); while

(*c*) Hyde Hist. Religionis vet. Persarum, Cap. xix. and xxxiii.
(*d*) Ross's Religions, Sect. 6.
(*e*) Koran, Chap. ii. iii. xxii.
(*f*) Mahomet Baradan.

the

the Christian institution gives no sanction to perjury, and allows no profanation of the name of God. The Koran enjoins charity and good works, but limits them to Mahometans; while the gospel extends works of charity and loving kindness to all men, of whatever religion. The Mahometan code threatens wilful murder with severe penalties in the next world, but allows it to be compounded for in this, by paying a fine, and redeeming a Moslem from captivity. *(g)*; while the Mosaic law, which evidently suggested the idea to the impostor, accepted of no composition; but required the life of the deliberate murderer. I have enumerated those rites, precepts, and prohibitions of the Koran to prove, that many of them were borrowed from the Mosaic and evangelical writings; and that they which differ from the scriptures are far inferior to them in justice and utility. This observation is of some importance; as it evinces, that the Mahometan code has no claim to originality; because then it would improve on, and not fall short of those revelations which preceded it, and which the impostor allowed to have God for their author. Hence we may perceive the falshood of an assertion in the History of the Roman Empire, that " the authority and station of Adam, Noah, Moses, Christ and Mahomet, rise in just gradation above each other *(h)*." If the historian means

(g) Mod. Univ. Hist. Vol. I. folio.
(h) Gibbon, Chap. l. p. 205. quarto.

SECT. IV. temporal authority and station, it is evident that there was no such gradation; as Christ was inferior to Adam, Noah, and Moses in both these respects. If he means, that they rose in spiritual authority and station by just gradation from Moses up to Mahomet, the opinion is fallacious; as Mahomet was inferior to his predecessors, having wrought no miracles similar to those of Moses, Christ, and others who preceded him.

His unborrowed opinions false, contradictory, and ridiculous.

Those parts of the Koran, in which the prophet indulges his own fancy, and in which alone he could justly pretend to inspiration, are a rhapsody of lies, contradictions and ridiculous fables, which could impose only on the ignorant Arabs. He speaks of the books of Abraham, though he wrote none; says, that Christ spoke in his cradle as a man of forty or fifty years (*i*); and that Pharaoh's wife prayed, " Lord build me an house in paradise (*k*)." He affirms, that Ishmael was one of the prophets, and that Zacharias was dumb only for three days, though history acquaints us, that he was so for nine months. He makes the Virgin Mary the sister of Moses; calls the apostles his own scholars, though they flourished about six hundred years before he was born: and tells us, that Noah, Isaac, and Jacob, believed in the Koran. He alleges, that Solomon had an army composed of men, devils, and birds; and that a pis-

(*i*) Koran, Chap. iv. (*k*) Koran, Chap. lxvi.

mire cried out, "O pifmires, pifmires, haften to your cells, left Solomon's army tread you under foot (*l*):" that the queen of Sheba fent Solomon a meffage by the whoop; which bird Solomon difpatched back again to the queen, to know whether fhe fent it. He affirms, that a mountain was raifed to overfhadow the Ifraelites (*m*); that the winds were fubject to Solomon, and blew at his command; that fome devils built his palaces, that others dived into the fea, to bring him pearls, while fome attended to execute his orders (*n*). Mahomet reckoned revenge among the attributes of God; and in the fame chapter afks, who but God forgiveth fins (*o*)? Sometimes he affirms, that all devils fhall be faved, and elfewhere thofe devils only, who obey his precepts (*p*). He afferts, that Solomon divided the moon into two parts, one of which fell into his lap, and the other on the ground, and that he foldered them again (*q*). He affirms, that in Noah's ark, the hog was generated of the elephant's dung, and a rat of the hog's dung; that a rat, having gnawed a hole in the ark, was put to flight by a cat, which leaped out of the brains of the lion (*r*). He fays, he was the firft that ever entered paradife; and elfewhere, that he found it inhabited by men and women. In fome paffages he affures us, that all

(*l*) Koran, Chap. xxvii.   (*m*) Ibid. Chap. ii.   (*n*) Ibid. Chap. xxxviii.   (*o*) Ibid. Chap. iii.   (*p*) Ibid. Chap. xii. (*q*) Ibid. Chap. xxxviii.   (*r*) Mahomet Baradan.

SECT. IV. who live well, whether Jews, or Christians, may be saved; and in another passage, that none can be saved, except they embrace the Koran (s). He requires his followers to believe, that when a corpse is laid in the grave, two angels examine it, concerning the Unity of God, and the mission of Mahomet. If the body answers right, it is suffered to rest in peace, and admitted into paradise; if not, it is beaten with iron maces, pressed with earth, and gnawed by ninety-nine dragons with seven heads each (t). He blasphemously boasts, that he has more knowledge than men and angels; ascribes to God all his impieties and impostures; and affirms the Koran to be inspired by the Holy Ghost; and Christ to be conceived by the smell of a rose. One general effect of this short abstract of the doctrines of the Koran, on the minds of Christians, must be, to render them enamoured of their own religion, and to convince them of the absurdity and falshood of the Mahometan. The God of truth could never dictate such gross contradictions, such shocking blasphemies, such romantic fables, and palpable falshoods. Where the Koran corresponds with the gospels, it tends to promote the welfare of society, and the happiness of individuals; where it differs from them, it is false, trifling, or contradictory, and teaches maxims pernicious to states. It is admitted, that

(s) Koran, Chap. xii.   (t) Broughton, Art. Mahomedan.

this impostor abolished several abominable cus- **SECT. IV.** toms prevalent in Arabia, and was beneficial to his country, as a reformer of abuses and idolatrous practices. Yet it is undeniable, that his religion was in many instances absurd, and that some of its doctrines have produced direful effects, in all the societies where it has been adopted. These, to which he was most indebted for his conquests, were revenge, predestination, and a sensual paradise: these were the chief instruments in the hands of him and his successors, in disseminating his religion, and extending their conquests, as will presently appear from the history of the first Caliphs.

Some have imagined, that Mahomet's idea of paradise was borrowed from the Jews (*u*); but it seems more probable that he derived it from the Persians, who believed in an earthly paradise, with beautiful virgins, gardens and rivers, into which none are admitted, until their actions are weighed in a scale: if the bad actions preponderate, they are flung into hell; if the good, they are admitted into paradise (*w*). This false prophet adapted his promises to the desires of men, who lived in a sultry climate; and who were delighted with women, rivers, shady groves, and delicious fruits. As the country was excessively hot and dry, and the people lewd and licentious, he

His paradise and hell.

(*u*) Sale, Sect. 4.   (*w*) Hyde's Sadder.

SECT. IV. promised to indulge them with gardens " where many rivers flow;" where they shall repose themselves under the shadow of the trees of paradise, be clothed in richest silks, and adorned with bracelets of gold and precious stones. " They shall, says this sensualist, enter into gardens, where they shall repose on fine beds lined with crimson:" " have wives, who shall not cast a look but upon them; and whom neither men or angels may touch before them." " They shall resemble coral and rubies. There are in those gardens women, that have eyes exceedingly black, and bodies exceedingly white, covered with vermilion (*x*)." Paradise affords its inhabitants so many pleasures and delights, that man would sink under them, did not God give unto every person the strength of an hundred for the enjoyment of them. There men shall be allowed to drink freely of wine, which will not intoxicate; enjoy perpetual youth, at whatever age they die; and shall be delighted with music, surpassing any thing ever heard by mortals (*y*). Mr. Gibbon assures us, that " instead of inspiring the blessed inhabitants of Paradise with a liberal taste for harmony and science, conversation and friendship; Mahomet idly celebrates the pearls and diamonds, the robes of silk, palaces of marble, dishes of gold, rich wines, artificial dainties, numerous attendants, and the whole train

(*x*) Koran, Chap. iv. xxxvi. xxxvii. xliii. ii. lv. lxxvi.
(*y*) Sale, Sect. 4.

of

of sensual and costly luxury." "Seventy-two Houris, or black-eyed girls of resplendent beauty, blooming youth, virgin purity, and exquisite sensibility, will be created for the use of the meanest believer; a moment of pleasure will be prolonged to a thousand years, and his faculties will be encreased an hundred fold to render him worthy of his felicity (z)." The favourites of God shall see his face morning and evening, a pleasure far exceeding all the pleasures of paradise (a): so that the happiness of the blessed, in the next life, according to the Mahometan system, consists not merely in corporeal enjoyments and sensual delights, but also in those, which are spiritual and refined. But we may easily guess, which of them was most likely to captivate a carnal people, who apprehended, beyond the grave, the same wants which they experienced in this life; and who tied camels at the tombs of the deceased, for their masters to ride on, as has been already observed. The Arabian impostor does not hint, that those pleasures are to be understood figuratively; and all orthodox Mahometans hope to enjoy them literally; while others are too refined for such gross ideas; and understand his descriptions in an allegorical sense. The epistles and gospels, on the contrary, convey no sensual or impure idea, nor attempt any thing puerile or particular, like Ma-

(z) Hist. Roman Empire, Chap. l. p. 218. Quarto.
(a) Sale, Sect. 4.

homet's

SECT. IV. homet's paradife; the pleafures offered by thefe, being reprefented to be fuch, "as eye hath not feen, nor ear heard, nor hath it entered into the heart of man to conceive." And as Mahomet accommodated his rewards to the appetites of the fenfual, fo did he threaten them with torments grievous and infupportable. He thus defcribes the punifhments of hell; they fhall drink nothing but boiling, ftinking water; breathe nothing but hot winds, dwell for ever in continual burning fire and fmoke; eat nothing but briars and thorns, and the fruit of a tree that rifeth out of the bottom of hell, whofe branches refemble the heads of devils, and whofe fruits fhall be in their bellies like burning pitch (*b*).

Parad'fe and other doctrines contributed to his fuccefies in Arabia.

Mahomet repeatedly enjoined his followers to wage war againft infidels, declared it meritorious to rob, murder, and extirpate unbelievers, and promifed a crown of martyrdom, and immediate admittance into paradife, to thofe flain in defence of the faith. The prophet prohibited his difciples to difpute about the Koran (*c*), but enjoins them to fight for it (*d*): "When you meet with unbelievers, fays he, cut off their heads, kill them, make them prifoners, and never ceafe to perfecute them, until they have laid down their arms and fubmitted to you (*e*)." "O ye that are true believers, be patient in your adverfities, fight for

(*b*) Koran, Chap. vii. xxxvii. xliii. (*c*) Ibid. Chap. iv.
(*d*) Ibid. Chap. ii.   (*e*) Ibid. Chap. of Battles.

the

the faith, fear God, and you shall be happy (*f*)." "O ye that believe in God, esteem no man to be elected of God, that is not of your religion:" "I will cover the offences of them that assemble to fight for the faith, I will open to them the gates of paradise, wherein flow many rivers, to recompense their good works (*g*)." In consequence of these doctrines, and the practice of the first publishers of the Koran, Mahometan divines call the sword the key of heaven and hell, and maintain that the least drop of blood, spilled in the cause of God and religion, is acceptable to him: whereas severe threats are denounced against those who desert, or refuse to engage in, or contribute to the support of holy wars (*h*). The effects of those doctrines were sensibly felt in the battles of Bedar and Muta: the ambition of dying in the cause of God and his prophet, and the hope of admission into heaven, inspired them with courage, and rendered them irresistible (*i*). The Saracens buried those, who fought for religion, covered with blood, from a persuasion that all martyrs shall be raised, on the day of judgment, with blood upon their throats, and led directly to paradise, without being called to an account (*k*). In consequence of this, and other doctrines of the Koran, the Saracens endured the greatest hardships, rather than

---

(*f*) Koran, Chap. iii.   (*g*) Ibid. Chap. iii.   (*h*) Ibid. Chap. iii. and ix.   (*i*) Smyth's Manners of the Turks.
(*k*) Ockley's Hist. of the Saracens.

SECT. IV. surrender a fortification, and submitted to certain death, not only without murmur, but even with joy, rather than religion should suffer (*l*). In the infancy of Mahometanism, they who opposed the Koran, if taken in battle, were put to death without mercy; but when that religion was established, beyond all danger of being subverted, Mahometans gave the vanquished their choice of three offers: to embrace the Koran, and be entitled to all the privileges of Moslems; to pay tribute, and profess their own religion, provided it was not idolatrous nor immoral; or decide the quarrel by the sword. In this latter case, if Moslems prevailed, captive women and children were reduced to absolute servitude; and men, taken in battle, were slain, or disposed of, at the pleasure of the prince (*m*). It would be tedious to enumerate the several battles fought by the impostor, and the various means employed by him, in establishing his religion, and reducing his countrymen to an obedience of his authority. We have recited the doctrines which assisted him in defeating the Coreshites, the most powerful of all the Arabian tribes; and shall only add that, in consequence of his victory over these, the other tribes readily submitted to his authority, in civil and ecclesiastical affairs. The different tribes, before divided, now united their efforts, to extend their conquests

---

(*l*) Smyth's Manners of the Turks.   (*m*) Sale, Sect. 6.

and religion; nor can we be furprifed at the fucceffes of a fierce people, united under fuch a general as Mahomet, when influenced by his doctrines, and oppofed by the enemies which his fucceffors had to encounter.

Mahomet, finding himfelf eftablifhed in regal and pontifical power in Arabia, difpatched embaffadors to neighbouring princes, to invite them to embrace his religion; and was furnifhed with a pretext of commencing hoftilities againft them if they fhould refufe to comply. This was the firft ftep towards the extenfion of the empire of the Arabs, and the foundation of the conquefts afterwards obtained by him, and the caliphs who fucceeded him. He died meditating further conquefts, and bequeathed to his fucceffors the Koran and its doctrines, and alfo an example that they fhould follow his fteps. He died prince and pontiff, head in temporal and fpiritual affairs, under the title of caliph, a title tranfmitted to his fucceffors, who were kings and high priefts for three hundred years. When the empire was overturned by the Tartars, the caliphs loft both the name and authority; were ftripped of all temporal jurifdiction; and confined to the difcharge of the facred function only (*n*). In Turkey, Perfia, and the Mogul empire, thofe minifters of religion are appointed by the refpective princes

Death of Mahomet, and eftablifhment of the Caliphat.

(*n*) Prideaux's Life of Mahomet.

as interpreters of the laws, and depofed by them at pleafure (o). In the Ottoman empire, the mufti is a mere inftrument in the hands of the emperor, obliged to ratify all his mandates, and regularly attends his retinue to confirm his edicts (p). The foltan encourages a veneration for the mufti, pays him great external homage himfelf, and pretends to confult him in all doubts and difficulties (q). When he has refolved to make war or peace, to put to death a bafhaw or vizier, or meditates any other important bufinefs, he afks his opinion: if the mufti fhould refufe to approve of his moft iniquitous orders, he is depofed, degraded, and put to death, and another is appointed, more flexible and complying. The concurrence of the mufti, juftifies the foltan's conduct, and filences the difcontents of the people, who are perfuaded, that whatever he confents to is approved by the Deity. Such is the final iffue of the facerdotal office, eftablifhed by Mahomet, and the caliphs who fucceeded him. At its firft inftitution it was united with defpotifm, and when almoft annihilated itfelf, lent its feeble aid to fupport defpotic power, acquired by impofture. We fhall now examine the means by which the caliphs were enabled to extend their conquefts and religion, after the death of the prophet, and

---

(o) Prideaux's Life of Mahomet.   (p) Smyth's Manners.   (q) Ricaut's Maxims, Book II. Ch. iv.

the influence of his doctrines on the state of society.

After Mahomet's death, the Arabs being a restless people, and not sufficiently impressed with a sense of his religion, rebelled against Abubeker, and refused to pay him the usual tribute of tithes and alms, and perform other rites required by the prophet (*r*). The new caliph sent an able general, named Caled, to suppress this rebellion; and to his courage and conduct we are chiefly to attribute the conquest of Syria, and the establishment of Mahometanism. He defeated the rebels in a set battle, obtained considerable plunder, and reduced them to servitude. This general had an implacable aversion for the enemies of his religion, or apostates from it; and refused to spare even those who expressed the strongest marks of renouncing their errors. The Greek emperor, and other princes, who paid little regard to the Saracens during their domestic quarrels, now experienced the force of their arms. When Abubeker had reduced rebels and apostates to submission, he resolved to compel his neighbours to embrace his religion, or pay tribute (*s*), in compliance with an injunction of the prophet, who commanded his followers to fight until all men were converted (*t*). The caliph dispatched Caled with

Mahometanism assisted Caled in reducing Persia and other places.

(*r*) Ockley. Ch. viii. (*s*) Koran, Ch. ix. (*t*) Ibid.

troops

SECT. IV.

troops to Irak, and this zealous officer obliged the Persians to submit to the empire of the Saracens (u). Abubeker, having assembled some of his friends, was advised to invade Syria, and to acquaint his adherents in different parts of Arabia, that he intended to send true believers into that country to rescue it from infidels. They who received intelligence of his intentions, expressed great readiness of complying with his commands; and a considerable army was levied from the different provinces of Arabia to march into Syria. In this expedition the Arabs defeated the emperor Heraclius, and obtained great booty; and their successes prompted the inhabitants of Mecca, who had hitherto stood neuter, chearfully to take up arms in order to partake of the spoil. Amrou is dispatched, at the head of troops, to Palestine, and Obeidah into Syria, on pretence of compelling men to embrace the Mahometan faith. The latter of those generals, being worsted by the Greek emperor, is recalled, and Caled is appointed in his room; a successful leader, who took several important places in Syria, and obliged the inhabitants to pay tribute (w). At the siege of Bostra, Caled cried out, " Fight, fight; paradise, paradise:" in consequence of this speech the Saracens fought like lions; took this wealthy town, and reduced its inhabitants to the yoke; while priests

(u) Ockley.   (w) Ibid.

and

and monks ran about the streets, in vain calling upon God, whose laws they had violated, and whose providence had delivered them into the hands of their enemies (x).

The emperor Heraclius sends Verdan, with an army, to the relief of Damascus, which was besieged by Caled; and this general dispatches Derar with a small force to make a diversion. Derar, notwithstanding the disparity of numbers, advanced against Verdan's troops, on a principle advanced by one of his soldiers, and founded on experience; that " it was common for Mussulmen to rout a great army with an handful of men." In the beginning of the engagement, Derar was taken prisoner, and his troops would have fled, had not Omeirah cried out with a loud voice, " What! don't you know that whosoever turns his back upon his enemies offends God and his prophet? That the gates of paradise shall be open to none but such as fight for religion?" These words revived the spirits of the soldiers, and prevailed on them to rally, and maintain their ground, until succours had arrived. Caled soon came to their assistance, entirely defeated the Grecians, and returned immediately to the siege of Damascus. Heraclius dispatched Verdan a second time, with seventy thousand men, to raise the siege, which so alarmed Caled that he summoned all the great officers,

It assisted him in reducing Damascus.

(x) Ockley.

SECT. IV. officers, employed in different quarters, to hasten to his assistance. When the two armies were in sight of each other, Caled rode through the ranks, and exhorted them to "fight in earnest in the cause of religion, and to be sure not to turn their backs, and so be damned for their pains," as the prophet expresses it (*y*). The Greek general, though his army far surpassed that of the Saracens in number, wished to decline the combat, knowing that his soldiers would not fight so desperately as enthusiasts, who were sure of martyrdom if slain in the propagation of the Mahometan religion. His apprehensions were well founded; the Saracens entirely defeated the Christians; killed in one day fifty thousand of them; and obtained plunder of inestimable value. When some hungry Arabs, particularly those of Mecca, heard of the successes of their countrymen, they solicited permission to go into Syria, from a desire of sharing in the plunder, and of exchanging the uncultivated deserts of Arabia Petrea for the delicacies of Damascus. The Saracens returned to the siege of this city, elated with success, and almost certain of victory, while the besieged deliberated whether they should surrender, and pay tribute for the preservation of their lives. Thomas, the emperor's son-in-law, objected to the proposal, and inveighed against the Arabs as poor, naked,

(*y*) Koran, Ch. viii.

and barefooted wretches, far inferior to the Damascenes in numbers and discipline. He was told in answer, that "these men fought desperately under the greatest disadvantages, and believed stedfastly that every man who is slain, enters immediately into paradise, and every man of the enemy, into hell." Thomas however prevailed on the Damascenes to resist the Saracens, and even forced them to retire a little, notwithstanding a speech of Caled previous to the engagement. This general exhorts his soldiers to persevere, "since they shall rest after death;" and adds, "that is the best rest, which shall never be succeeded by any labour." We find even a Mahometan woman, whose husband was slain, solicit death, fired by enthusiasm, and by the cant of generals. " Happy art thou, said she, my dear; thou art gone to thy Lord, who first joined us together, and then parted us asunder; I will revenge thy death, and endeavour, to the utmost of my power, to come to the place where thou art." Having spoken these words, she neither wept nor wailed, but armed herself for the battle, and fought desperately until she was slain. The inhabitants of Damascus, pressed hard by the Saracens, were ready to capitulate when the city was betrayed to Caled, who attacked them immediately, in order to anticipate a surrender, and obtain booty for his soldiers. All the inhabitants of Damascus were obliged to quit the city, except such

SECT. IV. such as consented to pay tribute. Abubeker died the day on which it was taken, and was succeeded by Omar, to whom he bequeathed the Caliphat (z).

It assisted Obeidah in reducing Hems, Jerusalem, and other places.

Omar sent some of his generals to invade the Persian empire, and make conquests in Irak: this caliph took the command from Caled, who was too violent and fierce, and conferred it on Abu Obeidah, who was mild and gentle. Abdolla, surrounded by an host of Christians, exhorts his troops in words to this purpose: " Either we shall succeed, and have all the plunder, or else die, and so the next way to paradise:" having uttered these words, he fell upon the Christians, and made havock among them. The soldiers of Obeidah sustained great damages at the siege of Balbec, from the engines planted on the walls of that city, and from a sally of its inhabitants. This general told his chief officers, that the slaughter of the soldiers was decreed by God, and enjoined patience and perseverance to his troops; since God promised success to those who persevered, and the degree of martyrdom to those who were slain in the propagation of the faith. The Saracens having, as usual, prevailed, seized on Herbis, governor of that city, and brought him before Obeidah. When the governor saw the condition to which he was reduced, and the smallness of the

(z) Ockley.

enemies

enemies number, "he bit his fingers with rage and indignation." The Mahometan leader took advantage of this circumstance, and acquainted Herbis, that the number of true believers always appears greater in the eyes of idolators than it really is; that angels help *them*, as they did Mahomet at the battle of Bedar (*a*); that they depend on those heavenly auxiliaries for assistance; and though they never saw them themselves, it was sufficient for them that they were seen by their enemies (*b*).

Such was the influence of enthusiasm in the wars of the first caliphs, that a Mahometan officer signalized himself in the battle of Hems, from a prospect of the joys of Mahomet's paradise. He thus expressed himself aloud, "Methinks I see the black-eyed girls looking upon me, one of which, if she should appear in the world, all mankind would die for love of her." Having spoken these words, he charged his enemies with violence, and made havock wherever he went, until he was killed by a javelin from the hands of the governor. The emperor Heraclius, exerted all his strength to conquer those enthusiasts, and appointed Mahon general of such an army as never appeared in Syria since the invasion of the Saracens. The Greeks began the onset with such valour and impetuosity, that the Mahometans

All Syria, Egypt, and part of Persia, submit to the Saracens in the Caliphat of Omar.

(*a*) Koran, Ch. ix. (*b*) Ockley, p. 204.

turned their backs; and were prevailed on to rally by women, posted in the rear, who attacked them so warmly with blows and invective, that they chose to face their enemies rather than endure them. They were so hard pressed by the Greeks, that they forgot the cant of their generals, who told them, before the engagement, that paradise was before them, and hell-fire behind them; and even Obeidah, who used those words, was forced to retreat. Night at length separated the combatants, and in the mean time, Obeidah told his men, that their enemies suffered the same pain that they did, but had not the same reward to expect for their labours (c). The Saracens, who were victorious in the end, killed one hundred and fifty thousand Christians, took forty thousand prisoners, and lost, comparatively, but few of their own soldiers. Obeidah marches to the siege of Jerusalem, and proposes the usual conditions, of fighting, embracing Mahometanism, or paying tribute. The inhabitants of that city having resolved on resistance, that general strengthened himself with a reinforcement of fresh troops, again offers the above terms, and threatens those who shall reject them, with men who love death better than Christians do wine, or hogs flesh, as that leader sarcastically expressed it. Each of the Saracen generals, in their prayers before Jerusa-

(c) Ockley, p. 237.

lem, ufes the words which Mahomet puts into the mouth of Mofes to the children of Ifrael: " O people, enter ye into the holy land, which God hath decreed for you (d)." Thefe words, which accorded with their prefent defigns, were underftood by the Saracens to relate to themfelves as well as to the Ifraelites, and animated the foldiers to perfevere in the fiege. At the end of four months the befieged, able to make no further refiftance, capitulate and fubmit to the payment of tribute, and to other fevere conditions, for the protection of their lives and fortunes, and a liberty of confcience (e). The fame year in which Jerufalem was taken, the Saracens defeated the Perfians, and obtained confiderable booty, clothes adorned with gold and jewels, vaft fums of money, and an armoury ftored with all forts of ammunition.

The next place they laid fiege to was Aleppo, which they took by furprife, after a fiege of five months, and marched immediately to Antioch, the refidence of the Greek emperor. Heraclius was vanquifhed by the treachery of his own people, the metropolis of Syria furrendered to Obeidah, and that prince efcaped privately to Conftantinople with few friends. In the mean time, Caled was fuccefsful in another quarter; and feveral towns furrendered to him as far as the Euphrates.

Other places fubmit to them in his Caliphat.

(d) Koran, Ch. v.   (e) Ockley, p. 246.

SECT. IV. After the capitulation of Jerusalem, Omar dispatched Amrou to conquer Egypt, and propagate religion in that country; Constantine the emperor's son opposed his progress, but was not successful. The Saracens displayed their accustomed valour, and were, as usual, victorious: such was the zeal of those enthusiasts, that even a beardless youth had the rashness to fight one of Constantine's officers, who was far more robust, and who killed not only him, but two or three more. This stripling used to say, that he was not influenced by the delicacies of Syria to go thither, but that his desire was to fight for the service of God, seeking his favour, and that of his apostle. Before he engaged the Christian officer, he took leave of his friends, and told them, they should meet again, and drink of the waters which belong to the apostle of God in paradise (*f*). Tripoli, Tyre, Cæsarea, and all other places of Syria, which had hitherto maintained an opposition, surrendered at length to the Saracens; and Amrou besieged Pharmah, Cairo, and other parts of Egypt, and took them by force, stratagem, or treachery. After the surrender of Alexandria, all Egypt submitted, and each inhabitant compounded for his life, fortune, and liberty of conscience, for two ducats a year. Omar, during his caliphat, banished all Jews and Christians from

(*f*) Ockley, p. 333.

Arabia, and subdued Syria, Egypt, and other territories of Africa, with great part of Persia. At his death, Othman, who succeeded him, turned his arms against Persia, entirely destroyed that country, and transferred it to the caliphs. We now see the origin of the great empire founded by the Saracens, and enlarged by the authority and wealth of the caliphs; to whom the Koran (g) allocates a fifth of the spoils taken in war, together with a part of the tribute paid by the inhabitants of conquered towns and provinces. The caliphs were enabled by wealth, territory, and authority, thus acquired, by the cant of generals, and enthusiasm of soldiers, to extend their conquests still further, when backed by hardy, zealous, and temperate troops. Such were the doctrines and means employed by Mahomet and the other caliphs, in extending their conquests and propagating their religion: such were the immediate effects of primitive Mahometanism on the lives of its professors, and the welfare of communities!

The successes of Mahomet and his successors have arisen chiefly, but not entirely, from the doctrines of the impostor; other causes contributed to promote the victories of the Saracens, as I have already observed. The natural bravery of the Arabs, the imbecility of the neighbouring

<small>Other causes concurred with Mahometanism in advancing the conquests of the Saracens.</small>

(g) Ch. viii.

SECT. IV. nations, the perfidy of some Christians, who betrayed the rest in the course of those wars, and the virtues of the first Caliphs, all contributed to the conquests of the Saracens. The impostor himself was well fitted to impose a false religion on mankind, and richly furnished with natural endowments; "beautiful in his person, of a subtle wit, agreeable behaviour, liberal to the poor, courteous to all, valiant in fight (*h*)." According to the Mahometan religion, the duties of prayer, fasting, and almsgiving, were so pleasing to God, that Omar said, Prayer carries us half way to God, fasting brings us to the door of his palace, and alms procures us admission. The duty of fasting was deemed so momentous, that Mahomet used to say it was the gate of religion, and that the odour of the mouth of him that fasts, is more grateful to God than that of musk (*i*). Abubeker, Mahomet's successor in the caliphat, possessed many virtues; he was chaste, temperate, and disinterested; and divided all the money in the treasury every Friday, according to men's merits; while Omar distributed once a week to the necessitous, and maintained that his practice was preferable to that of Abubeker; since the things of this world were intended for the relief of men's necessities, and not for the reward of merit, which properly

(*h*) Sale, to the Reader.   (*i*) Broughton, Art. Mahomed.

belongs

belongs to another world. But besides those causes, which have contributed to the victories of the Saracens, we may find in the Koran (*k*) a doctrine that was extremely useful in promoting their conquests. Mahomet absolutely prohibited the use of wine to his followers; and to abstemiousness Sir Paul Ricaut (*l*) ascribes great part of the success which attended the caliphs. In times of primitive Mahometanism, they strictly abstained from wine; and the conscientious will still not drink, buy, nor sell it, nor even use money made by the sale of that liquor. The Persians and Turks in general, drink freely; and when reproached by Christians with drinking wine, contrary to the precepts of the Koran, they say it is with them, as with some Christians, whose religion forbids drunkenness, and who yet drink to excess, and even glory in their debaucheries (*m*).

Should we compare the doctrines of Mahomet, and the means which he employed in propagating his religion, with those made use of by Christ and his apostles; and the effects of primitive Mahometanism, and primitive Christianity; the contrast would appear striking, furnish a strong proof of the superior excellence of the Christian code, and point out the baleful influence of that religion, which was propagated by the sword, and founded

Comparison of Christianity and Mahometanism in the tendency and effects of their doctrines.

(*k*) Ch. ii. and v.   (*l*) Maxims, Book III. Ch. xi.
(*m*) Sale, Sect. 5.

SECT. IV.

on imposture. I shall refer my readers to the learned and elegant discourses of a late writer (*n*), for a comparison of Christianity and Mahometanism in their history, evidence, and effects; and shall make but few observations on a subject, so ably discussed by that author. The gospel was not published in times of ignorance, nor to a barbarous people; the sword was not the instrument, by which it was promulgated. Christianity had not its rise in an obscure part of the earth, inhabited by thieves, destitute of learning, but in the Augustan age, when science flourished. The doctrines of Christ were spiritual and refined; while those of Mahomet were adapted to the fancies and appetites of a sensual and ignorant people. Mahometanism was propagated by violence; while Christianity was disseminated by the homely discourses of a few simple and illiterate men, endued by God with miraculous gifts. The Koran was accommodated to the ruling passion of the Arabs; while the gospel opposed the prejudices of men, and enjoined actions most painful to the corruptions of our nature. Mahomet was not illiterate, as he pretended; and even if he was, he could more easily have imposed any doctrines on the ignorant Arabs, than the apostles could theirs on the learned and refined. The Mahometan religion led to conquest and glory; whereas the Christian pro-

(*n*) White's Sermons.

mised

mised nothing to its votaries except sufferings and tribulations. The Gentile world, who hated the Jews, were averse from Christianity, which originated among that people; while the Jews disliked a religion, that included all mankind; and reduced them from their boasted superiority to the same level with Heathen nations. Bayle acknowledges, that no force was employed in propagating the gospel for three centuries; but affirms, that it was disseminated by the sword from the third to the sixth century, as the Koran was afterwards. Though I might perhaps justly question the assertion of the gainsayer, I shall accede to it at present, and shew, that he can deduce no conclusion from that concession, which can in the smallest degree injure the credit of Christianity. The gospel was propagated, though not established, long before princes took up the sword in its defence; and was not indebted for its propagation to those, who established and supported it by their power. The internal evidence of the Christian system, and the miracles of its professors, made multitudes of converts in many countries, before the age of Constantine. Christianity was disseminated, though not established, when that emperor undertook its defence; no violence was employed for three hundred years in propagating it; whereas the Koran owed its progress and establishment, from the very beginning, entirely to the sword.

SECT. IV.

Comparison of the lives and doctrines of Christ and Mahomet.

If we compare the lives and doctrines of Christ, and the prophet of Arabia, the contrast will appear striking, at first view: the former did not promise brutal pleasures in Elysium, like Pagans and Mahometans, but pure and spiritual enjoyments, such as could not enter into the heart of man to conceive. Christ prohibited not only immodest looks, and obscene conversation, but even impure thoughts; and recommended self-denial, temperance, charity, forgiveness, and resignation, not only by precept, but also by example. Christ was spotless and without sin; Mahomet, though possessed of some shining qualities, was a robber, perjurer, murderer, adulterer, and fornicator. The former, inculcated peace, patience, and love; the latter, war, revenge, and hatred: the former, checked men's lusts by monogamy; the latter, inflamed them by indulging his followers with a plurality of wives. Christ permitted the moderate use of all God's creatures; the other prohibited wine and swines flesh. The former commanded men to search the scriptures; the other forbid the Koran to be translated into other languages, or read by the people. The one propagated his religion by his own virtues and those of his followers; the other by tyranny, and acts of violence: the disciples of one were innocent fishermen; while those of the other robbed and murdered, on pretence of propagating the religion of the prophet.

Humility

Humility and forgiveness were the characteristics of Christ; while, according to Mr. Gibbon, "the stern passions of pride and revenge were kindled in the bosom of the prophet of Arabia." The disciples of the former were honest and humane; while that historian denominates the followers of the latter "holy robbers, who were eager to execute or to prevent the order of a massacre (*o*)." The gospel was propagated by the miracles and virtues of its first professors; while "the use of fraud and perfidy, of cruelty and injustice, were often subservient to the propagation of Mahometanism," as Mr. Gibbon (*p*) expresses it. Tribulation was denounced against, and actually experienced by early converts to Christianity; while this writer affirms, that "the encreasing myriads, who acknowledged Mahomet as their king and prophet, had been compelled by his arms, or allured by his prosperity (*q*)." Sherlock (*r*), in one of his discourses proves, that the Christian and Mahometan are the only revelations which pretend to be a rule of religion to all countries. This learned writer appeals to natural religion, calls upon her to determine which of those two is most consonant to reason, and has God for its author, and proves that the Christian alone has any

(*o*) Hist. of the Roman Empire, Chap. l. p. 239 and 250.
(*p*) Ibid. Chap. l. p. 250, quarto.
(*q*) Ibid. Chap. li. p. 276.
(*r*) Vol. I. Serm. IX.

just claim to a divine revelation. His words are thefe: "Go to your natural religion; lay before her Mahomet and his difciples, arrayed in armour, and in blood; riding in triumph over the fpoils of thoufands and tens of thoufands who fell by his victorious fword. Shew her the cities which he fet in flames, the countries which he ravaged and deftroyed, and the miferable diftrefs of all the inhabitants of the earth. When fhe has viewed him in this fcene, carry her into his retirements; fhew her the prophet's chamber, his concubines and wives; let her fee his adultery, and hear him alledge revelation, and his divine commiffion to juftify his luft, and his oppreffion. When fhe is tired with this profpect, then fhew her the bleffed Jefus, humble and meek, doing good to all the fons of men, patiently inftructing both the ignorant and perverfe. Let her fee him in his moft retired privacies; let her follow him to the mount and hear his devotions, and fupplications unto God. Carry her to his table, to view his poor fare, and hear his heavenly difcourfes; let her fee him injured, but not provoked; let her attend him to the tribunal, and confider the patience with which he endured the fcoffs and reproaches of his enemies. Lead her to his crofs, and let her view him in the agony of death, and hear his laft prayer for his perfecutors, "Father forgive them, for they know not what they do." When natural religion has viewed both, afk, Which is the prophet of God? But her answer we have already had, when she saw part of this scene through the eyes of the Centurion, who attended at the cross; by him she spoke and said, Truly this was the Son of God."

SECT. IV.

We have the testimony of Kabizi Agam, a learned Turk, who was educated with prejudices against the Christian religion, that the precepts of the gospel are preferable to those of the Koran. Being called upon to abjure this opinion, and threatened with death in case of a refusal, he maintained it with firmness, and voluntarily endured death, rather than renounce it. In consequence of his obstinacy, as it was called, a terrifying edict was issued out, that all, who maintained similar doctrines, should share the same fate (*s*). Here we are furnished with one reason of Bayle's (*t*) assertion, that there are fewer converts from Mahometanism to Christianity, than from Christianity to Mahometanism. But several other causes have concurred, to prevent converts from the Mahometan to the Christian religion, and to make proselytes from the gospel to the Koran. Mahometans employ rewards and punishments for the purpose of making proselytes, and exempt from taxes converts from the gospel. According to the Mahometan faith, the wicked, after a certain time, are released from the torments of hell; out of

Difficulty of making apostates from Mahometanism.

(*s*) Mod. Univ. Hist. Vol. V. folio.
(*t*) Life of Mahomet.

which,

which, according to Christianity, there is no redemption. The Koran allows private revenge, so pleasing to the corruptions of human nature; and its professors speak respectfully of Moses and Christ, so that Jews and Christians are easily converted. As Mahometanism was propagated by the sword, and intended to derive its chief support from the ignorance of its votaries, the prophet prohibited the study of philosophy, and made it capital to dispute about the Koran, to sell it to strangers, to translate (*u*) it, or even to attempt to convert a Mussulman (*w*). Should Mahometans be allowed even to argue about the Koran, it would be next to impossible to convert or confute them. The prophet himself declared, that of twelve thousand sentences in the Koran, only four thousand are true; so that the clearest refutation in a thousand instances cannot induce a Mussulman to change his opinion; as these may possibly be some of the eight thousand falshoods (*x*). There is one reason which renders it extremely dangerous, to attempt to alter or oppose the Mahometan religion, in countries where it is professed. The authority of the supreme magistrate is founded upon the Koran; the doctrines of this book are the basis of his throne; so that any change in religion must disturb his government, and a religious innovator is considered as an enemy to the prince.

(*u*) Ross's Religions.   (*w*) Smyth's Manners.
(*x*) Sale, Sect. 3.

Having

Having examined the influence of Mahometanism in the time of the first caliphs, I proceed to point out its most remarkable effects, during its continuance and establishment. Primitive Mahometans looked on the victories, and extensive conquests of Mahomet, and his immediate successors, as happy effects of the doctrines of the impostor. But every man, who consults reason or history, must be convinced that extent of empire does not constitute the happiness of individuals or communities; and fatal experience may convince the subjects of the Grand Signior, that while their ancestors were extending their conquests, and disseminating their religion, they were fabricating chains for their descendants, and augmenting the authority of a despotic tyrant. The territories, acquired by the three first caliphs, are to be ascribed in a great degree to Mahometanism, and the foundation of the extensive conquests afterwards obtained by those who succeeded them. Sir Paul Ricaut (y) thus describes the extent of the Ottoman empire in his time, "all the delightful fields of Asia, says this historian, the pleasant plains of Tempe and Thrace, all the plenty of Egypt, and the fertility of the Nile, the luxury, the substance of Peloponnesus, Athens, Lemnos, Chios, and Mitylene, with other isles of the Egean sea; the spices of Arabia, the riches of a great part of

SECT. IV.

Despotism an effect of the conquests of the Saracens.

(y) Maxims, Book I, Chap. i.

Persia,

SECT. IV. Perſia, all Armenia, the provinces of Galatia, Bithynia, Phrygia, Lycia, Pamphylia, Paleſtine, Celoſyria and Phenicia; Colchis and a great part of Georgia; the tributary provinces of Moldavia, Valachia, Romania, Bulgaria and Servia, and the beſt part of Hungary; all the extent of this vaſt empire concur to ſatisfy the appetites of the Grand Signior." Such was the fruit and final iſſue of the ſyſtem of religion which originated from the impoſtor, and his immediate ſucceſſors! Servitude and violence were the natural effects of the government erected by Mahomet, and the caliphs who ſucceeded him. As the Ottoman empire was founded in time of war, its laws and polity were arbitrary and ſevere, agreeable to the principles of military diſcipline. Warriors became ſovereigns, and what was acquired by the ſword naturally became the property of their generals or princes. The Grand Signior can diſpoſe of lands, cattle, houſes, nay, of every thing in the empire, except lands appropriated to ſacred uſes. He was ſtyled God on Earth, the Shadow of God, Brother of the Sun and Moon, and the Giver of all earthly Crowns. It is a maxim among the Turks, that the Grand Signior can never be depoſed, or brought to an account for cruelty and oppreſſion; while he deſtroys leſs than one thouſand of his ſubjects in a day without a cauſe (z). Abſolute

(z) Maxims, Chap. iii.

power implies paſſive obedience; and great induſtry is employed to inſtil ſubmiſſion into thoſe, who are deſigned for great offices in the ſtate. To die by the hand or even command of the prince, when the blow is ſubmitted to with entire reſignation, is taught in the ſeraglio to be the higheſt pitch of martyrdom, and he, who is ſo fortunate to ſuffer in this manner, is ſuppoſed to be immediately tranſported to Paradiſe (*a*). In conſequence of this ſyſtem of education, ſubjects readily obey the commands of the emperor; anticipate his wiſhes; and would not heſitate to fling themſelves from a precipice, or kill each other, for his pleaſure or entertainment. A Grand Vizier, who was a favourite of the Sultan, and applauded as a fortunate miniſter, confeſſed there was not any thing wanting to complete his honours, except dying by the hand of the Grand Signior (*b*). To ſupport deſpotic power, the emperor employs none in high offices, but perſons educated in the principles of Mahometaniſm, and paſſive obedience: children of Chriſtian captives, unconnected in the ſtate, whom he may raiſe without envy, and deſtroy without danger. Deſpotic power prevails in all places, where Mahometaniſm is planted, and is every where accompanied with ſubjection and ſervitude. " Every free and gallant people, whom it has involved in the progreſs

(*a*) Maxims, Chap. iii.   (*b*) Ibid. Chap. iv.

SECT. IV.

of its power, says Mr. White, have abandoned their rights, the pride of independence, and security of freedom, as soon as they enlisted under the banner of the prophet (c)." A learned writer (d) asserts, that, in consequence of oppression and the doctrine of predestination, Egypt is less populous, and worse cultivated than formerly; that its inhabitants are reduced to a third of their former number; and that upwards of one third of the lands, cultivated in ancient times, is "metamorphosed into desarts, whose horrid aspect frights the traveller." The husbandman neglects to improve his farm, from an uncertainty of transmitting it to his children; and the peasant is so loaded with arbitrary taxes, that he frequently wants absolute necessaries in the most fertile country on earth.

The Koran secures private property to individuals.

In consequence of despotism in the Ottoman empire, succession to property is not hereditary, but depends primarily on the will of the Soltan: but still individuals can secure their lands to their descendants, by annexing them to the church, as the prophet commanded. Any man, who wishes to transmit property safely to his male issue, settles the reversion on some religious foundation, during the life of that direct male issue; and annually pays a small quit-rent, until it is extinct; at which time the whole devolves to that foundation. The religious and political systems, being blended to-

(c) Sermon IX.   (d) Savary's 43d Letter on Egypt.

gether in the Koran, every subject, who observes this law of the prophet, holds his possessions by the same right, that the sovereign does his throne; nor has any prince ever attempted to dispossess the man, who complied with this law (*e*). Mahomet has not limited this law to those of his own sect, but equally extended it to Jews and Christians; so that the revenues of the church, we may suppose, are immense, and must in time possess almost all the land in the Ottoman empire. In Sir Paul Ricaut's (*f*) time, it was computed that one third part of the lands of that great empire was destined and set apart for sacred uses. Their mosques are magnificent and richly endowed, and their emaums, or priests, maintained in opulence and splendor. The Caliphs transferred the whole property of Christian churches to Mahometan ecclesiastics; appropriating none of the ancient possessions to private uses; but made considerable additions to former donations. The founders of that empire were priests, as well as princes, and the civil laws of Mahometans are founded upon the Koran, as those of the Jews are on the Pentateuch. The Koran was at first considered as a political, as well as religious code; but being found defective in its civil institutes, lawyers, without derogating from its authority, have supplied its defects by commenting on the Koran, and explaining and extending the ideas of the prophet.

(*e*) Guthrie's Geography. (*f*) Maxims, Book II. Ch. vii.

SECT. IV.

Ignorance an effect of Mahometanism.

But besides the mischiefs experienced by the vanquished, and the servitude entailed on them and their descendants; those conquests were, in one particular instance, peculiarly destructive to the literary world. The Caliph Omar, by burning the famous library at Alexandria, that great repository of eastern erudition, robbed mankind in some measure of the discoveries of the ancients, which might have served posterity as materials of literature, and rudiments of science. This Caliph maintained that, if those books agreed with the Koran, they were useless; if they differed from it, they were pernicious, and ought to be destroyed (g). In consequence of this loss of books, and the despotic power established by the Caliphs, Mahometans, especially the Turks, are remarkably ignorant, rarely improve their intellectual faculties, despise literature, and value themselves upon their ignorance of arts and sciences, as enervating the mind, and rendering them less fit for the occupation of arms. The Koran is a political, as well as religious code, and Mahomet, by forbidding his disciples to dispute about or question it, excluded all that learning, which is necessary in other countries, for the acquisition of religious and political knowledge. By those restraints on information and genius, this servile people have lost all desire of recovering knowledge; are become too

(g) Mod. Univ. Hist. Vol. I. folio, Book I. Ch. ii. Sect. 2.

indolent

indolent to exert their own talents, and too proud and perverse to adopt, or regard the discoveries of others; while in countries, where the Christian religion is taught in its purity, we find its professors active, inquisitive and inventive, well acquainted with liberty and arts, and with the unalienable and immutable rights of mankind. A mind, accustomed to entertain sublime ideas of the attributes of the Deity, will be more apt to form exalted notions on other subjects, than the man, who fears to question the truth of contradictory passages in the Koran, and is obliged to assent to every thing in it, however absurd or ridiculous. It is acknowledged that the Koran represents the Deity in lively colours from the prophets and evangelists; but still the impostor often blends this sublimity, with the impure rites and superstitions of the Arabs; and sometimes makes this sublime Being dispense with the laws of morality, and descend to the meanest employments, for the indulgence of his favourite. So troublesome were Mahomet's wives, and so importunate in their demands for fine cloaths, that, in order to satisfy them, he introduces the Almighty regulating his domestic concerns, and silencing their clamours.

Renaudot doubts the burning of the library at Alexandria; and the historian of the Roman empire absolutely denies the fact, for the following reasons. The testimony of Abulpharagius, who relates that disaster, and who wrote six hundred years

Mr. Gibbon's idea of the Alexandrian library examined.

SECT. IV. years after Omar, is overbalanced by the silence of Eutychius and Elmacin, both Christians, and natives of Egypt (*h*). But I cannot comprehend why Mr. Gibbon should oppose the silence of these men to the positive assertion of Abulpharagius, who wrote an history that does honour to his memory (*i*), and who was more unexceptionable in his character and testimony, than either of these annalists. The former of them, when patriarch of Alexandria, was hated by his people; and relates several things not to be found elsewhere, together with many lying and fabulous wonders (*k*). Hence the historian of the Roman empire might easily have perceived, why an author, accustomed to relate new and marvellous events, was likely to be silent about the well-known fact of the burning of the library. Elmacin, having filled a post of distinction and trust under Mahometan princes, must reasonably have been attached to their religion and government. He calls the impostor himself Mahomet of glorious memory, emperor of the faithful, and his followers the orthodox: so that, if not a Mahometan, he must have been a time-serving Christian, and unlikely to relate a fact disgraceful to Omar, one of the most

(*h*) Ch. li. p. 342. quarto.
(*i*) Bayle's Life of Abulpharagius.
(*k*) A New and General Biographical Dictionary, Art. Eutychius.

renowned

renowned of the Caliphs. " They, says Bayle (*l*), who consider the measures Elmacin was obliged to keep in his high office, will not think it strange, that he speaks honourably of the Caliphs; and never difrespectfully of the Mahometan religion." Another reason why Mr. Gibbon denies the burning of the library, is the inconsistency of such conduct with certain opinions of Mahometan casuists, who allow the faithful to read profane authors, and do not suffer the books of Jews or Christians to be burned, from a respect which they entertain for the name of God (*m*). But let me ask, whether these opinions were entertained in the time of Omar? and whether it is not absurd to suppose this Caliph to be acquainted with Mahometan casuistry, which did not prevail until after his time? Even this historian admits, that some casuists were, on other occasions, extremely illiberal; and condemned some Caliphs who were encouragers of learning. " Superstition, says he, was alarmed at the introduction even of abstract sciences; and the more rigid doctors of the law condemned the rash and pernicious curiosity of Almamon (*n*)." If such men had flourished in the time of Omar, we cannot doubt, but they would encourage him to, rather than restrain him from burning the library. Mr. Gibbon denies the bad effects which are supposed to have arisen from

(*l*) Life of Elmacin.   (*m*) Gibbon, Ch. li. p. 340.
(*n*) Ibid. Ch. lii. p. 431.

SECT. IV. that event; since those classicks have been spared which Quintilian enumerates, and to which the suffrage of antiquity has adjudged the first place of genius and glory. "The contempt of the Greeks for barbaric science, says he, would scarcely admit the Indian or Ethiopic books into the library of Alexandria; nor is it proved, that philosophy has sustained any real loss from the exclusion of them (*o*)." But surely Quintilian does not pretend to enumerate all books of genius, judgment, or information, in the ancient world: he is silent about the works of the Egyptians, Chaldeans, Indians and Phenicians, from whom the Greeks borrowed, though with many of their writings they must have been little acquainted. Is it probable that the Greeks, who were notorious plagiaries, would exclude from their libraries the writings of Barbarians, from whom they derived knowledge, while they affected to despise them? If these writings were admitted and consumed by the flames, the loss of them to literature might be lamented, but cannot be ascertained.

Revenge, illiberality and extortion the effects of Mahometanism.

The Koran encourages revenge, and expresly enjoins retaliation of injuries; "We have ordained the talio, says Mahomet, a man for a man, an eye for an eye, a nose for a nose, an ear for an ear, a tooth for a tooth, a wound for a wound (*p*)." In another passage he thus expresses the same idea in general terms: "offend them that offend you,

(*o*) Gibbon, Ch. lii. p. 344.   (*p*) Koran, Ch. v.

in the same manner that they shall have offended you (*q*)." In consequence of those precepts, Turks are vindictive beyond expression; parents remind their children of any injury they have received, and excite them to revenge; so that this people seldom forget or forgive any injury which has been offered them (*r*). Here it is worthy of observation, that Mahomet built his law of retaliation, on a mistaken conception of the Mosaic code; the Hebrew lawgiver did not authorize individuals to pull out the eye, or tooth of those who injured them; but intended his law, as a direction to judges in the punishment of offences; while some Jews, and after them Mahomet and his followers, considered it as justifying individuals in avenging their own wrongs. The Koran has inspired its professors not only with a vindictive, but an unsocial spirit; and made it meritorious to destroy all, who disbelieve the prophet, as impious and profane. An hatred of other sects is the first idea impressed on the minds of Mahometans, and they manifest their aversion for Jews and Christians, by insulting them in their streets with the opprobrious titles of hogs and infidels (*s*). In consequence of the precepts of the Koran, and the practice of the first Caliphs, Turks consider all who

---

(*q*) Koran, Ch. ii.
(*r*) Observations on the Religion and Manners of Turks, Ch. i. Dubl. duod.
(*s*) Volney's Travels, Vol. II. Ch. xxxv.

refuse to adopt their religion as persons whom they may lawfully rob, murder, and extirpate; nor could any thing preserve other sects from their fury and enthusiasm, except political considerations, which, in some degree, abate their inveterate prejudices (*t*). We read of a worthy Mussulman, who could not divest himself of an illiberal and vindictive spirit, even in the act of recounting his virtues. " These are all my virtues, says he, and by the practice of these, I doubt not of finding entrance into paradise, where the faithful shall set their feet on the necks of the enemies of our holy law, and enjoy all sorts of happiness (*u*)." In Mahometan countries subject to the soltan, viceroys exercise all sorts of fraud and extortion on Christians, and never want evidences to justify them against their complaints. In Egypt the cadis are so partial in the distribution of justice, that it is scarcely possible for a Christian to gain a suit against a Mahometan; and the oaths of two Christians are reckoned but as one. If a Turk kill a Christian, he is only fined; while a Christian cannot even strike a Mussulman without risquing his life (*w*). Mr. Gibbon (*x*) acquaints us, that " Christians, in two hundred years after Mahomet, were separated from their fellow-subjects by

(*t*) On Manners of Turks. Dubl. duod.
(*u*) Turkish Spy, Book II. Lett. x.
(*w*) Volney's Travels to Syria and Egypt, Vol. II. Ch. xxxv.
(*x*) Hist. Ch. li. p. 388.

a turban,

a turban or girdle of a less honourable colour; instead of horses or mules they were condemned to ride on asses in the attitude of women. Their public and private buildings were measured by a diminutive standard; in the streets or baths it is their duty to give way or bow down before the meanest of the people, and their testimony is rejected, if it may tend to the prejudice of a true believer." The Mahometan code has operated powerfully on the private sentiments of its professors, and contracted the social affections within the narrow bounds of one religion or sect: while the Christian religion requires acts of loving-kindness, to all persons of whatever country or religion, whether friends or enemies; and has abated, if not abolished, national prejudices, formerly the source of enmity and dissension. We may appeal to experience, whether Christian nations, however they may differ in language, manners and national interest, do not observe the laws of courtesy and humanity, formerly unknown among different republics, and to which Mahometan countries at present are total strangers.

There is one doctrine of the Koran, which has been particularly destructive in those countries where it is professed. The prophet has told his followers, that God has numbered their days, and predestinated their fate; that every human event is irrevocably fixed; and not only the time, but even the manner and circumstances of man's death

SECT.
IV.
death so unalterably settled, that the devout Musfulman considers it criminal to attempt to alter what was preordained by God. In consequence of this maxim, Mahometans judge all precaution for saving life impious and vain; nor have they, until lately, been prevailed on in Constantinople, and other parts of the Ottoman empire, to employ any remedy against the plague, which makes havoc in those countries. They make use of medicines, not for the purpose of protracting life, but allaying pain; consider the plague as the dart of the Almighty, who infallibly hits his mark; and thinks it sinful to attempt to escape it, by changing infected for salubrious air (*t*). The Egyptians will even wear the apparel of infected persons, without the smallest apprehension; and as familiarly attend the beds, and frequent the company of pestilential persons, as we do the society of those who are gouty or rheumatic (*u*). We have the authority of Sir Paul Ricaut, that Constantinople would be depopulated by war and pestilence, if that city was not supplied with slaves annually imported thither from the Black Sea, and by incursions into Poland (*w*). Baron de Tott (*x*) assures us, that the plague at Constantinople is preserved and propagated by dealers in

---

(*t*) Smyth's Manners.   (*u*) Ricaut's Maxims, Book II. Ch. viii.   (*w*) Ibid. Book I. Ch. xiv.   (*x*) De Tott's Memoirs, Part I.

old

old clothes, who even fell the furs of those who have died of that disease. The plague does mischief also in Cairo every year; and would be more fatal if its violence had not been allayed by cooling breezes, which blow regularly from the north in that city, at the summer solstice (*y*). Though experience tells predestinarians, that Christians, who fly from infection, survive, while whole cities of them are depopulated; yet so firmly fixed is the opinion of fate, that they will not quit the apartments of the sick; where, especially in the families of great men, many servants, the healthy and diseased, lie promiscuously in the same room, and perish together. Men are positively forbid to abandon the city or their houses, or to shun the conversation of infectious persons, where business invites them; but are advised to avoid contagious places, where they have no business to transact. Many men of sense shun the plague, and retire from infectious to wholesome air, not confiding in the prophet's maxim contrary to experience (*z*). Savary proves, that the plague is not a native of Egypt, but is imported into that country by the infected goods of Turkish merchants; and maintains, that a disease, which did little mischief in ancient Lacedæmon, Athens, and Byzantium, would be equally harmless in

(*y*) Mod. Univ. Hist. Vol. VI. folio. Book II. Ch. viii.

(*z*) Ricaut,

SECT. IV. those countries in modern times, was it not for the doctrine of fate, and the disregard of Mahometan governments to the health of their subjects. In consequence of these two causes, this malady sometimes sweeps away, at Cairo, three hundred thousand souls; and has lately destroyed two hundred thousand at Moscow, being propagated by pestiferous merchandize from the warehouses of the Jews (*a*). Bashaws derive great emolument in Egypt from the doctrine of predestination, and from the evils which attend it. The Grand Signior governs that country by bashaws or viceroys, who pay him an exorbitant rent, and are obliged to support the temple of Mecca, maintain a certain number of troops, and supply him with slaves, of which there are multitudes in Africa. As the office of bashaw generally lasts but one year, he exercises every kind of extortion to pay the soltan his rent, and enrich himself in that time; but derives his principal emolument from the plague, which annually sweeps away thousands. Every person being only tenant for life, and life itself precarious, when a man dies, his property reverts to the emperor or his viceroy, who sells it immediately, and has sometimes sold the same estate to three or four persons in the course of one week (*b*). The doctrine of unalterable fate inspires an indif-

(*a*) Savary, Letter 44, on Egypt. Univ. Hist. Vol. VI. folio.

(*b*) Mod.

ference

ference for all things, and renders its professors dull and inactive to an extraordinary degree. Men, who are persuaded that every thing is predetermined by God, naturally indulge in ease; and think it vain, nay, impious, to interpose. As this doctrine destroys free agency, it renders reason useless, discourages industry, and prevents men from exercising their talents to obstruct or remedy evils, which may threaten or befal them. The disciple of Mahomet beholds, with stupid unconcern, his parents, children, and friends, languish or expire; and his country desolated by pestilence, without exerting a single effort to check its baleful influence, and mitigate its rage. The Mahometan feels none of the pious resignation of a good Christian under sufferings, and receives benefits from God, without feeling, or expressing any emotion of gratitude. A Turk, having narrowly escaped destruction from the fall of an house, instead of returning thanks for his deliverance from impending ruin, cries out, that " the hour is not yet come, which God has preordained for his departure from this life (c)."

Effects of Mahometan devotions on individuals and communities.

Let us consider the effects of Mahometan devotions on the state of individuals, and the welfare of society in Turkish countries. The prophet acquainted his followers, that God sent the Koran to the lowest heaven, on the month Ramadan;

(c) Smyth's Manners.

and

and that the angel Gabriel brought it down from thence, and delivered it to him chapter by chapter. In commemoration of this extraordinary event, the impostor ordered a fast on this month, which bears some resemblance to our Lent, but is more rigorously observed. The Mahometan fast consists in abstinence from meat, drink, and lying with their wives; and requires a constant attendance in places of worship, from sun rise to the end of evening twilight. Mussulmen reckon this month holy; and believe that, as long as it lasts, the gates of paradise are open, and those of hell shut. None are excused from fasting on this month, unless they are sick or on a journey, in which cases this fast is observed in another month (*d*). So great a veneration have Mahometans for their prophet, that every person, animal, or thing, which has any relation to him, are treated with the highest respect. Priests kiss the Koran, and bow to it; Mussulmen reverence the beast which carried it, and even the handkerchief that wiped off the sweat; nor is any person allowed to touch the Koran without washed hands and a clean napkin. Mahometans venerate every piece of paper; because, as some have imagined, the Koran is written on that substance; while others account for their veneration in a different manner. Busbequius affirms, that Turks respect

(*d*) Broughton, Art. Ramadan.

every piece of paper which comes in their way; as the name of God might be written upon it, and thruft it into some place where it cannot be trampled upon. They imagine, that when Mahomet shall summon his followers, on the day of judgment, into heaven, they must, in their way thither, walk over grates of hot iron barefooted; and that these pieces of paper, which they saved from being trodden upon, shall then be put under their feet to preserve them from the torture of red-hot bars (*e*). The descendants of the impostor are exempted from legal prosecutions in courts of justice; and in Cairo his shirt is preserved, and carried in procession on certain days, with great pomp and ceremony. Every person is required to visit the prophet's tomb at Mecca at least once in his life, except under particular circumstances. They who have performed this pilgrimage are confident they are absolved from all sin, and sure of being rewarded with the joys of paradise. Some pilgrims, at their return from the tomb, resolve on silence for three or four years; while others put out their eyes, as if every thing else was beneath their regard after a sight so divine (*f*). The grand signior draws great part of his revenues from the tribute, paid by pilgrims going to Mecca; and, as a mark of vene-

(*e*) Aug. Busbequii, Epist. I. p. 50. (*f*) Bayle's Life of Mahomet.

SECT. IV. ration for the prophet, annually sends into Arabia 500 sequins, a Koran covered with gold, and as much black stuff as serves for a tent in the mosque at Mecca (*g*). When the new tent is erected, pilgrims tear the old to pieces, and each of them carries home a rag, which is considered as a precious relic, having been so long near to the bones of the prophet (*h*). The Koran requires this pilgrimage from all who are in a condition to make it; and declares, that they who decline it might as well die Jews or Christians as in the Mahometan religion (*i*). In consequence of this command, the pilgrimage to Mecca is reckoned so essential a branch of practical religion, that " the Mussulman must leave his friends, family and country, and expose himself to the perils of a long journey through barren sands, and beneath a burning sky, to visit the temple of Mecca and the tomb of the prophet (*k*)." Such multitudes annually assemble at Mecca from different Mahometan countries, in honour of the prophet, that it is become a place of traffic; to which men carry the merchandize of their own country, and return home with the richest goods of Persia and the East Indies. Devotion has established a fair at Mecca; and caravans of forty thousand merchants and devotees

(*g*) Mod. Univ. Hist. Vol. I. folio, p. 355.
(*h*) Smyth's Manners.   (*i*) Broughton, Art. Ramadan.
(*k*) White, Serm. IX.

set

set out once a year from Cairo, Damascus, and other places, so as to meet on the way, and travel together unmolested to that city. Without such associations, no commerce could be carried on between countries so distant; nor could individuals, nor even small bodies of men, safely travel through barren desarts, where they were liable to be infested by Arabs, or destroyed by wild beasts (*l*).

From what has been delivered in this section, we may judge of the influence of the Mahometan institution in those countries in which it is professed. We have pointed out its principal bad effects, and may reduce them to the following heads; namely, a spirit of revenge, hatred of other sects, the despotism of rulers, the ignorance and servitude of subjects, the depopulation of countries by war and pestilence, and the inconveniences to individuals, and the public, from pilgrimages to Mecca. These evils are the natural offspring of the doctrines and practices of the preachers and professors of Mahometanism, and furnish a strong argument of the excellence of the Christian code, by the observance of whose precepts all those evils would vanish or disappear. If we may judge of the truth and divinity of any religious system, from the tendency and real effects of its doctrines, we must conclude that Mahome-

Effects of Mahometanism prove the excellent tendency of the gospel.

(*l*) Mod. Univ. Hist. Vol. VI. folio, Book XXI. Ch. iii.

tanifm could not have been infpired by a good and wife God, who never dictates what, upon the whole, is hoftile to the temporal happinefs of his creatures. We fhould not allow thofe doctrines to be of divine origin, which tend to the deftruction of mankind, while they pretend to advance men's eternal welfare. Having pointed out the happy effects of chriftianity in numerous inftances, we may, if we compare thefe effects with the evils that have arifen from Mahometanifm, form a general opinion of the truth or falfhood of thofe different fyftems of religion. Yet Mr. Gibbon approves the popular creed of Mahometans; " there is but one God, and Mahomet is his prophet;" and thinks it fo rational, that a philofophic Theift might be induced to fubfcribe it (*m*). I admit, that a philofophic Theift would not hefitate to fubfcribe the former part of this creed relative to the unity of God; but furely a philofopher could not readily be convinced, that Mahomet was a prophet commiffioned by that God. Even this philofophic hiftorian and Theift, though partial to this creed, doubts whether Mahomet was an enthufiaft or impoftor; and intimates, that he was indebted for his Koran to his own refearches, and not the affiftance of Jews or Chriftians, fince " the uniformity of a work denotes the hand of a fingle artift (*n*)." Admitting the

(*m*) Hift. Ch. l. p. 205. quarto. (*n*) Ch. l. p. 201, 202.

truth of this propofition, it neceffarily follows, that the Koran, which is a compound of heterogeneous materials of truth and falfhood, of low and fublime ideas, was not the work of one man. This writer, who attributes uniformity to Mahometanifm, admits, that in a verfion of the Koran, " the European infidel will perufe, with impatience, the endlefs incoherent rhapfody of fable, and precept, and declamation, which feldom excites a fentiment or an idea; which fometimes crawls in the duft, and is fometimes loft in the clouds (o)." Let me afk how the hiftorian can reconcile this incoherent rhapfody of fable, and precept, and declamation, &c. with the uniformity which he afcribed to the Mahometan fyftem a few pages before?

(o) Ch. 1. p. 209.

F I N I S.

E R R A T A.

Page 151, line 1, add *he* after the word *and*.
Page 209, laft line but one, *nine parts in ten*.
Page 215, line 7 from bottom, *Guinea* not *Guonia*.
Page 239, line 5 from bottom, read *encreafing* inftead of *encreafe*.
Page 281, line 11, read *declined* not *eclined*.
Page 318, line 6 from bottom, expunge the word *of*.

www.ingramcontent.com/pod-product-compliance
Lightning Source LLC
Chambersburg PA
CBHW032024220426
43664CB00006B/355